Computer and Information Science:
An Interdisciplinary Approach

Computer and Information Science: An Interdisciplinary Approach

Zoey Clark

WILLFORD PRESS

www.willfordpress.com

Published by Willford Press,
118-35 Queens Blvd., Suite 400,
Forest Hills, NY 11375, USA

ISBN: 978-1-68285-897-4

Cataloging-in-Publication Data

Computer and information science : an interdisciplinary approach / Zoey Clark.
    p. cm.
Includes bibliographical references and index.
ISBN 978-1-68285-897-4
1. Computer science. 2. Information science. 3. Information literacy. 4. Computers. I. Clark, Zoey.
QA76 .C66 2020
004--dc23

For information on all Willford Press publications
visit our website at www.willfordpress.com

Table of Contents

Preface

This book has been written, keeping in view that students want more practical information. Thus, my aim has been to make it as comprehensive as possible for the readers. I would like to extend my thanks to my family and co-workers for their knowledge, support and encouragement all along.

The branch of study which is concerned with the processes which can be represented as data in the form of programs and which interact with data is known as computer science. It focuses on the usage of algorithms for the manipulation, communication and storage of digital information. It also studies the theory of computing. Information science deals with the classification, collection, movement, retrieval, protection and storage of information. It seeks to study the usage and application of data and information for the purpose of improving, creating, understanding or replacing information systems. It is closely associated with computer science and technology. This textbook provides comprehensive insights into the field of computer and information science. It unfolds the innovative aspects of these fields which will be crucial for the progress in the future. Those in search of information to further their knowledge will be greatly assisted by this book.

A brief description of the chapters is provided below for further understanding:

Chapter – What is Computer Science?

Computer science is the study of computational systems and processes that interact with data and represent data as programs. Various algorithms are used to store and communicate digital information, and design software systems. This chapter has been carefully written to provide an easy introduction to computer science.

Chapter – Computer Architecture

The functioning, programming and implementation of a computer system is determined by a certain set of rules and methods which is termed as computer architecture. A few of its types are Von Neumann architecture, instruction set architecture, microarchitecture, etc. This chapter discusses in detail all these types of computer architecture.

Chapter – Computer Network and Security

A group of computers connected with each other for sharing information and other resources is defined as a computer network. The protection of computer systems and information from harm, unauthorized use and theft is termed as computer security. The topics elaborated in this chapter will help in gaining a better perspective about the different types of computer network as well as computer security.

Chapter – Information Science and Systems

The analysis, collection, retrieval, movement and protection of data and information falls under the field of information science. The information and communication technology that supports business processes by developing interaction between people and technology is termed as an information system. This chapter closely examines the important concepts of information science and systems such as information architecture and information management.

Chapter – Information Security: Threats and Protection

The process designed for the protection of private and confidential information from unauthorized access, misuse or disruption is referred to as information security. Some of the threats which are dealt within this field are malware, spyware, rootkit, ransomware, phishing, etc. This chapter dis-cusses in detail these threats related to information security.

Zoey Clark

1

What is Computer Science?

Computer science is the study of computational systems and processes that interact with data and represent data as programs. Various algorithms are used to store and communicate digital information, and design software systems. This chapter has been carefully written to provide an easy introduction to computer science.

Computer science is the study of computers and computing, including their theoretical and algorithmic foundations, hardware and software, and their uses for processing information. The discipline of computer science includes the study of algorithms and data structures, computer and network design, modeling data and information processes, and artificial intelligence. Computer science draws some of its foundations from mathematics and engineering and therefore incorporates techniques from areas such as queueing theory, probability and statistics, and electronic circuit design. Computer science also makes heavy use of hypothesis testing and experimentation during the conceptualization, design, measurement, and refinement of new algorithms, information structures, and computer architectures.

Computer science is considered as part of a family of five separate yet interrelated disciplines, computer engineering, computer science, information systems, information technology, and software engineering. This family has come to be known collectively as the discipline of computing. These five disciplines are interrelated in the sense that computing is their object of study, but they are separate since each has its own research perspective and curricular focus. (Since 1991 the Association for Computing Machinery [ACM], the IEEE Computer Society [IEEE-CS], and the Association for Information Systems [AIS] have collaborated to develop and update the taxonomy of these five interrelated disciplines and the guidelines that educational institutions worldwide use for their undergraduate, graduate, and research programs.)

The major subfields of computer science include the traditional study of computer architecture, programming languages, and software development. However, they also include computational science (the use of algorithmic techniques for modeling scientific data), graphics and visualization, human-computer interaction, databases and information systems, networks, and the social and professional issues that are unique to the practice of computer science. As may be evident, some of these subfields overlap in their activities with other modern fields, such as bioinformatics and computational chemistry. These overlaps are the consequence of a tendency among computer scientists to recognize and act upon their field's many interdisciplinary connections.

Algorithms and Complexity

An algorithm is a specific procedure for solving a well-defined computational problem. The development and analysis of algorithms is fundamental to all aspects of computer science: artificial intelligence, databases, graphics, networking, operating systems, security, and so on. Algorithm development is more than just programming. It requires an understanding of the alternatives available for solving a computational problem, including the hardware, networking, programming language, and performance constraints that accompany any particular solution. It also requires understanding what it means for an algorithm to be "correct" in the sense that it fully and efficiently solves the problem at hand.

An accompanying notion is the design of a particular data structure that enables an algorithm to run efficiently. The importance of data structures stems from the fact that the main memory of a computer (where the data is stored) is linear, consisting of a sequence of memory cells that are serially numbered 0, 1, 2,....etc. Thus, the simplest data structure is a linear array, in which adjacent elements are numbered with consecutive integer "indexes" and an element's value is accessed by its unique index. An array can be used, for example, to store a list of names, and efficient methods are needed to efficiently search for and retrieve a particular name from the array. For example, sorting the list into alphabetical order permits a so-called binary search technique to be used, in which the remainder of the list to be searched at each step is cut in half. This search technique is similar to searching a telephone book for a particular name. Knowing that the book is in alphabetical order allows one to turn quickly to a page that is close to the page containing the desired name. Many algorithms have been developed for sorting and searching lists of data efficiently.

Although data items are stored consecutively in memory, they may be linked together by pointers (essentially, memory addresses stored with an item to indicate where the next item or items in the structure are found) so that the data can be organized in ways similar to those in which they will be accessed. The simplest such structure is called the linked list, in which noncontiguously stored items may be accessed in a pre-specified order by following the pointers from one item in the list to the next. The list may be circular, with the last item pointing to the first, or each element may have pointers in both directions to form a doubly linked list. Algorithms have been developed for efficiently manipulating such lists by searching for, inserting, and removing items.

Pointers also provide the ability to implement more complex data structures. A graph, for example, is a set of nodes (items) and links (known as edges) that connect pairs of items. Such a graph might represent a set of cities and the highways joining them, the layout of circuit elements and connecting wires on a memory chip, or the configuration of persons interacting via a social network. Typical graph algorithms include graph traversal strategies, such as how to follow the links from node to node (perhaps searching for a node with a particular property) in a way that each node is visited only once. A related problem is the determination of the shortest path between two given nodes on an arbitrary graph. A problem of practical interest in network algorithms, for instance, is to determine how many "broken" links can be tolerated before communications begin to fail. Similarly, in very-large-scale integration (VLSI) chip design it is important to know whether the graph representing a circuit is planar, that is, whether it can be drawn in two dimensions without any links crossing (wires touching).

The (computational) complexity of an algorithm is a measure of the amount of computing resources (time and space) that a particular algorithm consumes when it runs. Computer scientists use mathematical measures of complexity that allow them to predict, before writing the code, how fast an algorithm will run and how much memory it will require. Such predictions are important guides for programmers implementing and selecting algorithms for real-world applications.

Computational complexity is a continuum, in that some algorithms require linear time (that is, the time required increases directly with the number of items or nodes in the list, graph, or network being processed), whereas others require quadratic or even exponential time to complete (that is, the time required increases with the number of items squared or with the exponential of that number). At the far end of this continuum lie the murky seas of intractable problems—those whose solutions cannot be efficiently implemented. For these problems, computer scientists seek to find heuristic algorithms that can almost solve the problem and run in a reasonable amount of time.

Further away still are those algorithmic problems that can be stated but are not solvable; that is, one can prove that no program can be written to solve the problem. A classic example of an unsolvable algorithmic problem is the halting problem, which states that no program can be written that can predict whether or not any other program halts after a finite number of steps. The unsolvability of the halting problem has immediate practical bearing on software development. For instance, it would be frivolous to try to develop a software tool that predicts whether another program being developed has an infinite loop in it (although having such a tool would be immensely beneficial).

Architecture and Organization

Computer architecture deals with the design of computers, data storage devices, and networking components that store and run programs, transmit data, and drive interactions between computers, across networks, and with users. Computer architects use parallelism and various strategies for memory organization to design computing systems with very high performance. Computer architecture requires strong communication between computer scientists and computer engineers, since they both focus fundamentally on hardware design.

At its most fundamental level, a computer consists of a control unit, an arithmetic logic unit (ALU), a memory unit, and input/output (I/O) controllers. The ALU performs simple addition, subtraction, multiplication, division, and logic operations, such as OR and AND. The memory stores the program's instructions and data. The control unit fetches data and instructions from memory and uses operations of the ALU to carry out those instructions using that data. (The control unit and ALU together are referred to as the central processing unit [CPU].) When an input or output instruction is encountered, the control unit transfers the data between the memory and the designated I/O controller. The operational speed of the CPU primarily determines the speed of the computer as a whole. All of these components—the control unit, the ALU, the memory, and the I/O controllers—are realized with transistor circuits.

Computers also have another level of memory called a cache, a small, extremely fast (compared with the main memory, or random access memory [RAM]) unit that can be used to store information that is urgently or frequently needed. Current research includes cache design and algorithms that can predict what data is likely to be needed next and preload it into the cache for improved performance.

I/O controllers connect the computer to specific input devices (such as keyboards and touch screen displays) for feeding information to the memory, and output devices (such as printers and displays) for transmitting information from the memory to users. Additional I/O controllers connect the computer to a network via ports that provide the conduit through which data flows when the computer is connected to the Internet.

Linked to the I/O controllers are secondary storage devices, such as a disk drive, that are slower and have a larger capacity than main or cache memory. Disk drives are used for maintaining permanent data. They can be either permanently or temporarily attached to the computer in the form of a compact disc (CD), a digital video disc (DVD), or a memory stick (also called a flash drive).

Flash-memory drive with USB on a laptop computer.

The operation of a computer, once a program and some data have been loaded into RAM, takes place as follows. The first instruction is transferred from RAM into the control unit and interpreted by the hardware circuitry. For instance, suppose that the instruction is a string of bits that is the code for LOAD 10. This instruction loads the contents of memory location 10 into the ALU. The next instruction, say ADD 15, is fetched. The control unit then loads the contents of memory location 15 into the ALU and adds it to the number already there. Finally, the instruction STORE 20 would store that sum into location 20. At this level, the operation of a computer is not much different from that of a pocket calculator.

In general, programs are not just lengthy sequences of load, store, and arithmetic operations. Most importantly, computer languages include conditional instructions—essentially, rules that say, "If memory location n satisfies condition a, do instruction number x next, otherwise do instruction y." This allows the course of a program to be determined by the results of previous operations—a critically important ability.

Finally, programs typically contain sequences of instructions that are repeated a number of times until a predetermined condition becomes true. Such a sequence is called a loop. For example, a loop would be needed to compute the sum of the first n integers, where n is a value stored in a separate memory location. Computer architectures that can execute sequences of instructions, conditional instructions, and loops are called "Turing complete," which means that they can carry out the execution of any algorithm that can be defined. Turing completeness is a fundamental and essential characteristic of any computer organization.

Logic design is the area of computer science that deals with the design of electronic circuits using the fundamental principles and properties of logic to carry out the operations of the control unit, the ALU, the I/O controllers, and other hardware. Each logical function (AND, OR, and NOT) is realized by a particular type of device called a gate. For example, the addition circuit of the ALU has inputs corresponding to all the bits of the two numbers to be added and outputs corresponding to the bits of the sum. The arrangement of wires and gates that link inputs to outputs is determined by the mathematical definition of addition. The design of the control unit provides the circuits that interpret instructions. Due to the need for efficiency, logic design must also optimize the circuitry to function with maximum speed and has a minimum number of gates and circuits.

An important area related to architecture is the design of microprocessors, which are complete CPUs—control unit, ALU, and memory—on a single integrated circuit chip. Additional memory and I/O control circuitry are linked to this chip to form a complete computer. These thumbnail-sized devices contain millions of transistors that implement the processing and memory units of modern computers.

VLSI microprocessor design occurs in a number of stages, which include creating the initial functional or behavioral specification, encoding this specification into a hardware description language, and breaking down the design into modules and generating sizes and shapes for the eventual chip components. It also involves chip planning, which includes building a "floor plan" to indicate where on the chip each component should be placed and connected to other components. Computer scientists are also involved in creating the computer-aided design (CAD) tools that support engineers in the various stages of chip design and in developing the necessary theoretical results, such as how to efficiently design a floor plan with near-minimal area that satisfies the given constraints.

Advances in integrated circuit technology have been incredible. For example, in 1971 the first microprocessor chip (Intel Corporation's 4004) had only 2,300 transistors, in 1993 Intel's Pentium chip had more than 3 million transistors, and by 2000 the number of transistors on such a chip was about 50 million. The Power7 chip introduced in 2010 by IBM contained approximately 1 billion transistors. The phenomenon of the number of transistors in an integrated circuit doubling about every two years is widely known as Moore's law.

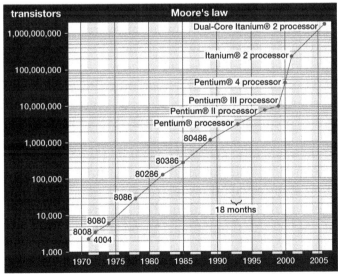

Moore's law: Gordon E. Moore observed that the number of transistors on a computer chip was doubling about every 18–24 months. As shown in the logarithmic graph of the number of transistors on Intel's processors at the time of their introduction, his "law" was being obeyed.

Fault tolerance is the ability of a computer to continue operation when one or more of its components fails. To ensure fault tolerance, key components are often replicated so that the backup component can take over if needed. Such applications as aircraft control and manufacturing process control run on systems with backup processors ready to take over if the main processor fails, and the backup systems often run in parallel so the transition is smooth. If the systems are critical in that their failure would be potentially disastrous (as in aircraft control), incompatible outcomes collected from replicated processes running in parallel on separate machines are resolved by a voting mechanism. Computer scientists are involved in the analysis of such replicated systems, providing theoretical approaches to estimating the reliability achieved by a given configuration and processor parameters, such as average time between failures and average time required to repair the processor. Fault tolerance is also a desirable feature in distributed systems and networks. For example, an advantage of a distributed database is that data replicated on different network hosts can provide a natural backup mechanism when one host fails.

Computational Science

Computational science applies computer simulation, scientific visualization, mathematical modeling, algorithms, data structures, networking, database design, symbolic computation, and high-performance computing to help advance the goals of various disciplines. These disciplines include biology, chemistry, fluid dynamics, archaeology, finance, sociology, and forensics. Computational science has evolved rapidly, especially because of the dramatic growth in the volume of data transmitted from scientific instruments. This phenomenon has been called the "big data" problem.

The mathematical methods needed for computational science require the transformation of equations and functions from the continuous to the discrete. For example, the computer integration of a function over an interval is accomplished not by applying integral calculus but rather by approximating the area under the function graph as a sum of the areas obtained from evaluating the function at discrete points. Similarly, the solution of a differential equation is obtained as a sequence of discrete points determined by approximating the true solution curve by a sequence of tangential line segments. When discretized in this way, many problems can be recast as an equation involving a matrix (a rectangular array of numbers) solvable using linear algebra. Numerical analysis is the study of such computational methods. Several factors must be considered when applying numerical methods: (1) the conditions under which the method yields a solution, (2) the accuracy of the solution, (3) whether the solution process is stable (i.e., does not exhibit error growth), and (4) the computational complexity of obtaining a solution of the desired accuracy.

The requirements of big-data scientific problems, including the solution of ever larger systems of equations, engage the use of large and powerful arrays of processors (called multiprocessors or supercomputers) that allow many calculations to proceed in parallel by assigning them to separate processing elements. These activities have sparked much interest in parallel computer architecture and algorithms that can be carried out efficiently on such machines.

Graphics and Visual Computing

Graphics and visual computing is the field that deals with the display and control of images on a computer screen. This field encompasses the efficient implementation of four interrelated computational tasks: rendering, modeling, animation, and visualization. Graphics techniques incorporate principles of linear algebra, numerical integration, computational geometry, special-purpose hardware, file formats, and graphical user interfaces (GUIs) to accomplish these complex tasks.

Applications of graphics include CAD, fine arts, medical imaging, scientific data visualization, and video games. CAD systems allow the computer to be used for designing objects ranging from automobile parts to bridges to computer chips by providing an interactive drawing tool and an engineering interface to simulation and analysis tools. Fine arts applications allow artists to use the computer screen as a medium to create images, cinematographic special effects, animated cartoons, and television commercials. Medical imaging applications involve the visualization of data obtained from technologies such as X-rays and magnetic resonance imaging (MRIs) to assist doctors in diagnosing medical conditions. Scientific visualization uses massive amounts of data to define simulations of scientific phenomena, such as ocean modeling, to produce pictures that provide more insight into the phenomena than would tables of numbers. Graphics also provide realistic visualizations for video gaming, flight simulation, and other representations of reality or fantasy. The term virtual reality has been coined to refer to any interaction with a computer-simulated virtual world.

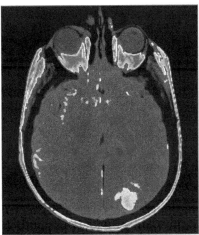

Brain cancer; magnetic resonance imaging (MRI). An image, produced by magnetic resonance imaging (MRI), of a human brain affected by cancer. The bright blue area indicates that the cancer spread to the occipital lobe (lower right).

A challenge for computer graphics is the development of efficient algorithms that manipulate the myriad of lines, triangles, and polygons that make up a computer image. In order for realistic on-screen images to be presented, each object must be rendered as a set of planar units. Edges must be smoothed and textured so that their underlying construction from polygons is not obvious to the naked eye. In many applications, still pictures are inadequate, and rapid display of real-time images is required. Both extremely efficient algorithms and state-of-the-art hardware are needed to accomplish real-time animation.

Human-computer Interaction

Human-computer interaction (HCI) is concerned with designing effective interaction between users and computers and the construction of interfaces that support this interaction. HCI occurs at an interface that includes both software and hardware. User interface design impacts the life cycle of software, so it should occur early in the design process. Because user interfaces must accommodate a variety of user styles and capabilities, HCI research draws on several disciplines including psychology, sociology, anthropology, and engineering. In the 1960s, user interfaces consisted of computer consoles that allowed an operator directly to type commands that could be executed immediately or at some future time. With the advent of more user-friendly personal computers in the 1980s, user interfaces became more sophisticated, so that the user could "point and click" to send a command to the operating system.

Thus, the field of HCI emerged to model, develop, and measure the effectiveness of various types of interfaces between a computer application and the person accessing its services. GUIs enable users to communicate with the computer by such simple means as pointing to an icon with a mouse or touching it with a stylus or forefinger. This technology also supports windowing environments on a computer screen, which allow users to work with different applications simultaneously, one in each window.

Information Management

Information management (IM) is primarily concerned with the capture, digitization, representation, organization, transformation, and presentation of information. Because a computer's main memory provides only temporary storage, computers are equipped with auxiliary disk storage devices that permanently store data. These devices are characterized by having much higher capacity than main memory but slower read/write (access) speed. Data stored on a disk must be read into main memory before it can be processed. A major goal of IM systems, therefore, is to develop efficient algorithms to store and retrieve specific data for processing.

IM systems comprise databases and algorithms for the efficient storage, retrieval, updating, and deleting of specific items in the database. The underlying structure of a database is a set of files residing permanently on a disk storage device. Each file can be further broken down into a series of records, which contains individual data items, or fields. Each field gives the value of some property (or attribute) of the entity represented by a record. For example, a personnel file may contain a series of records, one for each individual in the organization, and each record would contain fields that contain that person's name, address, phone number, e-mail address, and so forth.

Many file systems are sequential, meaning that successive records are processed in the order in which they are stored, starting from the beginning and proceeding to the end. This file structure was particularly popular in the early days of computing, when files were stored on reels of magnetic tape and these reels could be processed only in a sequential manner. Sequential files are generally stored in some sorted order (e.g., alphabetic) for printing of reports (e.g., a telephone directory) and for efficient processing of batches of transactions. Banking transactions (deposits and withdrawals), for instance, might be sorted in the same order as the accounts file, so that as each transaction is read the system need only scan ahead to find the accounts record to which it applies.

With modern storage systems, it is possible to access any data record in a random fashion. To facilitate efficient random access, the data records in a file are stored with indexes called keys. An index of a file is much like an index of a book; it contains a key for each record in the file along with the location where the record is stored. Since indexes might be long, they are usually structured in some hierarchical fashion so that they can be navigated efficiently. The top level of an index, for example, might contain locations of (point to) indexes to items beginning with the letters A, B, etc. The A index itself may contain not locations of data items but pointers to indexes of items beginning with the letters Ab, Ac, and so on. Locating the index for the desired record by traversing a treelike structure is quite efficient.

Many applications require access to many independent files containing related and even overlapping data. Their information management activities frequently require data from several files to be linked, and hence the need for a database model emerges. Historically, three different types of database models have been developed to support the linkage of records of different types: (1) the hierarchical model, in which record types are linked in a treelike structure (e.g., employee records might be grouped under records describing the departments in which employees work), (2) the network model, in which arbitrary linkages of record types may be created (e.g., employee records might be linked on one hand to employees' departments and on the other hand to their supervisors—that is, other employees), and (3) the relational model, in which all data are represented in simple tabular form.

In the relational model, each individual entry is described by the set of its attribute values (called a relation), stored in one row of the table. This linkage of n attribute values to provide a meaningful description of a real-world entity or a relationship among such entities forms a mathematical n-tuple. The relational model also supports queries (requests for information) that involve several tables by providing automatic linkage across tables by means of a "join" operation that combines records with identical values of common attributes. Payroll data, for example, can be stored in one table and personnel benefits data in another; complete information on an employee could be obtained by joining the two tables using the employee's unique identification number as a common attribute.

To support database processing, a software artifact known as a database management system (DBMS) is required to manage the data and provide the user with commands to retrieve information from the database. For example, a widely used DBMS that supports the relational model is MySQL.

Another development in database technology is to incorporate the object concept. In object-oriented databases, all data are objects. Objects may be linked together by an "is-part-of" relationship to represent larger, composite objects. Data describing a truck, for instance, may be stored as a composite of a particular engine, chassis, drive train, and so forth. Classes of objects may form a hierarchy in which individual objects may inherit properties from objects farther up in the hierarchy. For example, objects of the class "motorized vehicle" all have an engine; members of the subclasses "truck" or "airplane" will then also have an engine.

NoSQL, or non-relational databases, have also emerged. These databases are different from the classic relational databases because they do not require fixed tables. Many of them are document-oriented databases, in which voice, music, images, and video clips are stored along with traditional textual information. An important subset of NoSQL are the XML databases, which are widely used in the development of Android smartphone and tablet applications.

Data integrity refers to designing a DBMS that ensures the correctness and stability of its data across all applications that access the system. When a database is designed, integrity checking is enabled by specifying the data type of each column in the table. For example, if an identification number is specified to be nine digits, the DBMS will reject an update attempting to assign a value with more or fewer digits or one including an alphabetic character. Another type of integrity, known as referential integrity, requires that each entity referenced by some other entity must itself exist in the database. For example, if an airline reservation is requested for a particular flight number, then the flight referenced by that number must actually exist.

Access to a database by multiple simultaneous users requires that the DBMS include a concurrency control mechanism (called locking) to maintain integrity whenever two different users attempt to access the same data at the same time. For example, two travel agents may try to book the last seat on a plane at more or less the same time. Without concurrency control, both may think they have succeeded, though only one booking is actually entered into the database.

A key concept in studying concurrency control and the maintenance of data integrity is the transaction, defined as an indivisible operation that transforms the database from one state into another. To illustrate, consider an electronic transfer of funds of $5 from bank account A to account B. The operation that deducts $5 from account A leaves the database without integrity since the total over all accounts is $5 short. Similarly, the operation that adds $5 to account B in itself makes the total $5 too much. Combining these two operations into a single transaction, however, maintains data integrity. The key here is to ensure that only complete transactions are applied to the data and that multiple concurrent transactions are executed using locking so that serializing them would produce the same result. A transaction-oriented control mechanism for database access becomes difficult in the case of a long transaction, for example, when several engineers are working, perhaps over the course of several days, on a product design that may not exhibit data integrity until the project is complete.

A database may be distributed in that its data can be spread among different host computers on a network. If the distributed data contains duplicates, the concurrency control problem is more complex. Distributed databases must have a distributed DBMS to provide overall control of queries and updates in a manner that does not require that the user know the location of the data. A closely related concept is interoperability, meaning the ability of the user of one member of a group of disparate systems (all having the same functionality) to work with any of the systems of the group with equal ease and via the same interface.

Intelligent Systems

Artificial intelligence (AI) is an area of research that goes back to the very beginnings of computer science. The idea of building a machine that can perform tasks perceived as requiring human intelligence is an attractive one. The tasks that have been studied from this point of view include game playing, language translation, natural language understanding, fault diagnosis, robotics, and supplying expert advice.

Since the late 20th century, the field of intelligent systems has focused on the support of everyday applications—e-mail, word processing, and search—using nontraditional techniques. These techniques include the design and analysis of autonomous agents that perceive their environment and interact rationally with it. The solutions rely on a broad set of knowledge-representation schemes, problem-solving mechanisms, and learning strategies. They deal with sensing (e.g., speech recognition, natural language understanding, and computer vision), problem-solving (e.g., search and planning), acting (e.g., robotics), and the architectures needed to support them (e.g,. agents and multi-agents).

ASIMO, a two-legged "humanoid" robot developed by the Honda Motor Co. in the early 21st century, could walk independently and climb or descend stairs.

Networking and Communication

The field of networking and communication includes the analysis, design, implementation, and use of local, wide-area, and mobile networks that link computers together. The Internet itself is a network that makes it feasible for nearly all computers in the world to communicate.

A computer network links computers together via a combination of infrared light signals, radio wave transmissions, telephone lines, television cables, and satellite links. The challenge for computer scientists has been to develop protocols (standardized rules for the format and exchange of messages) that allow processes running on host computers to interpret the signals they receive and to engage in meaningful "conversations" in order to accomplish tasks on behalf of users. Network protocols also include flow control, which keeps a data sender from swamping a receiver with messages that it has no time to process or space to store, and error control, which involves transmission error detection and automatic resending of messages to correct such errors.

The standardization of protocols is an international effort. Since it would otherwise be impossible for different kinds of machines and operating systems to communicate with one another, the key concern has been that system components (computers) be "open." This terminology comes from the open systems interconnection (OSI) communication standards, established by the International Organization for Standardization. The OSI reference model specifies network protocol standards in seven layers. Each layer is defined by the functions it relies upon from the layer below it and by the services it provides to the layer above it.

The open systems interconnection (OSI) model for network communication. Established in 1983 by the International Organization for Standardization, the OSI model divides network protocols (standardized procedures for exchanging information) into seven functional "layers." This communications architecture enables end users employing different operating systems or working in different networks to communicate quickly and correctly.

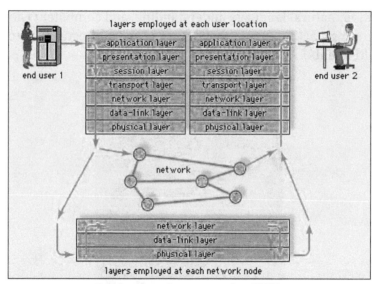

Open systems interconnection (OSI).

At the bottom of the protocol lies the physical layer, containing rules for the transport of bits across a physical link. The data-link layer handles standard-sized "packets" of data and adds reliability in the form of error detection and flow control bits. The network and transport layers break messages into the standard-size packets and route them to their destinations. The session layer supports interactions between applications on two communicating machines. For example, it provides a mechanism with which to insert checkpoints (saving the current status of a task) into a long file transfer so that, in case of a failure, only the data after the last checkpoint need to be retransmitted. The presentation layer is concerned with functions that encode data, so that heterogeneous systems may engage in meaningful communication. At the highest level are protocols that support specific applications. An example of such an application is the file transfer protocol (FTP), which governs the transfer of files from one host to another.

The development of networks and communication protocols has also spawned distributed systems, in which computers linked in a network share data and processing tasks. A distributed database system, for example, has a database spread among (or replicated at) different network sites. Data are replicated at "mirror sites," and replication can improve availability and reliability. A distributed DBMS manages a database whose components are distributed across several computers on a network.

A client-server network is a distributed system in which the database resides on one computer (the server) and the users connect to this computer over the network from their own computers (the clients). The server provides data and responds to requests from each client, while each client accesses the data on the server in a way that is independent and ignorant of the presence of other clients accessing the same database. Client-server systems require that individual actions from several clients to the same part of the server's database be synchronized, so that conflicts are resolved in a reasonable way. For example, airline reservations are implemented using a client-server model. The server contains all the data about upcoming flights, such as current bookings and seat assignments. Each client wants to access this data for the purpose of booking a flight, obtaining a seat assignment, and paying for the flight. During this process, it is likely that two or more client requests want to access the same flight and that there is only one seat left to be assigned. The software must synchronize these two requests so that the remaining seat is assigned in a rational way (usually to the person who made the request first).

Another popular type of distributed system is the peer-to-peer network. Unlike client-server networks, a peer-to-peer network assumes that each computer (user) connected to it can act both as a client and as a server; thus, everyone on the network is a peer. This strategy makes sense for groups that share audio collections on the Internet and for organizing social networks such as LinkedIn and Facebook. Each person connected to such a network both receives information from others and shares his or her own information with others.

Operating Systems

An operating system is a specialized collection of software that stands between a computer's hardware architecture and its applications. It performs a number of fundamental activities such as file system management, process scheduling, memory allocation, network interfacing, and resource sharing among the computer's users. Operating systems have evolved in their complexity over time, beginning with the earliest computers in the 1960s.

With early computers, the user typed programs onto punched tape or cards, which were read into the computer, assembled or compiled, and run. The results were then transmitted to a printer or a magnetic tape. These early operating systems engaged in batch processing; i.e., handling sequences of jobs that are compiled and executed one at a time without intervention by the user. Accompanying each job in a batch were instructions to the operating system (OS) detailing the resources needed by the job, such as the amount of CPU time required, the files needed, and the storage devices on which the files resided. From these beginnings came the key concept of an operating system as a resource allocator. This role became more important with the rise of multiprogramming, in which several jobs reside in the computer simultaneously and share resources, for example, by being allocated fixed amounts of CPU time in turn. More sophisticated hardware allowed one job to be reading data while another wrote to a printer and still another performed computations. The operating system thus managed these tasks in such a way that all the jobs were completed without interfering with one another.

The advent of time sharing, in which users enter commands and receive results directly at a terminal, added more tasks to the operating system. Processes known as terminal handlers were needed, along with mechanisms such as interrupts (to get the attention of the operating system to handle urgent tasks) and buffers (for temporary storage of data during input/output to make the transfer run more smoothly). Modern large computers interact with hundreds of users simultaneously, giving each one the perception of being the sole user.

Another area of operating system research is the design of virtual memory. Virtual memory is a scheme that gives users the illusion of working with a large block of contiguous memory space (perhaps even larger than real memory), when in actuality most of their work is on auxiliary storage (disk). Fixed-size blocks (pages) or variable-size blocks (segments) of the job are read into main memory as needed. Questions such as how much main memory space to allocate to users and which pages or segments should be returned to disk ("swapped out") to make room for incoming pages or segments must be addressed in order for the system to execute jobs efficiently.

The first commercially viable operating systems were developed by IBM in the 1960s and were called OS/360 and DOS/360. Unix was developed at Bell Laboratories in the early 1970s and since has spawned many variants, including Linux, Berkeley Unix, GNU, and Apple's iOS. Operating systems developed for the first personal computers in the 1980s included IBM's (and later Microsoft's) DOS, which evolved into various flavours of Windows. An important 21st-century development in operating systems was that they became increasingly machine-independent.

Parallel and Distributed Computing

The simultaneous growth in availability of big data and in the number of simultaneous users on the Internet places particular pressure on the need to carry out computing tasks "in parallel," or simultaneously. Parallel and distributed computing occurs across many different topic areas in computer science, including algorithms, computer architecture, networks, operating systems, and software engineering. During the early 21st century there was explosive growth in multiprocessor design and other strategies for complex applications to run faster. Parallel and distributed computing builds on fundamental systems concepts, such as concurrency, mutual exclusion, consistency in state/memory manipulation, message-passing, and shared-memory models.

Creating a multiprocessor from a number of single CPUs requires physical links and a mechanism for communication among the processors so that they may operate in parallel. Tightly coupled multiprocessors share memory and hence may communicate by storing information in memory accessible by all processors. Loosely coupled multiprocessors, including computer networks, communicate by sending messages to each other across the physical links. Computer scientists have investigated various multiprocessor architectures. For example, the possible configurations in which hundreds or even thousands of processors may be linked together are examined to find the geometry that supports the most efficient system throughput. A much-studied topology is the hypercube, in which each processor is connected directly to some fixed number of neighbours: two for the two-dimensional square, three for the three-dimensional cube, and similarly for the higher-dimensional hypercubes. Computer scientists also investigate methods for carrying out computations on such multiprocessor machines (e.g., algorithms to make optimal use of the architecture and techniques to avoid conflicts in data transmission). The machine-resident software that makes possible the use of a particular machine, in particular its operating system, is an integral part of this investigation.

Concurrency refers to the execution of more than one procedure at the same time (perhaps with the access of shared data), either truly simultaneously (as on a multiprocessor) or in an unpredictably interleaved order. Modern programming languages such as Java include both encapsulation and features called "threads" that allow the programmer to define the synchronization that occurs among concurrent procedures or tasks.

Two important issues in concurrency control are known as deadlocks and race conditions. Deadlock occurs when a resource held indefinitely by one process is requested by two or more other processes simultaneously. As a result, none of the processes that call for the resource can continue; they are deadlocked, waiting for the resource to be freed. An operating system can handle this situation with various prevention or detection and recovery techniques. A race condition, on the other hand, occurs when two or more concurrent processes assign a different value to a variable, and the result depends on which process assigns the variable first (or last).

Preventing deadlocks and race conditions is fundamentally important, since it ensures the integrity of the underlying application. A general prevention strategy is called process synchronization.

Synchronization requires that one process wait for another to complete some operation before proceeding. For example, one process (a writer) may be writing data to a certain main memory area, while another process (a reader) may want to read data from that area. The reader and writer must be synchronized so that the writer does not overwrite existing data until the reader has processed it. Similarly, the reader should not start to read until data has been written in the area.

With the advent of networks, distributed computing became feasible. A distributed computation is one that is carried out by a group of linked computers working cooperatively. Such computing usually requires a distributed operating system to manage the distributed resources. Important concerns are workload sharing, which attempts to take advantage of access to multiple computers to complete jobs faster; task migration, which supports workload sharing by efficiently distributing jobs among machines; and automatic task replication, which occurs at different sites for greater reliability.

Platform-based Development

Platform-based development is concerned with the design and development of applications for specific types of computers and operating systems ("platforms"). Platform-based development takes into account system-specific characteristics, such as those found in Web programming, multimedia development, mobile application development, and robotics. Platforms such as the Internet or an Android tablet enable students to learn within and about environments constrained by specific hardware, application programming interfaces (APIs), and special services. These environments are sufficiently different from "general purpose" programming to warrant separate research and development efforts.

For example, consider the development of an application for an Android tablet. The Android programming platform is called the Dalvic Virtual Machine (DVM), and the language is a variant of Java. However, an Android application is defined not just as a collection of objects and methods but, moreover, as a collection of "intents" and "activities," which correspond roughly to the GUI screens that the user sees when operating the application. XML programming is needed as well, since it is the language that defines the layout of the application's user interface. Finally, I/O synchronization in Android application development is more demanding than that found on conventional platforms, though some principles of Java file management carry over.

Real-time systems provide a broader setting in which platform-based development takes place. The term real-time systems refers to computers embedded into cars, aircraft, manufacturing assembly lines, and other devices to control processes in real time. Frequently, real-time tasks repeat at fixed-time intervals. For example, sensor data are gathered every second, and a control signal is generated. In such cases, scheduling theory is used to determine how the tasks should be scheduled on a given processor. A good example of a system that requires real-time action is the antilock braking system (ABS) on an automobile; because it is critical that the ABS instantly reacts to brake-pedal pressure and begins a program of pumping the brakes, such an application is said to have a hard deadline. Other real-time systems are said to have soft deadlines, in that no disaster will happen if the system's response is slightly delayed; an example is an order shipping and tracking system. The concept of "best effort" arises in real-time system design, because soft deadlines sometimes slip and hard deadlines are sometimes met by computing a less than optimal result. For example, most details on an air traffic controller's screen are approximations (e.g., altitude) that need not be computed more precisely (e.g., to the nearest inch) in order to be effective.

Programming Languages

Programming languages are the languages with which a programmer implements a piece of software to run on a computer. The earliest programming languages were assembly languages, not far removed from the binary-encoded instructions directly executed by the computer. By the mid-1950s, programmers began to use higher-level languages.

Two of the first higher-level languages were FORTRAN (Formula Translator) and ALGOL (Algorithmic Language), which allowed programmers to write algebraic expressions and solve scientific computing problems. As learning to program became increasingly important in the 1960s, a stripped-down version of FORTRAN called BASIC (Beginner's All-Purpose Symbolic Instruction Code) was developed at Dartmouth College. BASIC quickly spread to other academic institutions, and by 1980 versions of BASIC for personal computers allowed even students at elementary schools to learn the fundamentals of programming. Also, in the mid-1950s, COBOL (Common Business-Oriented Language) was developed to support business programming applications that involved managing information stored in records and files.

The trend since then has been toward developing increasingly abstract languages, allowing the programmer to communicate with the machine at a level ever more remote from machine code. COBOL, FORTRAN, and their descendants (Pascal and C, for example) are known as imperative languages, since they specify as a sequence of explicit commands how the machine is to go about solving the problem at hand. These languages were also known as procedural languages, since they allowed programmers to develop and reuse procedures, subroutines, and functions to avoid reinventing basic tasks for every new application.

Other high-level languages are called functional languages, in that a program is viewed as a collection of (mathematical) functions and its semantics are very precisely defined. The best-known functional language of this type is LISP (List Processing), which in the 1960s was the mainstay programming language for AI applications. Successors to LISP in the AI community include Scheme, Prolog, and C and C++. Scheme is similar to LISP except that it has a more formal mathematical definition. Prolog has been used largely for logic programming, and its applications include natural language understanding and expert systems such as MYCIN. Prolog is notably a so-called nonprocedural, or declarative, language in the sense that the programmer specifies what goals are to be accomplished but not how specific methods are to be applied to attain those goals. C and C++ have been used widely in robotics, an important application of AI research. An extension of logic programming is constraint logic programming, in which pattern matching is replaced by the more general operation of constraint satisfaction.

Another important development in programming languages through the 1980s was the addition of support for data encapsulation, which gave rise to object-oriented languages. The original object-oriented language was called Smalltalk, in which all programs were represented as collections of objects communicating with each other via message-passing. An object is a set of data together with the methods (functions) that can transform that data. Encapsulation refers to the fact that an object's data can be accessed only through these methods. Object-oriented programming has been very influential in computing. Languages for object-oriented programming include C++, Visual BASIC, and Java.

Java is unusual because its applications are translated not into a particular machine language but into an intermediate language called Java Bytecode, which runs on the Java Virtual Machine (JVM). Programs on the JVM can be executed on most contemporary computer platforms, including Intel-based systems, Apple Macintoshes, and various Android-based smartphones and tablets. Thus, Linux, iOS, Windows, and other operating systems can run Java programs, which makes Java ideal for creating distributed and Web-based applications. Residing on Web-based servers, Java programs may be downloaded and run in any standard Web browser to provide access to various services, such as a client interface to a game or entry to a database residing on a server.

At a still higher level of abstraction lie declarative and scripting languages, which are strictly interpreted languages and often drive applications running in Web browsers and mobile devices. Some declarative languages allow programmers to conveniently access and retrieve information from a database using "queries," which are declarations of what to do (rather than how to do it). A widely used database query language is SQL (Structured Query Language) and its variants (e.g., MySQL and SQLite). Associated with these declarative languages are those that describe the layout of a Web page on the user's screen. For example, HTML (HyperText Markup Language) supports the design of Web pages by specifying their structure and content. Gluing the Web page together with the database is the task of a scripting language (e.g., PHP), which is a vehicle for programmers to integrate declarative statements of HTML and MySQL with imperative actions that are required to effect an interaction between the user and the database. An example is an online book order with Amazon.com, where the user queries the database to find out what books are available and then initiates an order by pressing buttons and filling appropriate text areas with his or her ordering information. The software that underlies this activity includes HTML to describe the content of the Web page, MySQL to access the database according to the user's requests, and PHP to control the overall flow of the transaction.

Computer programs written in any language other than machine language must be either interpreted or translated into machine language ("compiled"). An interpreter is software that examines a computer program one instruction at a time and calls on code to execute the machine operations required by that instruction.

A compiler is software that translates an entire computer program into machine code that is saved for subsequent execution whenever desired. Much work has been done on making both the compilation process and the compiled code as efficient as possible. When a new language is developed, it is usually interpreted at first. If it later becomes popular, a compiler is developed for it, since compilation is more efficient than interpretation.

There is an intermediate approach, which is to compile code not into machine language but into an intermediate language (called a virtual machine) that is close enough to machine language that it is efficient to interpret, though not so close that it is tied to the machine language of a particular computer. It is this approach that provides the Java language with its computer platform independence via the JVM.

Security and Information Assurance

Security and information assurance refers to policy and technical elements that protect information systems by ensuring their availability, integrity, authentication, and appropriate levels of confidentiality. Information security concepts occur in many areas of computer science, including operating systems, computer networks, databases, and software.

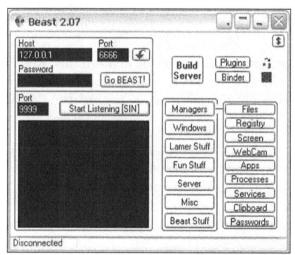

Malware: Trojan Screenshot of Beast, a Remote Administration
Tool, or trojan, software program.

Operating system security involves protection from outside attacks by malicious software that interferes with the system's completion of ordinary tasks. Network security provides protection of entire networks from attacks by outsiders. Information in databases is especially vulnerable to being stolen, destroyed, or modified maliciously when the database server is accessible to multiple users over a network. The first line of defense is to allow access to a computer only to authorized users by authenticating those users by a password or similar mechanism.

However, clever programmers (known as hackers) have learned how to evade such mechanisms by designing computer viruses, programs that replicate themselves, spread among the computers in a network, and "infect" systems by destroying resident files and applications. Data can be stolen by using devices such as "Trojan horses," programs that carry out a useful task but also contain hidden malicious code, or simply by eavesdropping on network communications. The need to protect sensitive data (e.g., to protect national security or individual privacy) has led to advances in cryptography and the development of encryption standards that provide a high level of confidence that the data is safe from decoding by even the most clever attacks.

Software Engineering

Software engineering is the discipline concerned with the application of theory, knowledge, and practice to building reliable software systems that satisfy the computing requirements of customers and users. It is applicable to small-, medium-, and large-scale computing systems and organizations. Software engineering uses engineering methods, processes, techniques, and measurements. Software development, whether done by an individual or a team, requires choosing the most appropriate tools, methods, and approaches for a given environment.

Software is becoming an ever larger part of the computer system and has become complicated to develop, often requiring teams of programmers and years of effort. Thus, the development of a large piece of software can be viewed as an engineering task to be approached with care and attention to cost, reliability, and maintainability of the final product. The software engineering process is usually described as consisting of several phases, called a life cycle, variously defined but generally consisting of requirements development, analysis and specification, design, construction, validation, deployment, operation, and maintenance.

Concern over the high failure rate of software projects has led to the development of nontraditional software development processes. Notable among these is the agile software process, which includes rapid development and involves the client as an active and critical member of the team. Agile development has been effectively used in the development of open-source software, which is different from proprietary software because users are free to download and modify it to fit their particular application needs. Particularly successful open-source software products include the Linux operating system, the Firefox Web browser, and the Apache Open Office word processing/spreadsheet/presentation suite.

Regardless of the development methodology chosen, the software development process is expensive and time-consuming. Since the early 1980s, increasingly sophisticated tools have been built to aid the software developer and to automate the development process as much as possible. Such computer-aided software engineering (CASE) tools span a wide range of types, from those that carry out the task of routine coding when given an appropriately detailed design in some specified language to those that incorporate an expert system to enforce design rules and eliminate software defects prior to the coding phase.

As the size and complexity of software has grown, the concept of reuse has become increasingly important in software engineering, since it is clear that extensive new software cannot be created cheaply and rapidly without incorporating existing program modules (subroutines, or pieces of computer code). One of the attractive aspects of object-oriented programming is that code written in terms of objects is readily reused. As with other aspects of computer systems, reliability (usually rather vaguely defined as the likelihood of a system to operate correctly over a reasonably long period of time) is a key goal of the finished software product.

Sophisticated techniques for testing software have also been designed. For example, unit testing is a strategy for testing every individual module of a software product independently before the modules are combined into a whole and tested using "integration testing" techniques.

2

Computer Architecture

The functioning, programming and implementation of a computer system is determined by a certain set of rules and methods which is termed as computer architecture. A few of its types are Von Neumann architecture, instruction set architecture, microarchitecture, etc. This chapter discusses in detail all these types of computer architecture.

Computer architecture is a specification describing how hardware and software technologies interact to create a computer platform or system. When we think of the word architecture, we think of building a house or a building. Keeping that same principle in mind, computer architecture involves building a computer and all that goes into a computer system. Computer architecture consists of three main categories:

- System design – This includes all the hardware parts, such as CPU, data processors, multi-processors, memory controllers and direct memory access. This part is the actual computer system.

- Instruction set architecture – The includes the CPU's functions and capabilities, the CPU's programming language, data formats, processor register types and instructions used by computer programmers. This part is the software that makes it run, such as Windows or Photoshop or similar programs.

- Microarchitecture – This defines the data processing and storage element or data paths and how they should be implemented into the instruction set architecture. These might include DVD storage devices or similar devices.

All these parts go together in a certain order and must be developed in a pattern so they will function correctly.

The main components in a typical computer system are the processor, memory, input/output devices, and the communication channels that connect them.

The processor is the workhorse of the system; it is the component that executes a program by performing arithmetic and logical operations on data. It is the only component that creates new information by combining or modifying current information. In a typical system there will be only one processor, known at the central processing unit, or CPU. Modern high performance systems, for example vector processors and parallel processors, often have more than one processor. Systems with only one processor are serial processors, or, especially among computational scientists, scalar processors.

Memory is a passive component that simply stores information until it is requested by another part of the system. During normal operations it feeds instructions and data to the processor, and at other times it is the source or destination of data transferred by I/O devices. Information in a memory is accessed by its address. In programming language terms, one can view memory as a one-dimensional array M. A processor's request to the memory might be "send the instruction at location M" or a disk controller's request might be "store the following block of data in locations M through M."

Input/output (I/O) devices transfer information without altering it between the external world and one or more internal components. I/O devices can be secondary memories, for example disks and tapes, or devices used to communicate directly with users, such as video displays, keyboards, and mouses.

The communication channels that tie the system together can either be simple links that connect two devices or more complex switches that interconnect several components and allow any two of them to communicate at a given point in time. When a switch is configured to allow two devices to exchange information, all other devices that rely on the switch are blocked, i.e. they must wait until the switch can be reconfigured.

A common convention used in drawing simple "stick figures" of computer systems is the PMS notation. In a PMS diagram each major component is represented by a single letter, e.g. P for processor, M for memory, or S for switch. A subscript on a letter distinguished different types of components, e.g. M_p for primary memory and M_c for cache memory. Lines connecting two components represent links, and lines connecting more than two components represent a switch. Although they are primitive and might appear at first glance to be too simple, PMS diagrams convey quite a bit of information and have several advantages, not the least of which is they are independent of any particular manufacturer's notations.

As an example of a PMS diagram and a relatively simple computer architecture. The first thing one notices is a single communication channel, known as the bus, that connects all the other major components. Since the bus is a switch, only two of these components can communicate at any time. When the switch is configured for an I/O transfer, for example from main memory (M_p) to the disk (via K*disk*), the processor is unable to fetch data or instructions and remains idle. This organization is typical of personal computers and low end workstations; mainframes, supercomputers, and other high performance systems have much richer (and thus more expensive) structures for connecting I/O devices to internal main memory that allow the processor to keep working at full speed during I/O operations.

VON NEUMANN ARCHITECTURE

The von Neumann architecture—also known as the von Neumann model or Princeton architecture—is a computer architecture based on a 1945 description by the mathematician and physicist John von Neumann and others in the *First Draft of a Report on the EDVAC*. That document describes a design architecture for an electronic digital computer with these components:

- A processing unit that contains an arithmetic logic unit and processor registers.

- A control unit that contains an instruction register and program counter.

- Memory that stores data and instructions.

- External mass storage.

- Input and output mechanisms.

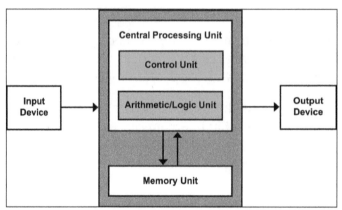

Von Neumann architecture scheme.

The term "von Neumann architecture" has evolved to mean any stored-program computer in which an instruction fetch and a data operation cannot occur at the same time because they share a common bus. This is referred to as the von Neumann bottleneck and often limits the performance of the system.

The design of a von Neumann architecture machine is simpler than a Harvard architecture machine—which is also a stored-program system but has one dedicated set of address and data buses for reading and writing to memory, and another set of address and data buses to fetch instructions.

A stored-program digital computer keeps both program instructions and data in read-write, random-access memory (RAM). Stored-program computers were an advancement over the program-controlled computers of the 1940s, such as the Colossus and the ENIAC. Those were programmed by setting switches and inserting patch cables to route data and control signals between various functional units. The vast majority of modern computers use the same memory for both data and program instructions. The von Neumann vs. Harvard distinction applies to the cache architecture, not the main memory (split cache architecture).

Capabilities

On a large scale, the ability to treat instructions as data is what makes assemblers, compilers, linkers, loaders, and other automated programming tools possible. It makes "programs that write programs" possible. This has made a sophisticated self-hosting computing ecosystem flourish around von Neumann architecture machines.

Some high level languages leverage the von Neumann architecture by providing an abstract, machine-independent way to manipulate executable code at runtime (e.g., LISP), or by using runtime information to tune just-in-time compilation (e.g. languages hosted on the Java virtual machine, or languages embedded in web browsers).

On a smaller scale, some repetitive operations such as BITBLT or pixel and vertex shaders can be accelerated on general purpose processors with just-in-time compilation techniques. This is one use of self-modifying code that has remained popular.

Early Von Neumann-architecture Computers

The *First Draft* described a design that was used by many universities and corporations to construct their computers. Among these various computers, only ILLIAC and ORDVAC had compatible instruction sets:

- ARC2 (Birkbeck, University of London) officially came online on May 12, 1948.

- Manchester Baby (Victoria University of Manchester, England) made its first successful run of a stored program on June 21, 1948.

- EDSAC (University of Cambridge, England) was the first practical stored-program electronic computer (May 1949).

- Manchester Mark 1 (University of Manchester, England) Developed from the Baby (June 1949).

- CSIRAC (Council for Scientific and Industrial Research) Australia (November 1949).

- EDVAC (Ballistic Research Laboratory, Computing Laboratory at Aberdeen Proving Ground 1951).

- ORDVAC (U-Illinois) at Aberdeen Proving Ground, Maryland (completed November 1951).

- IAS machine at Princeton University (January 1952).

- MANIAC I at Los Alamos Scientific Laboratory (March 1952).

- ILLIAC at the University of Illinois, (September 1952).

- BESM-1 in Moscow (1952).

- AVIDAC at Argonne National Laboratory (1953).

- ORACLE at Oak Ridge National Laboratory (June 1953).

- BESK in Stockholm (1953).

- JOHNNIAC at RAND Corporation (January 1954).

- DASK in Denmark (1955).

- WEIZAC at the Weizmann Institute of Science in Rehovot, Israel (1955).

- PERM in Munich (1956).

- SILLIAC in Sydney (1956).

Early Stored-program Computers

The date information in the following chronology is difficult to put into proper order. Some dates are for first running a test program, some dates are the first time the computer was demonstrated or completed, and some dates are for the first delivery or installation.

- The IBM SSEC had the ability to treat instructions as data, and was publicly demonstrated on January 27, 1948. This ability was claimed in a US patent. However it was partially electromechanical, not fully electronic. In practice, instructions were read from paper tape due to its limited memory.

- The ARC2 developed by Andrew Booth and Kathleen Booth at Birkbeck, University of London officially came online on May 12, 1948. It featured the first rotating drum storage device.

- The Manchester Baby was the first fully electronic computer to run a stored program. It ran a factoring program for 52 minutes on June 21, 1948, after running a simple division program and a program to show that two numbers were relatively prime.

- The ENIAC was modified to run as a primitive read-only stored-program computer (using the Function Tables for program ROM) and was demonstrated as such on September 16, 1948, running a program by Adele Goldstine for von Neumann.

- The BINAC ran some test programs in February, March, and April 1949, although was not completed until September 1949.

- The Manchester Mark 1 developed from the Baby project. An intermediate version of the Mark 1 was available to run programs in April 1949, but was not completed until October 1949.

- The EDSAC ran its first program on May 6, 1949.

- The EDVAC was delivered in August 1949, but it had problems that kept it from being put into regular operation until 1951.

- The CSIR Mk I ran its first program in November 1949.

- The SEAC was demonstrated in April 1950.

- The Pilot ACE ran its first program on May 10, 1950 and was demonstrated in December 1950.

- The SWAC was completed in July 1950.

- The Whirlwind was completed in December 1950 and was in actual use in April 1951.

- The first ERA Atlas (later the commercial ERA 1101/UNIVAC 1101) was installed in December 1950.

Evolution

Through the decades of the 1960s and 1970s computers generally became both smaller and faster, which led to evolutions in their architecture. For example, memory-mapped I/O lets input and output devices be treated the same as memory. A single system bus could be used to provide a modular system with lower cost. This is sometimes called a "streamlining" of the architecture. In subsequent decades, simple microcontrollers would sometimes omit features of the model to lower cost and size. Larger computers added features for higher performance.

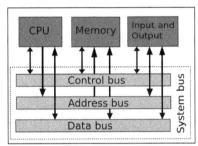

Single system bus evolution of the architecture.

Design Limitations

Von Neumann Bottleneck

The shared bus between the program memory and data memory leads to the *von Neumann bottleneck*, the limited throughput (data transfer rate) between the central processing unit (CPU) and memory compared to the amount of memory. Because the single bus can only access one of the two classes of memory at a time, throughput is lower than the rate at which the CPU can work. This seriously limits the effective processing speed when the CPU is required to perform minimal processing on large amounts of data. The CPU is continually forced to wait for needed data to move to or from memory. Since CPU speed and memory size have increased much faster than the throughput between them, the bottleneck has become more of a problem, a problem whose severity increases with every new generation of CPU.

The von Neumann bottleneck was described by John Backus in his 1977 ACM Turing Award lecture. According to Backus:

> "Surely there must be a less primitive way of making big changes in the store than by pushing vast numbers of words back and forth through the von Neumann bottleneck. Not only is this tube a literal bottleneck for the data traffic of a problem, but, more importantly, it is an intellectual bottleneck that has kept us tied to word-at-a-time thinking instead of encouraging us to think in terms of the larger conceptual units of the task at hand. Thus programming is basically planning and detailing the enormous traffic of words through the von Neumann bottleneck, and much of that traffic concerns not significant data itself, but where to find it".

Mitigations

There are several known methods for mitigating the Von Neumann performance bottleneck. For example, the following all can improve performance:

- Providing a cache between the CPU and the main memory.

- Providing separate caches or separate access paths for data and instructions (the so-called Modified Harvard architecture).

- Using branch predictor algorithms and logic.

- Providing a limited CPU stack or other on-chip scratchpad memory to reduce memory access.

- Implementing the CPU and the memory hierarchy as a system on chip, providing greater locality of reference and thus reducing latency and increasing throughput between processor registers and main memory.

The problem can also be sidestepped somewhat by using parallel computing, using for example the non-uniform memory access (NUMA) architecture—this approach is commonly employed by supercomputers. It is less clear whether the *intellectual bottleneck* that Backus criticized has changed much since 1977. Backus's proposed solution has not had a major influence. Modern functional programming and object-oriented programming are much less geared towards "pushing vast numbers of words back and forth" than earlier languages like FORTRAN were, but internally, that is still what computers spend much of their time doing, even highly parallel supercomputers.

As of 1996, a database benchmark study found that three out of four CPU cycles were spent waiting for memory. Researchers expect that increasing the number of simultaneous instruction streams with multithreading or single-chip multiprocessing will make this bottleneck even worse. In the context of multi-core processors, additional overhead is required to maintain cache coherence between processors and threads.

Self-modifying Code

Aside from the von Neumann bottleneck, program modifications can be quite harmful, either by accident or design. In some simple stored-program computer designs, a malfunctioning program can damage itself, other programs, or the operating system, possibly leading to a computer crash. Memory protection and other forms of access control can usually protect against both accidental and malicious program modification.

INSTRUCTION SET ARCHITECTURE

An instruction set architecture (ISA) is an abstract model of a computer. It is also referred to as architecture or computer architecture. A realization of an ISA is called an *implementation*. An ISA permits multiple implementations that may vary in performance, physical size, and monetary cost (among other things); because the ISA serves as the interface between software and hardware. Software that has been written for an ISA can run on different implementations of the same ISA. This has enabled binary compatibility between different generations of computers to be easily achieved, and the development of computer families. Both of these developments have helped to lower the cost of computers and to increase their applicability. For these reasons, the ISA is one of the most important abstractions in computing today.

An ISA defines everything a machine language programmer needs to know in order to program a computer. What an ISA defines differs between ISAs; in general, ISAs define the supported data types, what state there is (such as the main memory and registers) and their semantics (such as the memory consistency and addressing modes), the *instruction set* (the set of machine instructions that comprises a computer's machine language), and the input/output model.

An instruction set architecture is distinguished from a microarchitecture, which is the set of processor design techniques used, in a particular processor, to implement the instruction set. Processors with different microarchitectures can share a common instruction set. For example, the Intel Pentium and the Advanced Micro Devices Athlon implement nearly identical versions of the x86 instruction set, but have radically different internal designs.

The concept of an *architecture*, distinct from the design of a specific machine, was developed by Fred Brooks at IBM during the design phase of System/360.

Prior to NPL [System/360], the company's computer designers had been free to honor cost objectives not only by selecting technologies but also by fashioning functional and architectural refinements. The SPREAD compatibility objective, in contrast, postulated a single architecture for a series of five processors spanning a wide range of cost and performance. None of the five engineering design teams could count on being able to bring about adjustments in architectural specifications as a way of easing difficulties in achieving cost and performance objectives.

Some virtual machines that support bytecode as their ISA such as Smalltalk, the Java virtual machine, and Microsoft's Common Language Runtime, implement this by translating the bytecode for commonly used code paths into native machine code. In addition, these virtual machines execute less frequently used code paths by interpretation. Transmeta implemented the x86 instruction set atop VLIW processors in this fashion.

Classification of ISAs

An ISA may be classified in a number of different ways. A common classification is by architectural *complexity*. A complex instruction set computer (CISC) has many specialized instructions, some of which may only be rarely used in practical programs. A reduced instruction set computer (RISC) simplifies the processor by efficiently implementing only the instructions that are frequently used in programs, while the less common operations are implemented as subroutines, having their resulting additional processor execution time offset by infrequent use.

Other types include very long instruction word (VLIW) architectures, and the closely related *long instruction word* (LIW) and *explicitly parallel instruction computing* (EPIC) architectures. These architectures seek to exploit instruction-level parallelism with less hardware than RISC and CISC by making the compiler responsible for instruction issue and scheduling.

Architectures with even less complexity have been studied, such as the minimal instruction set computer (MISC) and one instruction set computer (OISC). These are theoretically important types, but have not been commercialized.

Instructions

Machine language is built up from discrete *statements* or *instructions*. On the processing architecture, a given instruction may specify:

- Particular registers (for arithmetic, addressing, or control functions).
- Particular memory locations (or offsets to them).
- Particular addressing modes (used to interpret the operands).

More complex operations are built up by combining these simple instructions, which are executed sequentially, or as otherwise directed by control flow instructions.

Instruction Types

Examples of operations common to many instruction sets include:

Data Handling and Memory Operations

- Set a register to a fixed constant value.
- Copy data from a memory location to a register, or vice versa (a machine instruction is often called move; however, the term is misleading). Used to store the contents of a register, the result of a computation, or to retrieve stored data to perform a computation on it later. Often called load and store operations.
- Read and write data from hardware devices.

Arithmetic and Logic Operations

- Add, subtract, multiply, or divide the values of two registers, placing the result in a register, possibly setting one or more condition codes in a status register.
- Increment, decrement in some ISAs, saving operand fetch in trivial cases.
- Perform bitwise operations, e.g., taking the conjunction and disjunction of corresponding bits in a pair of registers, taking the negation of each bit in a register.
- Compare two values in registers (for example, to see if one is less, or if they are equal).
- Floating-point instructions for arithmetic on floating-point numbers.

Control Flow Operations

- Branch to another location in the program and execute instructions there.
- Conditionally branch to another location if a certain condition holds.
- Indirectly branch to another location.
- Call another block of code, while saving the location of the next instruction as a point to return to.

Coprocessor Instructions

- Load/store data to and from a coprocessor or exchanging with CPU registers.
- Perform coprocessor operations.

Complex Instructions

Processors may include "complex" instructions in their instruction set. A single "complex" instruction does something that may take many instructions on other computers. Such instructions are typified by instructions that take multiple steps, control multiple functional units, or otherwise appear on a larger scale than the bulk of simple instructions implemented by the given processor. Some examples of "complex" instructions include:

- Transferring multiple registers to or from memory (especially the stack) at once.

- Moving large blocks of memory (e.g. string copy or DMA transfer).

- Complicated integer and floating-point arithmetic (e.g. square root, or transcendental functions such as logarithm, sine, cosine, etc.).

- SIMD instructions, a single instruction performing an operation on many homogeneous values in parallel, possibly in dedicated SIMD registers.

- Performing an atomic test-and-set instruction or other read-modify-write atomic instruction.

- Instructions that perform ALU operations with an operand from memory rather than a register.

Complex instructions are more common in CISC instruction sets than in RISC instruction sets, but RISC instruction sets may include them as well. RISC instruction sets generally do not include ALU operations with memory operands, or instructions to move large blocks of memory, but most RISC instruction sets include SIMD or vector instructions that perform the same arithmetic operation on multiple pieces of data at the same time. SIMD instructions have the ability of manipulating large vectors and matrices in minimal time. SIMD instructions allow easy parallelization of algorithms commonly involved in sound, image, and video processing. Various SIMD implementations have been brought to market under trade names such as MMX, 3DNow!, and AltiVec.

Instruction Encoding

One instruction may have several fields, which identify the logical operation, and may also include source and destination addresses and constant values. This is the MIPS "Add Immediate" instruction, which allows selection of source and destination registers and inclusion of a small constant.

On traditional architectures, an instruction includes an opcode that specifies the operation to perform, such as *add contents of memory to register*—and zero or more operand specifiers, which may specify registers, memory locations, or literal data. The operand specifiers may have addressing modes determining their meaning or may be in fixed fields. In very long instruction word (VLIW) architectures, which include many microcode architectures, multiple simultaneous opcodes and operands are specified in a single instruction.

Some exotic instruction sets do not have an opcode field, such as transport triggered architectures (TTA), only operands.

The Forth virtual machine and other "0-operand" instruction sets lack any operand specifier fields, such as some stack machines including NOSC.

Conditional instructions often have a predicate field—a few bits that encode the specific condition to cause the operation to be performed rather than not performed. For example, a conditional branch instruction will be executed, and the branch taken, if the condition is true, so that execution proceeds to a different part of the program, and not executed, and the branch not taken, if the condition is false, so that execution continues sequentially. Some instruction sets also have conditional moves, so that the move will be executed, and the data stored in the target location, if the condition is true, and not executed, and the target location not modified, if the condition is false. Similarly, IBM z/Architecture has a conditional store instruction. A few instruction sets include a predicate field in every instruction; this is called branch predication.

Number of Operands

Instruction sets may be categorized by the maximum number of operands *explicitly* specified in instructions.

(In the examples that follow, *a*, *b*, and *c* are (direct or calculated) addresses referring to memory cells, while *reg1* and so on refer to machine registers.)

```
C = A+B
```

- 0-operand (*zero-address machines*), so called stack machines: All arithmetic operations take place using the top one or two positions on the stack: `push a, push b, add, pop c`.

  - `C = A+B` needs *four instructions*. For stack machines, the terms "0-operand" and "zero-address" apply to arithmetic instructions, but not to all instructions, as 1-operand push and pop instructions are used to access memory.

- 1-operand (*one-address machines*), so called accumulator machines, include early computers and many small microcontrollers: most instructions specify a single right operand (that is, constant, a register, or a memory location), with the implicit accumulator as the left operand (and the destination if there is one): `load a, add b, store c`.

  - `C = A+B` needs *three instructions*.

- 2-operand — many CISC and RISC machines fall under this category:

  - CISC — `move` A to C; then `add` B to C.

    - `C = A+B` needs *two instructions*. This effectively 'stores' the result without an explicit *store* instruction.

  - CISC — Often machines are limited to one memory operand per instruction: `load a, reg1; add b, reg1; store reg1, c;` This requires a load/store pair for any memory movement regardless of whether the `add` result is an augmentation stored to a different place, as in `C = A+B`, or the same memory location: `A = A+B`.

- ◦ `C = A+B` needs *three instructions*.

- ◦ RISC — Requiring explicit memory loads, the instructions would be: `load a,reg1; load b,reg2; add reg1,reg2; store reg2,c`.

- ◦ `C = A+B` needs *four instructions*.

- 3-operand, allowing better reuse of data:

  - ◦ CISC — It becomes either a single instruction: `add a,b,c`

  - ◦ `C = A+B` needs *one instruction*.

  - ◦ CISC — Or, on machines limited to two memory operands per instruction, `move a,reg1; add reg1,b,c;`

  - ◦ `C = A+B` needs *two instructions*.

  - ◦ RISC — arithmetic instructions use registers only, so explicit 2-operand load/store instructions are needed: `load a,reg1; load b,reg2; add reg1+reg2->reg3; store reg3,c;`

  - ◦ `C = A+B` needs *four instructions*.

  - ◦ Unlike 2-operand or 1-operand, this leaves all three values a, b, and c in registers available for further reuse.

- More Operands—some CISC machines permit a variety of addressing modes that allow more than 3 operands (registers or memory accesses), such as the VAX "POLY" polynomial evaluation instruction.

Due to the large number of bits needed to encode the three registers of a 3-operand instruction, RISC architectures that have 16-bit instructions are invariably 2-operand designs, such as the Atmel AVR, TI MSP430, and some versions of ARM Thumb. RISC architectures that have 32-bit instructions are usually 3-operand designs, such as the ARM, AVR32, MIPS, Power ISA, and SPARC architectures.

Each instruction specifies some number of operands (registers, memory locations, or immediate values) *explicitly*. Some instructions give one or both operands implicitly, such as by being stored on top of the stack or in an implicit register. If some of the operands are given implicitly, fewer operands need be specified in the instruction. When a "destination operand" explicitly specifies the destination, an additional operand must be supplied. Consequently, the number of operands encoded in an instruction may differ from the mathematically necessary number of arguments for a logical or arithmetic operation (the arity). Operands are either encoded in the "opcode" representation of the instruction, or else are given as values or addresses following the instruction.

Register Pressure

Register pressure measures the availability of free registers at any point in time during the program execution. Register pressure is high when a large number of the available registers are in use; thus, the higher the register pressure, the more often the register contents must be spilled into memory. Increasing the number of registers in an architecture decreases register pressure but increases the cost.

While embedded instruction sets such as Thumb suffer from extremely high register pressure because they have small register sets, general-purpose RISC ISAs like MIPS and Alpha enjoy low register pressure. CISC ISAs like x86-64 offer low register pressure despite having smaller register sets. This is due to the many addressing modes and optimizations (such as sub-register addressing, memory operands in ALU instructions, absolute addressing, PC-relative addressing, and register-to-register spills) that CISC ISAs offer.

Instruction Length

The size or length of an instruction varies widely, from as little as four bits in some microcontrollers to many hundreds of bits in some VLIW systems. Processors used in personal computers, mainframes, and supercomputers have instruction sizes between 8 and 64 bits. The longest possible instruction on x86 is 15 bytes (120 bits). Within an instruction set, different instructions may have different lengths. In some architectures, notably most reduced instruction set computers (RISC), instructions are a fixed length, typically corresponding with that architecture's word size. In other architectures, instructions have variable length, typically integral multiples of a byte or a halfword. Some, such as the ARM with *Thumb-extension* have *mixed* variable encoding, that is two fixed, usually 32-bit and 16-bit encodings, where instructions cannot be mixed freely but must be switched between on a branch (or exception boundary in ARMv8).

A RISC instruction set normally has a fixed instruction length (often 4 bytes = 32 bits), whereas a typical CISC instruction set may have instructions of widely varying length (1 to 15 bytes for x86). Fixed-length instructions are less complicated to handle than variable-length instructions for several reasons (not having to check whether an instruction straddles a cache line or virtual memory page boundary, for instance), and are therefore somewhat easier to optimize for speed.

Code Density

In early computers, memory was expensive, so minimizing the size of a program to make sure it would fit in the limited memory was often central. Thus the combined size of all the instructions needed to perform a particular task, the *code density*, was an important characteristic of any instruction set. Computers with high code density often have complex instructions for procedure entry, parameterized returns, loops, etc. (therefore retroactively named *Complex Instruction Set Computers*, CISC). However, more typical, or frequent, "CISC" instructions merely combine a basic ALU operation, such as "add", with the access of one or more operands in memory (using addressing modes such as direct, indirect, indexed, etc.). Certain architectures may allow two or three operands (including the result) directly in memory or may be able to perform functions such as automatic pointer increment, etc. Software-implemented instruction sets may have even more complex and powerful instructions.

Reduced instruction-set computers, RISC, were first widely implemented during a period of rapidly growing memory subsystems. They sacrifice code density to simplify implementation circuitry, and try to increase performance via higher clock frequencies and more registers. A single RISC instruction typically performs only a single operation, such as an "add" of registers or a "load" from a memory location into a register. A RISC instruction set normally has a fixed instruction length, whereas a typical CISC instruction set has instructions of widely varying length. However, as RISC computers normally require more and often longer instructions to implement a given task, they inherently make less optimal use of bus bandwidth and cache memories.

Certain embedded RISC ISAs like Thumb and AVR32 typically exhibit very high density owing to a technique called code compression. This technique packs two 16-bit instructions into one 32-bit instruction, which is then unpacked at the decode stage and executed as two instructions.

Minimal instruction set computers (MISC) are a form of stack machine, where there are few separate instructions (16-64), so that multiple instructions can be fit into a single machine word. These types of cores often take little silicon to implement, so they can be easily realized in an FPGA or in a multi-core form. The code density of MISC is similar to the code density of RISC; the increased instruction density is offset by requiring more of the primitive instructions to do a task.

There has been research into executable compression as a mechanism for improving code density. The mathematics of Kolmogorov complexity describes the challenges and limits of this.

Representation

The instructions constituting a program are rarely specified using their internal, numeric form (machine code); they may be specified by programmers using an assembly language or, more commonly, may be generated from programming languages by compilers.

Design

The design of instruction sets is a complex issue. There were two stages in history for the microprocessor. The first was the CISC (Complex Instruction Set Computer), which had many different instructions. In the 1970s, however, places like IBM did research and found that many instructions in the set could be eliminated. The result was the RISC (Reduced Instruction Set Computer), an architecture that uses a smaller set of instructions. A simpler instruction set may offer the potential for higher speeds, reduced processor size, and reduced power consumption. However, a more complex set may optimize common operations, improve memory and cache efficiency, or simplify programming.

Some instruction set designers reserve one or more opcodes for some kind of system call or software interrupt. For example, MOS Technology 6502 uses 00_H, Zilog Z80 uses the eight codes C7, CF, D7, DF, E7, EF, F7, FF_H while Motorola 68000 use codes in the range $A000..AFFF_H$.

Fast virtual machines are much easier to implement if an instruction set meets the Popek and Goldberg virtualization requirements.

The NOP slide used in immunity-aware programming is much easier to implement if the "unprogrammed" state of the memory is interpreted as a NOP.

On systems with multiple processors, non-blocking synchronization algorithms are much easier to implement if the instruction set includes support for something such as "fetch-and-add", "load-link/store-conditional" (LL/SC), or "atomic compare-and-swap".

Instruction Set Implementation

Any given instruction set can be implemented in a variety of ways. All ways of implementing a particular instruction set provide the same programming model, and all implementations of that instruction set are able to run the same executables. The various ways of implementing an instruction set give different tradeoffs between cost, performance, power consumption, size, etc.

When designing the microarchitecture of a processor, engineers use blocks of "hard-wired" electronic circuitry (often designed separately) such as adders, multiplexers, counters, registers, ALUs, etc. Some kind of register transfer language is then often used to describe the decoding and sequencing of each instruction of an ISA using this physical microarchitecture. There are two basic ways to build a control unit to implement this description (although many designs use middle ways or compromises):

1. Some computer designs "hardwire" the complete instruction set decoding and sequencing (just like the rest of the microarchitecture).

2. Other designs employ microcode routines or tables (or both) to do this—typically as on-chip ROMs or PLAs or both (although separate RAMs and ROMs have been used historically). The Western Digital MCP-1600 is an older example, using a dedicated, separate ROM for microcode.

Some designs use a combination of hardwired design and microcode for the control unit.

Some CPU designs use a writable control store—they compile the instruction set to a writable RAM or flash inside the CPU (such as the Rekursiv processor and the Imsys Cjip), or an FPGA (reconfigurable computing).

An ISA can also be emulated in software by an interpreter. Naturally, due to the interpretation overhead, this is slower than directly running programs on the emulated hardware, unless the hardware running the emulator is an order of magnitude faster. Today, it is common practice for vendors of new ISAs or microarchitectures to make software emulators available to software developers before the hardware implementation is ready.

Often the details of the implementation have a strong influence on the particular instructions selected for the instruction set. For example, many implementations of the instruction pipeline only allow a single memory load or memory store per instruction, leading to a load-store architecture (RISC). For another example, some early ways of implementing the instruction pipeline led to a delay slot.

The demands of high-speed digital signal processing have pushed in the opposite direction—forcing instructions to be implemented in a particular way. For example, to perform digital filters fast enough, the MAC instruction in a typical digital signal processor (DSP) must use a kind of Harvard architecture that can fetch an instruction and two data words simultaneously, and it requires a single-cycle multiply–accumulate multiplier.

MICROARCHITECTURE

In computer engineering, microarchitecture, also called computer organization and sometimes abbreviated as *μarch* or *uarch*, is the way a given instruction set architecture (ISA) is implemented in a particular processor. A given ISA may be implemented with different microarchitectures; implementations may vary due to different goals of a given design or due to shifts in technology.

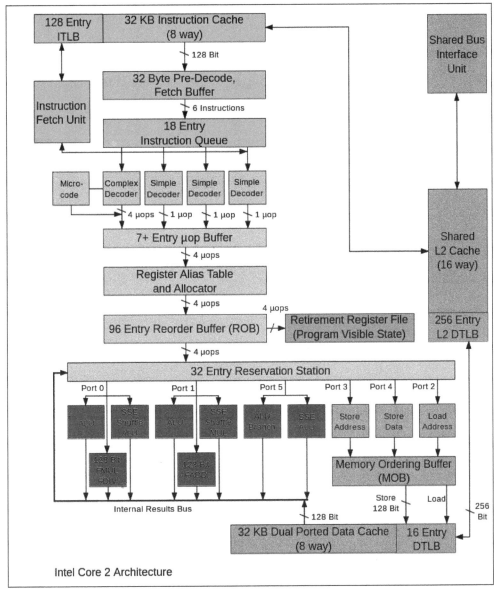

Intel Core microarchitecture.

Computer architecture is the combination of microarchitecture and instruction set architecture.

Relation to Instruction Set Architecture

The ISA is roughly the same as the programming model of a processor as seen by an assembly language programmer or compiler writer. The ISA includes the execution model, processor registers, address and data formats among other things. The microarchitecture includes the constituent parts of the processor and how these interconnect and interoperate to implement the ISA.

The microarchitecture of a machine is usually represented as (more or less detailed) diagrams that describe the interconnections of the various microarchitectural elements of the machine, which may be anything from single gates and registers, to complete arithmetic logic units (ALUs) and even larger elements. These diagrams generally separate the datapath (where data is placed) and the control path (which can be said to steer the data).

The person designing a system usually draws the specific microarchitecture as a kind of data flow diagram. Like a block diagram, the microarchitecture diagram shows microarchitectural elements such as the arithmetic and logic unit and the register file as a single schematic symbol. Typically, the diagram connects those elements with arrows, thick lines and thin lines to distinguish between three-state buses (which require a three-state buffer for each device that drives the bus), unidirectional buses (always driven by a single source, such as the way the address bus on simpler computers is always driven by the memory address register), and individual control lines. Very simple computers have a single data bus organization – they have a single three-state bus. The diagram of more complex computers usually shows multiple three-state buses, which help the machine do more operations simultaneously.

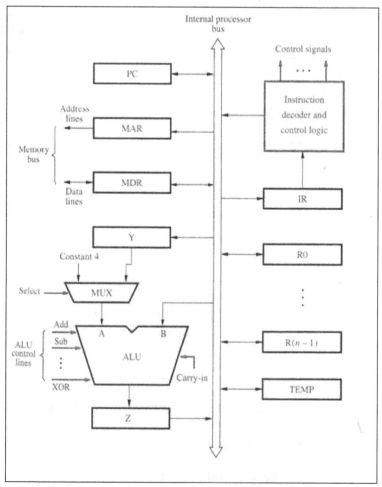

A microarchitecture organized around a single bus.

Each microarchitectural element is in turn represented by a schematic describing the interconnections of logic gates used to implement it. Each logic gate is in turn represented by a circuit diagram describing the connections of the transistors used to implement it in some particular logic family. Machines with different microarchitectures may have the same instruction set architecture, and thus be capable of executing the same programs. New microarchitectures and circuitry solutions, along with advances in semiconductor manufacturing, are what allows newer generations of processors to achieve higher performance while using the same ISA.

In principle, a single microarchitecture could execute several different ISAs with only minor changes to the microcode.

Aspects of Microarchitecture

The pipelined datapath is the most commonly used datapath design in microarchitecture today. This technique is used in most modern microprocessors, microcontrollers, and DSPs. The pipelined architecture allows multiple instructions to overlap in execution, much like an assembly line. The pipeline includes several different stages which are fundamental in microarchitecture designs. Some of these stages include instruction fetch, instruction decode, execute, and write back. Some architectures include other stages such as memory access. The design of pipelines is one of the central microarchitectural tasks.

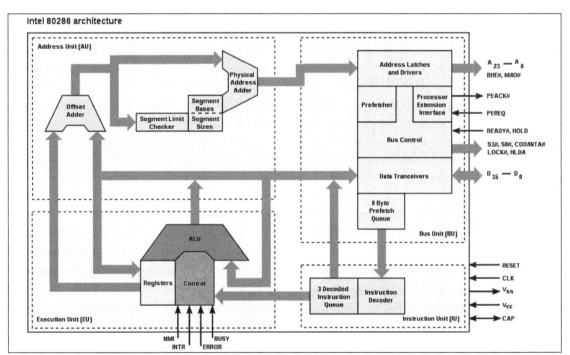

Intel 80286 microarchitecture.

Execution units are also essential to microarchitecture. Execution units include arithmetic logic units (ALU), floating point units (FPU), load/store units, branch prediction, and SIMD. These units perform the operations or calculations of the processor. The choice of the number of execution units, their latency and throughput is a central microarchitectural design task. The size, latency, throughput and connectivity of memories within the system are also microarchitectural decisions.

System-level design decisions such as whether or not to include peripherals, such as memory controllers, can be considered part of the microarchitectural design process. This includes decisions on the performance-level and connectivity of these peripherals.

Unlike architectural design, where achieving a specific performance level is the main goal, microarchitectural design pays closer attention to other constraints. Since microarchitecture design decisions directly affect what goes into a system, attention must be paid to issues such as chip area/cost, power consumption, logic complexity, ease of connectivity, manufacturability, ease of debugging, and testability.

Microarchitectural Concepts

Instruction Cycles

In general, all CPUs, single-chip microprocessors or multi-chip implementations run programs by performing the following steps:

1. Read an instruction and decode it.
2. Find any associated data that is needed to process the instruction.
3. Process the instruction.
4. Write the results out.

The instruction cycle is repeated continuously until the power is turned off.

Multicycle Microarchitecture

Historically, the earliest computers were multicycle designs. The smallest, least-expensive computers often still use this technique. Multicycle architectures often use the least total number of logic elements and reasonable amounts of power. They can be designed to have deterministic timing and high reliability. In particular, they have no pipeline to stall when taking conditional branches or interrupts. However, other microarchitectures often perform more instructions per unit time, using the same logic family. When discussing "improved performance," an improvement is often relative to a multicycle design.

In a multicycle computer, the computer does the four steps in sequence, over several cycles of the clock. Some designs can perform the sequence in two clock cycles by completing successive stages on alternate clock edges, possibly with longer operations occurring outside the main cycle. For example, stage one on the rising edge of the first cycle, stage two on the falling edge of the first cycle, etc.

In the control logic, the combination of cycle counter, cycle state (high or low) and the bits of the instruction decode register determine exactly what each part of the computer should be doing. To design the control logic, one can create a table of bits describing the control signals to each part of the computer in each cycle of each instruction. Then, this logic table can be tested in a software simulation running test code. If the logic table is placed in a memory and used to actually run a real computer, it is called a microprogram. In some computer designs, the logic table is optimized into the form of combinational logic made from logic gates, usually using a computer program that optimizes logic. Early computers used ad-hoc logic design for control until Maurice Wilkes invented this tabular approach and called it microprogramming.

Increasing Execution Speed

Complicating this simple-looking series of steps is the fact that the memory hierarchy, which includes caching, main memory and non-volatile storage like hard disks (where the program instructions and data reside), has always been slower than the processor itself. Step (2) often introduces a lengthy (in CPU terms) delay while the data arrives over the computer bus. A considerable amount of research has been put into designs that avoid these delays as much as possible. Over the years, a central goal was to execute more instructions in parallel, thus increasing the effective execution speed of a program. These efforts introduced complicated logic and circuit structures. Initially, these techniques could only be implemented on expensive mainframes or supercomputers due to the amount of circuitry needed for these techniques. As semiconductor manufacturing progressed, more and more of these techniques could be implemented on a single semiconductor chip.

Instruction Set Choice

Instruction sets have shifted over the years, from originally very simple to sometimes very complex (in various respects). In recent years, load-store architectures, VLIW and EPIC types have been in fashion. Architectures that are dealing with data parallelism include SIMD and Vectors. Some labels used to denote classes of CPU architectures are not particularly descriptive, especially so the CISC label; many early designs retroactively denoted "CISC" are in fact significantly simpler than modern RISC processors (in several respects).

However, the choice of instruction set architecture may greatly affect the complexity of implementing high-performance devices. The prominent strategy, used to develop the first RISC processors, was to simplify instructions to a minimum of individual semantic complexity combined with high encoding regularity and simplicity. Such uniform instructions were easily fetched, decoded and executed in a pipelined fashion and a simple strategy to reduce the number of logic levels in order to reach high operating frequencies; instruction cache-memories compensated for the higher operating frequency and inherently low code density while large register sets were used to factor out as much of the (slow) memory accesses as possible.

Instruction Pipelining

One of the first, and most powerful, techniques to improve performance is the use of instruction pipelining. Early processor designs would carry out all of the steps above for one instruction before moving onto the next. Large portions of the circuitry were left idle at any one step; for instance, the instruction decoding circuitry would be idle during execution and so on.

Pipelining improves performance by allowing a number of instructions to work their way through the processor at the same time. In the same basic example, the processor would start to decode (step 1) a new instruction while the last one was waiting for results. This would allow up to four instructions to be "in flight" at one time, making the processor look four times as fast. Although any one instruction takes just as long to complete (there are still four steps) the CPU as a whole "retires" instructions much faster.

RISC makes pipelines smaller and much easier to construct by cleanly separating each stage of the instruction process and making them take the same amount of time—one cycle. The processor as a whole operates in an assembly line fashion, with instructions coming in one side and results out the other. Due to the reduced complexity of the classic RISC pipeline, the pipelined core and an instruction cache could be placed on the same size die that would otherwise fit the core alone on a CISC design. This was the real reason that RISC was faster. Early designs like the SPARC and MIPS often ran over 10 times as fast as Intel and Motorola CISC solutions at the same clock speed and price.

Pipelines are by no means limited to RISC designs. By 1986 the top-of-the-line VAX implementation (VAX 8800) was a heavily pipelined design, slightly predating the first commercial MIPS and SPARC designs. Most modern CPUs (even embedded CPUs) are now pipelined, and microcoded CPUs with no pipelining are seen only in the most area-constrained embedded processors. Large CISC machines, from the VAX 8800 to the modern Pentium 4 and Athlon, are implemented with both microcode and pipelines. Improvements in pipelining and caching are the two major microarchitectural advances that have enabled processor performance to keep pace with the circuit technology on which they are based.

Cache

It was not long before improvements in chip manufacturing allowed for even more circuitry to be placed on the die, and designers started looking for ways to use it. One of the most common was to add an ever-increasing amount of cache memory on-die. Cache is simply very fast memory. It can be accessed in a few cycles as opposed to many needed to "talk" to main memory. The CPU includes a cache controller which automates reading and writing from the cache. If the data is already in the cache it simply "appears", whereas if it is not the processor is "stalled" while the cache controller reads it in.

RISC designs started adding cache in the mid-to-late 1980s, often only 4 KB in total. This number grew over time, and typical CPUs now have at least 512 KB, while more powerful CPUs come with 1 or 2 or even 4, 6, 8 or 12 MB, organized in multiple levels of a memory hierarchy. Generally speaking, more cache means more performance, due to reduced stalling.

Caches and pipelines were a perfect match for each other. Previously, it didn't make much sense to build a pipeline that could run faster than the access latency of off-chip memory. Using on-chip cache memory instead, meant that a pipeline could run at the speed of the cache access latency, a much smaller length of time. This allowed the operating frequencies of processors to increase at a much faster rate than that of off-chip memory.

Branch Prediction

One barrier to achieving higher performance through instruction-level parallelism stems from pipeline stalls and flushes due to branches. Normally, whether a conditional branch will be taken isn't known until late in the pipeline as conditional branches depend on results coming from a register. From the time that the processor's instruction decoder has figured out that it has encountered a conditional branch instruction to the time that the deciding register value can be read out, the pipeline needs to be stalled for several cycles, or if it's not and the branch is taken, the pipeline needs to be flushed. As clock speeds increase the depth of the pipeline increases with it, and some modern processors may have 20 stages or more. On average, every fifth instruction executed is a branch, so without any intervention, that's a high amount of stalling.

Techniques such as branch prediction and speculative execution are used to lessen these branch penalties. Branch prediction is where the hardware makes educated guesses on whether a particular branch will be taken. In reality one side or the other of the branch will be called much more often than the other. Modern designs have rather complex statistical prediction systems, which watch the results of past branches to predict the future with greater accuracy. The guess allows the hardware to prefetch instructions without waiting for the register read. Speculative execution is a further enhancement in which the code along the predicted path is not just prefetched but also executed before it is known whether the branch should be taken or not. This can yield better performance when the guess is good, with the risk of a huge penalty when the guess is bad because instructions need to be undone.

Superscalar

Even with all of the added complexity and gates needed to support the concepts outlined above, improvements in semiconductor manufacturing soon allowed even more logic gates to be used.

In the outline above the processor processes parts of a single instruction at a time. Computer programs could be executed faster if multiple instructions were processed simultaneously. This is what superscalar processors achieve, by replicating functional units such as ALUs. The replication of functional units was only made possible when the die area of a single-issue processor no longer stretched the limits of what could be reliably manufactured. By the late 1980s, superscalar designs started to enter the market place.

In modern designs it is common to find two load units, one store (many instructions have no results to store), two or more integer math units, two or more floating point units, and often a SIMD unit of some sort. The instruction issue logic grows in complexity by reading in a huge list of instructions from memory and handing them off to the different execution units that are idle at that point. The results are then collected and re-ordered at the end.

Out-of-Order Execution

The addition of caches reduces the frequency or duration of stalls due to waiting for data to be fetched from the memory hierarchy, but does not get rid of these stalls entirely. In early designs a *cache miss* would force the cache controller to stall the processor and wait. Of course there may be some other instruction in the program whose data *is* available in the cache at that point. Out-of-order execution allows that ready instruction to be processed while an older instruction waits on the cache, then re-orders the results to make it appear that everything happened in the programmed order. This technique is also used to avoid other operand dependency stalls, such as an instruction awaiting a result from a long latency floating-point operation or other multi-cycle operations.

Register Renaming

Register renaming refers to a technique used to avoid unnecessary serialized execution of program instructions because of the reuse of the same registers by those instructions. Suppose we have two groups of instruction that will use the same register. One set of instructions is executed first to leave the register to the other set, but if the other set is assigned to a different similar register, both sets of instructions can be executed in parallel (or) in series.

Multiprocessing and Multithreading

Computer architects have become stymied by the growing mismatch in CPU operating frequencies and DRAM access times. None of the techniques that exploited instruction-level parallelism (ILP) within one program could make up for the long stalls that occurred when data had to be fetched from main memory. Additionally, the large transistor counts and high operating frequencies needed for the more advanced ILP techniques required power dissipation levels that could no longer be cheaply cooled. For these reasons, newer generations of computers have started to exploit higher levels of parallelism that exist outside of a single program or program thread.

This trend is sometimes known as *throughput computing*. This idea originated in the mainframe market where online transaction processing emphasized not just the execution speed of one transaction, but the capacity to deal with massive numbers of transactions. With transaction-based applications such as network routing and web-site serving greatly increasing in the last decade, the computer industry has re-emphasized capacity and throughput issues.

One technique of how this parallelism is achieved is through multiprocessing systems, computer systems with multiple CPUs. Once reserved for high-end mainframes and supercomputers, small-scale (2–8) multiprocessors servers have become commonplace for the small business market. For large corporations, large scale (16–256) multiprocessors are common. Even personal computers with multiple CPUs have appeared since the 1990s.

With further transistor size reductions made available with semiconductor technology advances, multi-core CPUs have appeared where multiple CPUs are implemented on the same silicon chip. Initially used in chips targeting embedded markets, where simpler and smaller CPUs would allow multiple instantiations to fit on one piece of silicon. By 2005, semiconductor technology allowed dual high-end desktop CPUs *CMP* chips to be manufactured in volume. Some designs, such as Sun Microsystems' UltraSPARC T1 have reverted to simpler (scalar, in-order) designs in order to fit more processors on one piece of silicon.

Another technique that has become more popular recently is multithreading. In multithreading, when the processor has to fetch data from slow system memory, instead of stalling for the data to arrive, the processor switches to another program or program thread which is ready to execute. Though this does not speed up a particular program/thread, it increases the overall system throughput by reducing the time the CPU is idle.

Conceptually, multithreading is equivalent to a context switch at the operating system level. The difference is that a multithreaded CPU can do a thread switch in one CPU cycle instead of the hundreds or thousands of CPU cycles a context switch normally requires. This is achieved by replicating the state hardware (such as the register file and program counter) for each active thread.

A further enhancement is simultaneous multithreading. This technique allows superscalar CPUs to execute instructions from different programs/threads simultaneously in the same cycle.

SYSTEMS DESIGN

Systems design is the process of defining the architecture, modules, interfaces, and data for a system to satisfy specified requirements. Systems design could be seen as the application of systems theory to product development. There is some overlap with the disciplines of systems analysis, systems architecture and systems engineering.

If the broader topic of product development "blends the perspective of marketing, design, and manufacturing into a single approach to product development," then design is the act of taking the marketing information and creating the design of the product to be manufactured. Systems design is therefore the process of defining and developing systems to satisfy specified requirements of the user.

Until the 1990s, systems design had a crucial and respected role in the data processing industry. In the 1990s, standardization of hardware and software resulted in the ability to build modular systems. The increasing importance of software running on generic platforms has enhanced the discipline of software engineering.

Architectural Design

The architectural design of a system emphasizes the design of the system architecture that describes the structure, behavior and more views of that system and analysis.

Logical Design

The logical design of a system pertains to an abstract representation of the data flows, inputs and outputs of the system. This is often conducted via modelling, using an over-abstract (and sometimes graphical) model of the actual system. In the context of systems, designs are included. Logical design includes entity-relationship diagrams (ER diagrams).

Physical Design

The physical design relates to the actual input and output processes of the system. This is explained in terms of how data is input into a system, how it is verified/authenticated, how it is processed, and how it is displayed. In physical design, the following requirements about the system are decided:

- Input requirement,
- Output requirements,
- Storage requirements,
- Processing requirements,
- System control and backup or recovery.

Put another way, the physical portion of system design can generally be broken down into three sub-tasks:

- User Interface Design
- Data Design
- Process Design

User Interface Design is concerned with how users add information to the system and with how the system presents information back to them. Data Design is concerned with how the data is represented and stored within the system. Finally, Process Design is concerned with how data moves through the system, and with how and where it is validated, secured and transformed as it flows into, through and out of the system. At the end of the system design phase, documentation describing the three sub-tasks is produced and made available for use in the next phase.

Physical design, in this context, does not refer to the tangible physical design of an information system. To use an analogy, a personal computer's physical design involves input via a keyboard, processing within the CPU, and output via a monitor, printer, etc. It would not concern the actual layout of the tangible hardware, which for a PC would be a monitor, CPU, motherboard, hard drive, modems, video/graphics cards, USB slots, etc. It involves a detailed design of a user and a product database structure processor and a control processor. The H/S personal specification is developed for the proposed system.

Related Disciplines

- Benchmarking – Is an effort to evaluate how current systems perform.
- Computer programming and debugging in the software world, or detailed design in the consumer, enterprise or commercial world - specifies the final system components.
- Design – Designers will produce one or more 'models' of what they see a system eventually looking like, with ideas from the analysis section either used or discarded. A document will be produced with a description of the system, but nothing is specific – they might say 'touchscreen' or 'GUI operating system', but not mention any specific brands.
- Requirements analysis – Analyzes the needs of the end users or customers.
- System architecture – Creates a blueprint for the design with the necessary structure and behavior specifications for the hardware, software, people and data resources. In many cases, multiple architectures are evaluated before one is selected.
- System testing – Evaluates the system's actual functionality in relation to expected or intended functionality, including all integration aspects.

Alternative Design Methodologies

Rapid Application Development (RAD)

Rapid application development (RAD) is a methodology in which a system designer produces prototypes for an end-user. The end-user reviews the prototype, and offers feedback on its suitability. This process is repeated until the end-user is satisfied with the final system.

Joint Application Design (JAD)

Joint application design (JAD) is a methodology which evolved from RAD, in which a system designer consults with a group consisting of the following parties:

- Executive sponsor
- System Designer
- Managers of the system

JAD involves a number of stages, in which the group collectively develops an agreed pattern for the design and implementation of the system.

COMPUTER HARDWARE

Computer hardware includes the physical, tangible parts or components of a computer, such as the cabinet, central processing unit, monitor, keyboard, computer data storage, graphics card, sound card, speakers and motherboard. By contrast, software is instructions that can be stored and run by hardware. Hardware is so-termed because it is "hard" or rigid with respect to changes or modifications; whereas software is "soft" because it is easy to update or change. Intermediate between software and hardware is "firmware", which is software that is strongly coupled to the particular hardware of a computer system and thus the most difficult to change but also among the most stable with respect to consistency of interface. The progression from levels of "hardness" to "softness" in computer systems parallels a progression of layers of abstraction in computing.

PDP-11 CPU board.

Hardware is typically directed by the software to execute any command or instruction. A combination of hardware and software forms a usable computing system, although other systems exist with only hardware components.

Types of Computer Systems

Personal Computer

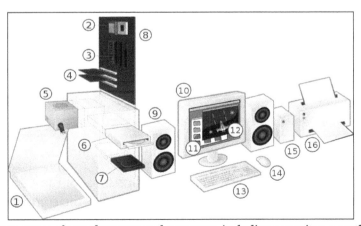

Basic hardware components of a modern personal computer, including a monitor, a motherboard, a CPU, a RAM, two expansion cards, a power supply, an optical disc drive, a hard disk drive, a keyboard and a mouse.

The personal computer, also known as the PC, is one of the most common types of computer due to its versatility and relatively low price. Laptops are generally very similar, although they may use lower-power or reduced size components, thus lower performance.

Inside a custom-built computer: power supply at the bottom has its own cooling fan.

Case

The computer case encloses and holds most of the components of the system. It provides mechanical support and protection for internal elements such as the motherboard, disk drives, and power supplies, and controls and directs the flow of cooling air over internal components. The case is also part of the system to control electromagnetic interference radiated by the computer, and protects internal parts from electrostatic discharge. Large tower cases provide extra internal space for multiple disk drives or other peripherals and usually stand on the floor, while desktop cases provide less expansion room. All-in-one style designs include a video display built into the same case. Portable and laptop computers require cases that provide impact protection for the unit. A current development in laptop computers is a detachable keyboard, which allows the system to be configured as a touch-screen tablet. Hobbyists may decorate the cases with colored lights, paint, or other features, in an activity called case modding.

Power Supply

A power supply unit (PSU) converts alternating current (AC) electric power to low-voltage direct current (DC) power for the internal components of the computer. Laptops are capable of running from a built-in battery, normally for a period of hours.

Motherboard

The motherboard is the main component of a computer. It is a board with integrated circuitry that connects the other parts of the computer including the CPU, the RAM, the disk drives (CD, DVD, hard disk, or any others) as well as any peripherals connected via the ports or the expansion slots.

Components directly attached to or to part of the motherboard include:

- The CPU (central processing unit), which performs most of the calculations which enable a computer to function, and is referred to as the brain of the computer which get a hold of program instruction from RAM,interprets and processes it and then send it backs to computer result so that the releavent components can carry out the instructions. It is usually cooled by a heat sink and fan, or water-cooling system. Most newer CPU include an on-die graphics processing unit (GPU). The clock speed of CPU governs how fast it executes instructions, and is measured in GHz; typical values lie between 1 GHz and 5 GHz. Many modern computers have the option to overclock the CPU which enhances performance at the expense of greater thermal output and thus a need for improved cooling.

- The chipset, which includes the north bridge, mediates communication between the CPU and the other components of the system, including main memory; as well as south bridge, which is connected to the north bridge, and supports auxiliary interfaces and buses; and, finally, a Super I/O chip, connected through the south bridge, which supports the slowest and most legacy components like serial ports, hardware monitoring and fan control.

- Random-access memory (RAM), which stores the code and data that are being actively accessed by the CPU. For example, when a web browser is opened on the computer it takes up memory; this is stored in the RAM until the web browser is closed. RAM usually comes on DIMMs in the sizes 2GB, 4GB, and 8GB, but can be much larger.

- Read-only memory (ROM), which stores the BIOS that runs when the computer is powered on or otherwise begins execution, a process known as Bootstrapping, or "booting" or "booting up". The BIOS (Basic Input Output System) includes boot firmware and power management firmware. Newer motherboards use Unified Extensible Firmware Interface (UEFI) instead of BIOS.

- Buses that connect the CPU to various internal components and to expand cards for graphics and sound.

- The CMOS battery, which powers the memory for date and time in the BIOS chip. This battery is generally a watch battery.

- The video card (also known as the graphics card), which processes computer graphics. More powerful graphics cards are better suited to handle strenuous tasks, such as playing intensive video games.

- Power MOSFETs make up the voltage regulator module (VRM), which controls how much voltage other hardware components receive.

Expansion Cards

An expansion card in computing is a printed circuit board that can be inserted into an expansion slot of a computer motherboard or backplane to add functionality to a computer system via the expansion bus. Expansion cards can be used to obtain or expand on features not offered by the motherboard.

Storage Devices

A storage device is any computing hardware and digital media that is used for storing, porting and extracting data files and objects. It can hold and store information both temporarily and permanently, and can be internal or external to a computer, server or any similar computing device. Data storage is a core function and fundamental component of computers.

Fixed Media

Data is stored by a computer using a variety of media. Hard disk drives are found in virtually all older computers, due to their high capacity and low cost, but solid-state drives are faster and more power efficient, although currently more expensive than hard drives in terms of dollar per gigabyte, so are often found in personal computers built post-2007. Some systems may use a disk array controller for greater performance or reliability.

Removable Media

To transfer data between computers, a USB flash drive or optical disc may be used. Their usefulness depends on being readable by other systems; the majority of machines have an optical disk drive, and virtually all have at least one USB port.

Input and Output Peripherals

Input and output devices are typically housed externally to the main computer chassis. The following are either standard or very common to many computer systems.

Input

Input devices allow the user to enter information into the system, or control its operation. Most personal computers have a mouse and keyboard, but laptop systems typically use a touchpad instead of a mouse. Other input devices include webcams, microphones, joysticks, and image scanners.

Output Device

Output devices display information in a human readable form. Such devices could include printers, speakers, monitors or a Braille embosser.

Mainframe Computer

A mainframe computer is a much larger computer that typically fills a room and may cost many hundreds or thousands of times as much as a personal computer. They are designed to perform large numbers of calculations for governments and large enterprises.

Departmental Computing

In the 1960s and 1970s, more and more departments started to use cheaper and dedicated systems for specific purposes like process control and laboratory automation.

Supercomputer

A supercomputer is superficially similar to a mainframe, but is instead intended for extremely demanding computational tasks. As of June 2018, the fastest supercomputer on the TOP500supercomputer list is the Summit, in the United States, with a LINPACK benchmarkscore of 122.3 PFLOPS Light, by around 29 PFLOPS.

The term supercomputer does not refer to a specific technology. Rather it indicates the fastest computations available at any given time. In mid 2011, the fastest supercomputers boasted speeds exceeding one petaflop, or 1 quadrillion (10^{15} or 1,000 trillion) floating point operations per second. Supercomputers are fast but extremely costly, so they are generally used by large organizations to execute computationally demanding tasks involving large data sets. Supercomputers typically run military and scientific applications. Although costly, they are also being used for commercial applications where huge amounts of data must be analyzed. For example, large banks employ supercomputers to calculate the risks and returns of various investment strategies, and healthcare organizations use them to analyze giant databases of patient data to determine optimal treatments for various diseases and problems incurring to the country.

Hardware Upgrade

When using computer hardware, an upgrade means adding new hardware to a computer that improves its performance, adds capacity or new features. For example, a user could perform a hardware upgrade to replace the hard drive with a SSD to get a boost in performance or increase the amount of files that may be stored. Also, the user could increase the RAM so the computer may run more smoothly. The user could add a USB 3.0 expansion card in order to fully use USB 3.0 devices, or could upgrade the GPU for extra rendering power. Performing such hardware upgrades may be necessary for older computers to meet a programs' system requirements.

Central Processing Unit

An Intel 80486DX2 CPU.

Bottom side of an Intel 80486DX2.

A central processing unit (CPU), also called a central processor or main processor, is the electronic circuitry within a computer that carries out the instructions of a computer program by performing the basic arithmetic, logic, controlling, and input/output (I/O) operations specified by the instructions. The computer industry has used the term "central processing unit" at least since the early 1960s. Traditionally, the term "CPU" refers to a processor, more specifically to its processing unit and control unit (CU), distinguishing these core elements of a computer from external components such as main memory and I/O circuitry.

The form, design, and implementation of CPUs have changed over the course of their history, but their fundamental operation remains almost unchanged. Principal components of a CPU include the arithmetic logic unit (ALU) that performs arithmetic and logic operations, processor registers that supply operands to the ALU and store the results of ALU operations, and a control unit that orchestrates the fetching (from memory) and execution of instructions by directing the coordinated operations of the ALU, registers and other components.

Most modern CPUs are microprocessors, where the CPU is contained on a single metal-oxide-semiconductor (MOS) integrated circuit (IC) chip. An IC that contains a CPU may also contain memory, peripheral interfaces, and other components of a computer; such integrated devices are variously called microcontrollers or systems on a chip (SoC). Some computers employ a multi-core processor, which is a single chip containing two or more CPUs called "cores"; in that context, one can speak of such single chips as "sockets".

Array processors or vector processors have multiple processors that operate in parallel, with no unit considered central. There also exists the concept of virtual CPUs which are an abstraction of dynamical aggregated computational resources.

Operation

The fundamental operation of most CPUs, regardless of the physical form they take, is to execute a sequence of stored instructions that is called a program. The instructions to be executed are kept in some kind of computer memory. Nearly all CPUs follow the fetch, decode and execute steps in their operation, which are collectively known as the instruction cycle.

After the execution of an instruction, the entire process repeats, with the next instruction cycle normally fetching the next-in-sequence instruction because of the incremented value in the program counter. If a jump instruction was executed, the program counter will be modified to contain the address of the instruction that was jumped to and program execution continues normally. In more complex CPUs, multiple instructions can be fetched, decoded and executed simultaneously. This topic describes what is generally referred to as the "classic RISC pipeline", which is quite common among the simple CPUs used in many electronic devices (often called microcontroller). It largely ignores the important role of CPU cache, and therefore the access stage of the pipeline.

Some instructions manipulate the program counter rather than producing result data directly; such instructions are generally called "jumps" and facilitate program behavior like loops, conditional program execution (through the use of a conditional jump), and existence of functions. In some processors, some other instructions change the state of bits in a "flags" register. These flags can be used to influence how a program behaves, since they often indicate the outcome of various operations. For example, in such processors a "compare" instruction evaluates two values and sets or clears bits in the flags register to indicate which one is greater or whether they are equal; one of these flags could then be used by a later jump instruction to determine program flow.

Fetch

The first step, fetch, involves retrieving an instruction (which is represented by a number or sequence of numbers) from program memory. The instruction's location (address) in program memory is determined by a program counter (PC), which stores a number that identifies the address of the next instruction to be fetched. After an instruction is fetched, the PC is incremented by the length of the instruction so that it will contain the address of the next instruction in the sequence. Often, the instruction to be fetched must be retrieved from relatively slow memory, causing the CPU to stall while waiting for the instruction to be returned. This issue is largely addressed in modern processors by caches and pipeline architectures.

Decode

The instruction that the CPU fetches from memory determines what the CPU will do. In the decode step, performed by the circuitry known as the *instruction decoder*, the instruction is converted into signals that control other parts of the CPU.

The way in which the instruction is interpreted is defined by the CPU's instruction set architecture (ISA). Often, one group of bits (that is, a "field") within the instruction, called the opcode, indicates which operation is to be performed, while the remaining fields usually provide supplemental information required for the operation, such as the operands. Those operands may be specified as a constant value (called an immediate value), or as the location of a value that may be a processor register or a memory address, as determined by some addressing mode.

In some CPU designs the instruction decoder is implemented as a hardwired, unchangeable circuit. In others, a microprogram is used to translate instructions into sets of CPU configuration signals that are applied sequentially over multiple clock pulses. In some cases the memory that stores the microprogram is rewritable, making it possible to change the way in which the CPU decodes instructions.

Execute

After the fetch and decode steps, the execute step is performed. Depending on the CPU architecture, this may consist of a single action or a sequence of actions. During each action, various parts of the CPU are electrically connected so they can perform all or part of the desired operation and then the action is completed, typically in response to a clock pulse. Very often the results are written to an internal CPU register for quick access by subsequent instructions. In other cases results may be written to slower, but less expensive and higher capacity main memory.

For example, if an addition instruction is to be executed, the arithmetic logic unit (ALU) inputs are connected to a pair of operand sources (numbers to be summed), the ALU is configured to perform an addition operation so that the sum of its operand inputs will appear at its output, and the ALU output is connected to storage (e.g., a register or memory) that will receive the sum. When the clock pulse occurs, the sum will be transferred to storage and, if the resulting sum is too large (i.e., it is larger than the ALU's output word size), an arithmetic overflow flag will be set.

Structure and Implementation

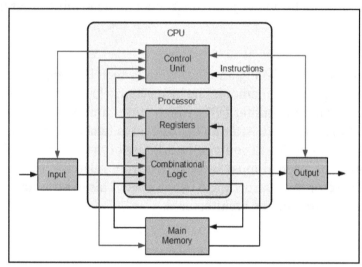

Block diagram of a basic uniprocessor-CPU computer. Black lines indicate data flow, whereas red lines indicate control flow; arrows indicate flow directions.

Hardwired into a CPU's circuitry is a set of basic operations it can perform, called an instruction set. Such operations may involve, for example, adding or subtracting two numbers, comparing two numbers, or jumping to a different part of a program. Each basic operation is represented by a particular combination of bits, known as the machine language opcode; while executing instructions in a machine language program, the CPU decides which operation to perform by "decoding" the opcode. A complete machine language instruction consists of an opcode and, in many cases, additional bits that specify arguments for the operation (for example, the numbers to be summed in the case of an addition operation). Going up the complexity scale, a machine language program is a collection of machine language instructions that the CPU executes.

The actual mathematical operation for each instruction is performed by a combinational logic circuit within the CPU's processor known as the arithmetic logic unit or ALU. In general, a CPU executes an instruction by fetching it from memory, using its ALU to perform an operation, and then storing the result to memory. Beside the instructions for integer mathematics and logic operations, various other machine instructions exist, such as those for loading data from memory and storing it back, branching operations, and mathematical operations on floating-point numbers performed by the CPU's floating-point unit (FPU).

Control Unit

The control unit (CU) is a component of the CPU that directs the operation of the processor. It tells the computer's memory, arithmetic and logic unit and input and output devices how to respond to the instructions that have been sent to the processor.

It directs the operation of the other units by providing timing and control signals. Most computer resources are managed by the CU. It directs the flow of data between the CPU and the other devices. John von Neumann included the control unit as part of the von Neumann architecture. In modern computer designs, the control unit is typically an internal part of the CPU with its overall role and operation unchanged since its introduction.

Arithmetic Logic Unit

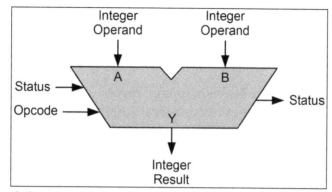

Symbolic representation of an ALU and its input and output signals.

The arithmetic logic unit (ALU) is a digital circuit within the processor that performs integer arithmetic and bitwise logic operations. The inputs to the ALU are the data words to be operated on (called operands), status information from previous operations, and a code from the control unit indicating which operation to perform. Depending on the instruction being executed, the operands may come from internal CPU registers or external memory, or they may be constants generated by the ALU itself.

When all input signals have settled and propagated through the ALU circuitry, the result of the performed operation appears at the ALU's outputs. The result consists of both a data word, which may be stored in a register or memory, and status information that is typically stored in a special, internal CPU register reserved for this purpose.

Address Generation Unit

Address generation unit (AGU), sometimes also called address computation unit (ACU), is an execution unit inside the CPU that calculates addresses used by the CPU to access main memory. By having address calculations handled by separate circuitry that operates in parallel with the rest of the CPU, the number of CPU cycles required for executing various machine instructions can be reduced, bringing performance improvements.

While performing various operations, CPUs need to calculate memory addresses required for fetching data from the memory; for example, in-memory positions of array elements must be calculated before the CPU can fetch the data from actual memory locations. Those address-generation calculations involve different integer arithmetic operations, such as addition, subtraction, modulo operations, or bit shifts. Often, calculating a memory address involves more than one general-purpose machine instruction, which do not necessarily decode and execute quickly. By incorporating an AGU into a CPU design, together with introducing specialized instructions that use the AGU, various address-generation calculations can be offloaded from the rest of the CPU, and can often be executed quickly in a single CPU cycle.

Capabilities of an AGU depend on a particular CPU and its architecture. Thus, some AGUs implement and expose more address-calculation operations, while some also include more advanced specialized instructions that can operate on multiple operands at a time. Furthermore, some CPU architectures include multiple AGUs so more than one address-calculation operation can be executed simultaneously, bringing further performance improvements by capitalizing on the superscalar nature of advanced CPU designs. For example, Intel incorporates multiple AGUs into its Sandy Bridge and Haswell microarchitectures, which increase bandwidth of the CPU memory subsystem by allowing multiple memory-access instructions to be executed in parallel.

Memory Management Unit (MMU)

Most high-end microprocessors (in desktop, laptop, server computers) have a memory management unit, translating logical addresses into physical RAM addresses, providing memory protection and paging abilities, useful for virtual memory. Simpler processors, especially microcontrollers, usually don't include an MMU.

Cache

A CPU cache is a hardware cache used by the central processing unit (CPU) of a computer to reduce the average cost (time or energy) to access data from the main memory. A cache is a smaller, faster memory, closer to a processor core, which stores copies of the data from frequently used main memory locations. Most CPUs have different independent caches, including instruction and data caches, where the data cache is usually organized as a hierarchy of more cache levels (L1, L2, L3, L4, etc.).

All modern (fast) CPUs (with few specialized exceptions) have multiple levels of CPU caches. The first CPUs that used a cache had only one level of cache; unlike later level 1 caches, it was not split into L1d (for data) and L1i (for instructions). Almost all current CPUs with caches have a split L1 cache. They also have L2 caches and, for larger processors, L3 caches as well. The L2 cache is usually not split and acts as a common repository for the already split L1 cache. Every core of a multi-core processor has a dedicated L2 cache and is usually not shared between the cores. The L3 cache, and higher-level caches, are shared between the cores and are not split. An L4 cache is currently uncommon, and is generally on dynamic random-access memory (DRAM), rather than on static random-access memory (SRAM), on a separate die or chip. That was also the case historically with L1, while bigger chips have allowed integration of it and generally all cache levels, with the possible exception of the last level. Each extra level of cache tends to be bigger and be optimized differently.

Other types of caches exist (that are not counted towards the "cache size" of the most important caches mentioned above), such as the translation lookaside buffer (TLB) that is part of the memory management unit (MMU) that most CPUs have.

Caches are generally sized in powers of two: 4, 8, 16 etc. KiB or MiB (for larger non-L1) sizes, although the IBM z13 has a 96 KiB L1 instruction cache.

Clock Rate

Most CPUs are synchronous circuits, which means they employ a clock signal to pace their sequential operations. The clock signal is produced by an external oscillator circuit that generates a consistent number of pulses each second in the form of a periodic square wave. The frequency of the clock pulses determines the rate at which a CPU executes instructions and, consequently, the faster the clock, the more instructions the CPU will execute each second.

To ensure proper operation of the CPU, the clock period is longer than the maximum time needed for all signals to propagate (move) through the CPU. In setting the clock period to a value well above the worst-case propagation delay, it is possible to design the entire CPU and the way it moves data around the "edges" of the rising and falling clock signal. This has the advantage of simplifying the CPU significantly, both from a design perspective and a component-count perspective. However, it also carries the disadvantage that the entire CPU must wait on its slowest elements, even though some portions of it are much faster. This limitation has largely been compensated for by various methods of increasing CPU parallelism.

However, architectural improvements alone do not solve all of the drawbacks of globally synchronous CPUs. For example, a clock signal is subject to the delays of any other electrical signal. Higher clock rates in increasingly complex CPUs make it more difficult to keep the clock signal in phase (synchronized) throughout the entire unit. This has led many modern CPUs to require multiple identical clock signals to be provided to avoid delaying a single signal significantly enough to cause the CPU to malfunction. Another major issue, as clock rates increase dramatically, is the amount of heat that is dissipated by the CPU. The constantly changing clock causes many components to switch regardless of whether they are being used at that time. In general, a component that is switching uses more energy than an element in a static state. Therefore, as clock rate increases, so does energy consumption, causing the CPU to require more heat dissipation in the form of CPU cooling solutions.

One method of dealing with the switching of unneeded components is called clock gating, which involves turning off the clock signal to unneeded components (effectively disabling them). However, this is often regarded as difficult to implement and therefore does not see common usage outside of very low-power designs. One notable recent CPU design that uses extensive clock gating is the IBM PowerPC-based Xenon used in the Xbox 360; that way, power requirements of the Xbox 360 are greatly reduced. Another method of addressing some of the problems with a global clock signal is the removal of the clock signal altogether. While removing the global clock signal makes the design process considerably more complex in many ways, asynchronous (or clockless) designs carry marked advantages in power consumption and heat dissipation in comparison with similar synchronous designs. While somewhat uncommon, entire asynchronous CPUs have been built without using a global clock signal. Two notable examples of this are the ARM compliant AMULET and the MIPS R3000 compatible MiniMIPS.

Rather than totally removing the clock signal, some CPU designs allow certain portions of the device to be asynchronous, such as using asynchronous ALUs in conjunction with superscalar pipelining to achieve some arithmetic performance gains. While it is not altogether clear whether totally asynchronous designs can perform at a comparable or better level than their synchronous counterparts, it is evident that they do at least excel in simpler math operations. This, combined with their excellent power consumption and heat dissipation properties, makes them very suitable for embedded computers.

Integer Range

Every CPU represents numerical values in a specific way. For example, some early digital computers represented numbers as familiar decimal (base 10) numeral system values, and others have employed more unusual representations such as ternary (base three). Nearly all modern CPUs represent numbers in binary form, with each digit being represented by some two-valued physical quantity such as a "high" or "low" voltage.

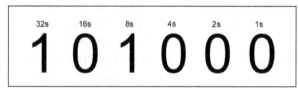

A six-bit word containing the binary encoded representation of
decimal value 40. Most modern CPUs employ word sizes that are a power of two,
for example 8, 16, 32 or 64 bits.

Related to numeric representation is the size and precision of integer numbers that a CPU can represent. In the case of a binary CPU, this is measured by the number of bits (significant digits of a binary encoded integer) that the CPU can process in one operation, which is commonly called *word size, bit width, data path width, integer precision,* or *integer size*. A CPU's integer size determines the range of integer values it can directly operate on.For example, an 8-bit CPU can directly manipulate integers represented by eight bits, which have a range of 256 (2^8) discrete integer values.

Integer range can also affect the number of memory locations the CPU can directly address (an address is an integer value representing a specific memory location). For example, if a binary CPU uses 32 bits to represent a memory address then it can directly address 2^{32} memory locations. To circumvent this limitation and for various other reasons, some CPUs use mechanisms (such as bank switching) that allow additional memory to be addressed.

CPUs with larger word sizes require more circuitry and consequently are physically larger, cost more and consume more power (and therefore generate more heat). As a result, smaller 4- or 8-bit microcontrollers are commonly used in modern applications even though CPUs with much larger word sizes (such as 16, 32, 64, even 128-bit) are available. When higher performance is required, however, the benefits of a larger word size (larger data ranges and address spaces) may outweigh the disadvantages. A CPU can have internal data paths shorter than the word size to reduce size and cost. For example, even though the IBM System/360 instruction set was a 32-bit instruction set, the System/360 Model 30 and Model 40 had 8-bit data paths in the arithmetic logical unit, so that a 32-bit add required four cycles, one for each 8 bits of the operands, and, even though the Motorola 68000 series instruction set was a 32-bit instruction set, the Motorola 68000 and Motorola 68010 had 16-bit data paths in the arithmetic logical unit, so that a 32-bit add required two cycles.

To gain some of the advantages afforded by both lower and higher bit lengths, many instruction sets have different bit widths for integer and floating-point data, allowing CPUs implementing that instruction set to have different bit widths for different portions of the device. For example, the IBM System/360 instruction set was primarily 32 bit, but supported 64-bit floating point values to facilitate greater accuracy and range in floating point numbers. The System/360 Model 65 had an 8-bit adder for decimal and fixed-point binary arithmetic and a 60-bit adder for floating-point arithmetic. Many later CPU designs use similar mixed bit width, especially when the processor is meant for general-purpose usage where a reasonable balance of integer and floating point capability is required.

Parallelism

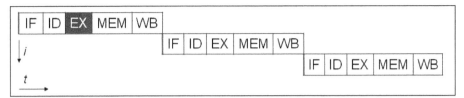

Model of a subscalar CPU, in which it takes fifteen clock cycles to complete three instructions.

This type of CPU, usually referred to as *subscalar*, operates on and executes one instruction on one or two pieces of data at a time, that is less than one instruction per clock cycle (IPC < 1).

This process gives rise to an inherent inefficiency in subscalar CPUs. Since only one instruction is executed at a time, the entire CPU must wait for that instruction to complete before proceeding to the next instruction. As a result, the subscalar CPU gets "hung up" on instructions which take more than one clock cycle to complete execution. Even adding a second execution unit does not improve performance much; rather than one pathway being hung up, now two pathways are hung up and the number of unused transistors is increased. This design, wherein the CPU's execution resources can operate on only one instruction at a time, can only possibly reach *scalar* performance (one instruction per clock cycle, IPC = 1). However, the performance is nearly always subscalar (less than one instruction per clock cycle, IPC < 1).

Attempts to achieve scalar and better performance have resulted in a variety of design methodologies that cause the CPU to behave less linearly and more in parallel. When referring to parallelism in CPUs, two terms are generally used to classify these design techniques:

- Instruction-level parallelism (ILP), which seeks to increase the rate at which instructions are executed within a CPU (that is, to increase the use of on-die execution resources);

- Task-level parallelism (TLP), which purposes to increase the number of threads or processes that a CPU can execute simultaneously.

Each methodology differs both in the ways in which they are implemented, as well as the relative effectiveness they afford in increasing the CPU's performance for an application.

Instruction-level Parallelism

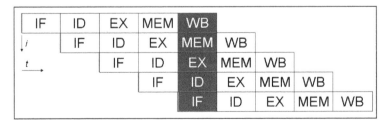

Basic five-stage pipeline. In the best case scenario, this pipeline can sustain a completion rate of one instruction per clock cycle.

One of the simplest methods used to accomplish increased parallelism is to begin the first steps of instruction fetching and decoding before the prior instruction finishes executing. This is the simplest form of a technique known as instruction pipelining, and is used in almost all modern general-purpose CPUs. Pipelining allows more than one instruction to be executed at any given time by breaking down the execution pathway into discrete stages. This separation can be compared to an assembly line, in which an instruction is made more complete at each stage until it exits the execution pipeline and is retired.

Pipelining does, however, introduce the possibility for a situation where the result of the previous operation is needed to complete the next operation; a condition often termed data dependency conflict. To cope with this, additional care must be taken to check for these sorts of conditions and delay a portion of the instruction pipeline if this occurs. Naturally, accomplishing this requires additional circuitry, so pipelined processors are more complex than subscalar ones (though not very significantly so). A pipelined processor can become very nearly scalar, inhibited only by pipeline stalls (an instruction spending more than one clock cycle in a stage).

Further improvement upon the idea of instruction pipelining led to the development of a method that decreases the idle time of CPU components even further. Designs that are said to be *superscalar* include a long instruction pipeline and multiple identical execution units, such as load-store units, arithmetic-logic units, floating-point units and address generation units. In a superscalar pipeline, multiple instructions are read and passed to a dispatcher, which decides whether or not the instructions can be executed in parallel (simultaneously). If so they are dispatched to available execution units, resulting in the ability for several instructions to be executed simultaneously. In general, the more instructions a superscalar CPU is able to dispatch simultaneously to waiting execution units, the more instructions will be completed in a given cycle.

A simple superscalar pipeline. By fetching and dispatching two instructions at a time, a maximum of two instructions per clock cycle can be completed.

Most of the difficulty in the design of a superscalar CPU architecture lies in creating an effective dispatcher. The dispatcher needs to be able to quickly and correctly determine whether instructions can be executed in parallel, as well as dispatch them in such a way as to keep as many execution units busy as possible. This requires that the instruction pipeline is filled as often as possible and gives rise to the need in superscalar architectures for significant amounts of CPU cache. It also makes hazard-avoiding techniques like branch prediction, speculative execution, register renaming, out-of-order execution and transactional memory crucial to maintaining high levels of performance. By attempting to predict which branch (or path) a conditional instruction will take, the CPU can minimize the number of times that the entire pipeline must wait until a conditional instruction is completed. Speculative execution often provides modest performance increases by executing portions of code that may not be needed after a conditional operation completes. Out-of-order execution somewhat rearranges the order in which instructions are executed to reduce delays due to data dependencies. Also in case of single instruction stream, multiple data stream—a case when a lot of data from the same type has to be processed, modern processors can disable parts of the pipeline so that when a single instruction is executed many times, the CPU skips the fetch and decode phases and thus greatly increases performance on certain occasions, especially in highly monotonous program engines such as video creation software and photo processing.

In the case where a portion of the CPU is superscalar and part is not, the part which is not suffers a performance penalty due to scheduling stalls. The Intel P5 Pentium had two superscalar ALUs which could accept one instruction per clock cycle each, but its FPU could not accept one instruction per clock cycle. Thus the P5 was integer superscalar but not floating point superscalar. Intel's successor to the P5 architecture, P6, added superscalar capabilities to its floating point features, and therefore afforded a significant increase in floating point instruction performance.

Both simple pipelining and superscalar design increase a CPU's ILP by allowing a single processor to complete execution of instructions at rates surpassing one instruction per clock cycle. Most modern CPU designs are at least somewhat superscalar, and nearly all general purpose CPUs designed in the last decade are superscalar. In later years some of the emphasis in designing high-ILP computers has been moved out of the CPU's hardware and into its software interface, or ISA. The strategy of the very long instruction word (VLIW) causes some ILP to become implied directly by the software, reducing the amount of work the CPU must perform to boost ILP and thereby reducing the design's complexity.

Task-level Parallelism

Another strategy of achieving performance is to execute multiple threads or processes in parallel. This area of research is known as parallel computing. In Flynn's taxonomy, this strategy is known as multiple instruction stream, multiple data stream (MIMD).

One technology used for this purpose was multiprocessing (MP). The initial flavor of this technology is known as symmetric multiprocessing (SMP), where a small number of CPUs share a coherent view of their memory system. In this scheme, each CPU has additional hardware to maintain a constantly up-to-date view of memory. By avoiding stale views of memory, the CPUs can cooperate on the same program and programs can migrate from one CPU to another. To increase the number of cooperating CPUs beyond a handful, schemes such as non-uniform memory access (NUMA) and directory-based coherence protocols were introduced in the 1990s. SMP systems are limited to a small number of CPUs while NUMA systems have been built with thousands of processors. Initially, multiprocessing was built using multiple discrete CPUs and boards to implement the interconnect between the processors. When the processors and their interconnect are all implemented on a single chip, the technology is known as chip-level multiprocessing (CMP) and the single chip as a multi-core processor.

It was later recognized that finer-grain parallelism existed with a single program. A single program might have several threads (or functions) that could be executed separately or in parallel. Some of the earliest examples of this technology implemented input/output processing such as direct memory access as a separate thread from the computation thread. A more general approach to this technology was introduced in the 1970s when systems were designed to run multiple computation threads in parallel. This technology is known as multi-threading (MT). This approach is considered more cost-effective than multiprocessing, as only a small number of components within a CPU is replicated to support MT as opposed to the entire CPU in the case of MP. In MT, the execution units and the memory system including the caches are shared among multiple threads. The downside of MT is that the hardware support for multithreading is more visible to software than that of MP and thus supervisor software like operating systems have to undergo larger changes to support MT. One type of MT that was implemented is known as temporal multithreading, where one thread is executed until it is stalled waiting for data to return from external memory. In this scheme, the CPU would then quickly context switch to another thread which is ready to run, the switch often done in one CPU clock cycle, such as the UltraSPARC T1. Another type of MT is simultaneous multithreading, where instructions from multiple threads are executed in parallel within one CPU clock cycle.

For several decades from the 1970s to early 2000s, the focus in designing high performance general purpose CPUs was largely on achieving high ILP through technologies such as pipelining, caches, superscalar execution, out-of-order execution, etc. This trend culminated in large, power-hungry CPUs such as the Intel Pentium 4. By the early 2000s, CPU designers were thwarted from achieving higher performance from ILP techniques due to the growing disparity between CPU operating frequencies and main memory operating frequencies as well as escalating CPU power dissipation owing to more esoteric ILP techniques.

CPU designers then borrowed ideas from commercial computing markets such as transaction processing, where the aggregate performance of multiple programs, also known as throughput computing, was more important than the performance of a single thread or process.

This reversal of emphasis is evidenced by the proliferation of dual and more core processor designs and notably, Intel's newer designs resembling its less superscalar P6 architecture. Late designs in several processor families exhibit CMP, including the x86-64 Opteron and Athlon 64 X2, the SPARC UltraSPARC T1, IBM POWER4 and POWER5, as well as several video game console CPUs like the Xbox 360's triple-core PowerPC design, and the PlayStation 3's 7-core Cell microprocessor.

Data Parallelism

A less common but increasingly important paradigm of processors (and indeed, computing in general) deals with data parallelism. The processors discussed earlier are all referred to as some type of scalar device. As the name implies, vector processors deal with multiple pieces of data in the context of one instruction. This contrasts with scalar processors, which deal with one piece of data for every instruction. Using Flynn's taxonomy, these two schemes of dealing with data are generally referred to as single instruction stream, multiple data stream (SIMD) and single instruction stream, single data stream (SISD), respectively. The great utility in creating processors that deal with vectors of data lies in optimizing tasks that tend to require the same operation (for example, a sum or a dot product) to be performed on a large set of data. Some classic examples of these types of tasks include multimedia applications (images, video and sound), as well as many types of scientific and engineering tasks. Whereas a scalar processor must complete the entire process of fetching, decoding and executing each instruction and value in a set of data, a vector processor can perform a single operation on a comparatively large set of data with one instruction. This is only possible when the application tends to require many steps which apply one operation to a large set of data.

Most early vector processors, such as the Cray-1, were associated almost exclusively with scientific research and cryptography applications. However, as multimedia has largely shifted to digital media, the need for some form of SIMD in general-purpose processors has become significant. Shortly after inclusion of floating-point units started to become commonplace in general-purpose processors, specifications for and implementations of SIMD execution units also began to appear for general-purpose processors. Some of these early SIMD specifications - like HP's Multimedia Acceleration eXtensions (MAX) and Intel's MMX - were integer-only. This proved to be a significant impediment for some software developers, since many of the applications that benefit from SIMD primarily deal with floating-point numbers. Progressively, developers refined and remade these early designs into some of the common modern SIMD specifications, which are usually associated with one ISA. Some notable modern examples include Intel's SSE and the PowerPC-related AltiVec (also known as VMX).

Virtual CPUs

Cloud computing can involve subdividing CPU operation into virtual central processing units (vCPUs).

A host is the virtual equivalent of a physical machine, on which a virtual system is operating. When there are several physical machines operating in tandem and managed as a whole, the grouped computing and memory resources form a cluster. In some systems, it is possible to dynamically add and remove from a cluster. Resources available at a host and cluster level can be partitioned out into resources pools with fine granularity.

Performance

The *performance* or *speed* of a processor depends on, among many other factors, the clock rate (generally given in multiples of hertz) and the instructions per clock (IPC), which together are the factors for the instructions per second (IPS) that the CPU can perform. Many reported IPS values have represented "peak" execution rates on artificial instruction sequences with few branches, whereas realistic workloads consist of a mix of instructions and applications, some of which take longer to execute than others. The performance of the memory hierarchy also greatly affects processor performance, an issue barely considered in MIPS calculations. Because of these problems, various standardized tests, often called "benchmarks" for this purpose—such as SPECint— have been developed to attempt to measure the real effective performance in commonly used applications.

Processing performance of computers is increased by using multi-core processors, which essentially is plugging two or more individual processors (called *cores* in this sense) into one integrated circuit. Ideally, a dual core processor would be nearly twice as powerful as a single core processor. In practice, the performance gain is far smaller, only about 50%, due to imperfect software algorithms and implementation. Increasing the number of cores in a processor (i.e. dual-core, quad-core, etc.) increases the workload that can be handled. This means that the processor can now handle numerous asynchronous events, interrupts, etc. which can take a toll on the CPU when overwhelmed. These cores can be thought of as different floors in a processing plant, with each floor handling a different task. Sometimes, these cores will handle the same tasks as cores adjacent to them if a single core is not enough to handle the information.

Due to specific capabilities of modern CPUs, such as simultaneous multithreading and uncore, which involve sharing of actual CPU resources while aiming at increased utilization, monitoring performance levels and hardware use gradually became a more complex task. As a response, some CPUs implement additional hardware logic that monitors actual use of various parts of a CPU and provides various counters accessible to software; an example is Intel's *Performance Counter Monitor* technology.

COMPUTER SOFTWARE

Computer software is a program that enables a computer to perform a specific task, as opposed to the physical components of the system (hardware). This includes application software such as a word processor, which enables a user to perform a task, and system software such as an operating system, which enables other software to run properly, by interfacing with hardware and with other software.

The term "software" was first used in this sense by John W. Tukey in 1957. In computer science and software engineering, computer software is all computer programs. The concept of reading different sequences of instructions into the memory of a device to control computations was invented by Charles Babbage as part of his difference engine. The theory that is the basis for most modern software was first proposed by Alan Turing in his 1935 essay, Computable Numbers with an Application to the Entscheidungsproblem.

Relationship to Hardware

Computer software is so called in contrast to computer hardware, which encompasses the physical interconnections and devices required to store and execute (or run) the software. In computers, software is loaded into random access memory (RAM) and executed in the central processing unit. At the lowest level, software consists of a machine language specific to an individual processor. The machine language consists of groups of binary values signifying processor instructions (object code), which change the state of the computer from its preceding state.

Software is an ordered sequence of instructions for changing the state of the computer hardware in a particular sequence. It is usually written in high-level programming languages that are easier and more efficient for humans to use (closer to natural language) than machine language. High-level languages are compiled or interpreted into machine language object code. Software may also be written in an assembly language, essentially, a mnemonic representation of a machine language using a natural language alphabet. Assembly language must be assembled into object code via an assembler.

Relationship to Data

Software has historically been considered an intermediary between electronic hardware and data, which are defined by the instructions defined by the software. As computational math becomes increasingly complex, the distinction between software and data becomes less precise. Data has generally been considered as either the output or input of executed software. However, data is not the only possible output or input. For example, (system) configuration information may also be considered input, although not necessarily considered data (and certainly not applications data). The output of a particular piece of executed software may be the input for another executed piece of software. Therefore, software may be considered an interface between hardware, data, and (other) software.

Types

Practical computer systems divide software into three major classes: System software, programming software, and application software, although the distinction is arbitrary and often blurred.

- System software helps run the computer hardware and computer system. It includes operating systems, device drivers, diagnostic tools, servers, windowing systems, utilities, and more. The purpose of systems software is to insulate the applications programmer as much as possible from the details of the particular computer complex being used, especially memory and other hardware features, and such accessory devices as communications, printers, readers, displays, keyboards, etc.

- Programming software usually provides tools to assist a programmer in writing computer programs and software using different programming languages in a more convenient way. The tools include text editors, compilers, interpreters, linkers, debuggers, and so on. An Integrated development environment (IDE) merges those tools into a software bundle, and a programmer may not need to type multiple commands for compiling, interpreter, debugging, tracing, and etc., because the IDE usually has an advanced graphical user interface (GUI).

- Application software allows humans to accomplish one or more specific (non-computer related) tasks. Typical applications include industrial automation, business software, educational software, medical software, databases, and computer games. Businesses are probably the biggest users of application software, but almost every field of human activity now uses some form of application software. It is used to automate all sorts of functions.

Computer Viruses

Computer viruses are a malignant type of computer program even though they might not be considered software. They can be created as any of the three types of software. Some viruses cause minor problems, such as slowing down a computer or using email to spread. Other viruses can cause more serious problems, such as destroying data or damaging hardware.

Program and Library

A program may not be sufficiently complete for execution by a computer. In particular, it may require additional software from a software library to be complete. Such a library may include software components used by stand-alone programs, but which cannot be executed on their own. Thus, programs may include standard routines that are common to many programs, extracted from these libraries. Libraries may also include stand-alone programs that are activated by some computer event and perform some function (such as computer "housekeeping") but do not return data to their activating program. Programs may be called by other programs and may call other programs.

Three Layers

Users often see things differently than programmers. People who use modern general purpose computers (as opposed to embedded systems, analog computers, supercomputers, and so forth) usually see three layers of software performing a variety of tasks: Platform, application, and user software.

- Platform software: Platform includes the basic input-output system (often described as firmware rather than software), device drivers, an operating system, and typically a graphical user interface which, in total, allow a user to interact with the computer and its peripherals (associated equipment). Platform software often comes bundled with the computer, and users may not realize that it exists or that they have a choice to use different platform software.

- Application software: Application software or simply, "Applications" are what most people think of when they think of software. Typical examples include office suites and video games. Application software is often purchased separately from computer hardware. Sometimes applications are bundled with the computer, but that does not change the fact that they run as independent applications. Applications are almost always independent programs from the operating system, though they are often tailored for specific platforms. Most users think of compilers, databases, and other "system software" as applications.

- User-written software: User software tailors systems to meet the users specific needs. User software include spreadsheet templates, word processor macros, scientific simulations, graphics and animation scripts. Even email filters are a kind of user software. Users create this software themselves and often overlook how important it is. Depending on how competently the user-written software has been integrated into purchased application packages, many users may not be aware of the distinction between the purchased packages, and what has been added by fellow co-workers.

Operation

Computer software has to be "loaded" into the computer's storage (also known as memory and RAM).

Once the software is loaded, the computer is able to execute the software. Computers operate by executing the computer program. This involves passing instructions from the application software, through the system software, to the hardware which ultimately receives the instruction as machine code. Each instruction causes the computer to carry out an operation—moving data, carrying out a computation, or altering the control flow of instructions.

Data movement is typically from one place in memory to another. Sometimes it involves moving data between memory and registers which enable high-speed data access in the CPU.

A simple example of the way software operates is what happens when a user selects an entry such as "Copy" from a menu. In this case, a conditional instruction is executed to copy text from data in a "document" area residing in memory, perhaps to an intermediate storage area known as a "clipboard" data area. If a different menu entry such as "Paste" is chosen, the software may execute the instructions to copy the text from the clipboard data area to a specific location in the same or another document in memory.

Currently, almost the only limitations on the use of computer software in applications is the ingenuity of the designer/programmer. Consequently, large areas of activities (such as playing grand master level chess) formerly assumed to be impossible if done by software simulation are now routinely programmed. The only area that has so far proved reasonably secure from software simulation is the realm of human art—especially, pleasing music and literature.

Quality and Reliability

Software reliability considers the errors, faults, and failures related to the creation and operation of software. A lot of the quality and reliability of a program has to do with the Application software being written for a specific System software. One example is that an application for an older System software may not work on a newer one.

Software Architecture

The software architecture of a system comprises its software components, their external properties, and their relationships with one another. The term also refers to documentation of a system's software architecture.

Describing Architectures

Architecture Description Languages

Architecture Description Languages (ADLs) are used to describe a Software Architecture. Several different ADLs have been developed by different organizations, including Wright (developed by Carnegie Mellon), Acme (developed by Carnegie Mellon), xADL (developed by UCI), Darwin (developed by Imperial College London), and DAOP-ADL (developed by University of Málaga). Common elements of an ADL are component, connector and configuration.

Views

Software architecture is commonly organized in views, which are analogous to the different types of blueprints made in building architecture.

License

Software license gives the user the right to use the software in the licensed environment, some software comes with the license when purchased off the shelf, or OEM license when bundled with hardware. Software can also be in the form of freeware or shareware.

Proprietary Software

Proprietary software is software that has restrictions on using and copying it, usually enforced by a proprietor. The prevention of use, copying, or modification can be achieved by legal or technical means. Technical means include releasing machine-readable binaries only, and withholding the human-readable source code. Legal means can involve software licensing, copyright, and patent law. Proprietary software can be sold for money as commercial software or available at zero-price as freeware. The monopoly provided by proprietary software allows a distributor of commercial copies to charge any price for those copies. Distributors of proprietary software have more control over what users can do with the software than nonproprietary software.

Free Software

Free software, as defined by the Free Software Foundation, is software which can be used, copied, studied, modified, and redistributed without restriction. Freedom from such restrictions is central to the concept, with the opposite of free software being proprietary software (a distinction unrelated to whether a fee is charged). The usual way for software to be distributed as free software is for the software to be licensed to the recipient with a free software license (or be in the public domain), and the source code of the software to be made available (for a compiled language). Most free software is distributed online without charge, or off-line at the marginal cost of distribution, but this is not required, and people may sell copies for any price.

To help distinguish libre (freedom) software from gratis (zero price) software, Richard Stallman, founder of the free software movement, developed the following explanation: "Free software is a matter of liberty, not price. To understand the concept, you should think of 'free' as in 'free speech', not as in 'free beer' ". More specifically, free software means that computer users have the freedom to cooperate with whom they choose, and to control the software they use.

Open-source Software

Open-source software is computer software whose source code is available under a copyright license that permits users to study, change, and improve the software, and to redistribute it in modified or unmodified form. It is the most prominent example of open source development.

In 1998, a group of individuals advocated that the term "free software" be replaced by open-source software (OSS) as an expression which is less ambiguous and more comfortable for the corporate world. Software developers may want to publish their software with an open-source software license, so that anybody may also develop the same software or understand how it works. Open-source software generally allows anybody to make a new version of the software, port it to new operating systems and processor architectures, share it with others or market it. The aim of open source is to let the product be more understandable, modifiable, duplicable, reliable, or simply accessible, while it is still marketable.

The Open Source Definition, notably, presents an open-source philosophy, and further defines a boundary on the usage, modification and redistribution of open-source software. Software licenses grant rights to users which would otherwise be prohibited by copyright. These include rights on usage, modification and redistribution. Several open-source software licenses have qualified within the boundary of the Open Source Definition. The most prominent example is the popular GNU General Public License (GPL). While open source presents a way to broadly make the sources of a product publicly accessible, the open-source licenses allow the authors to fine tune such access.

Freeware

Freeware is copyrighted computer software which is made available for use free of charge, for an unlimited time, as opposed to shareware, in which the user is required to pay (for example, after some trial period). The only criterion for being classified as "freeware" is that the software must be made available for use for an unlimited time at no cost. The software license may impose one or more other restrictions on the type of use including personal use, individual use, non-profit use, non-commercial use, academic use, commercial use. or any combination of these. For instance, the license may be "free for personal, non-commercial use." There is some software that may be considered freeware, but that have limited distribution; that is, they may only be downloaded from a specific site, and they can not be redistributed. Hence, such software wouldn't be freely redistributable software. According to the basic definition, that software would be freeware; according to stricter definitions, they wouldn't be. Everything created with the freeware programs can be distributed at no cost (for example graphic, documents, waves made by user).

Freeware contrasts with free software, because of the different meanings of the word "free." Freeware is gratis and refers to zero price, versus free software that is described as "libre," which means free to study, change, copy, redistribute, share, and use the software in any purpose. However, many programs are both freeware and free software. They are available for zero price, provide the source code and are distributed with free software permissions. This software would exclusively be called free software to avoid confusion with freeware that usually does not come with the source code and is therefore proprietary software.

Shareware

Shareware is a marketing method for commercial software, whereby a trial version is distributed in advance and without payment, as is common for proprietary software. Shareware software is typically obtained free of charge, either by downloading from the Internet or on magazine cover-disks. A user tries out the program, and thus shareware has also been known as "try before you buy," demoware, trialware, and by many other names. A shareware program is accompanied by a request for payment, and the software's distribution license often requires such a payment. Payment is often required once a set period of time has elapsed after installation.

References

- Johnson, Roger (April 2008). "School of Computer Science & Information Systems: A Short History" (PDF). Birkbeck College. University of London. Retrieved July 23, 2017

- What-is-computer-architecture: computersciencedegreehub.com

- "Electronic Digital Computers", Nature, 162: 487, September 25, 1948, doi:10.1038/162487a0, archived from the original on April 6, 2009, retrieved April 10, 2009

- Lavington, Simon, ed. (2012). Alan Turing and his Contemporaries: Building the World's First Computers. London: British Computer Society. P. 61. ISBN 9781906124908

- Crystal Chen; Greg Novick; Kirk Shimano (December 16, 2006). "RISC Architecture: RISC vs. CISC". Cs.stanford.edu. Retrieved February 21, 2015

- Page, Daniel (2009). "11. Compilers". A Practical Introduction to Computer Architecture. Springer. P. 464. Bibcode:2009pica.book.....P. ISBN 978-1-84882-255-9

- Thomas Willhalm; Roman Dementiev; Patrick Fay (December 18, 2014). "Intel Performance Counter Monitor – A better way to measure CPU utilization". Software.intel.com. Retrieved February 17, 2015

- Liebowitz, Kusek, Spies, Matt, Christopher, Rynardt (2014). Vmware vsphere Performance: Designing CPU, Memory, Storage, and Networking for Performance-Intensive Workloads. Wiley. P. 68. ISBN 978-1-118-00819-5

3

Computer Network and Security

A group of computers connected with each other for sharing information and other resources is defined as a computer network. The protection of computer systems and information from harm, unauthorized use and theft is termed as computer security. The topics elaborated in this chapter will help in gaining a better perspective about the different types of computer network as well as computer security.

COMPUTER NETWORK

During 20th century the most important technology has been the information gathering, its processing and distribution. The computers and communications have been merged together and their merger has had a profound effect on the manner in which computer systems are organized.

The old model in which a single computer used to serve all the computational needs of an organization has been replaced by a new one in which a large number of separate but interconnected computers do the job. Such systems are called as computer networks.

- Two computers are said to be interconnected if they interchange information. The connection between the separate computers can be done via a copper wire, fiber optics, microwaves or communication satellite.

- A printer, computer, or any machine that is capable of communicating on the network is referred to as a device or node.

- We can also say that computer network is an interconnection of various computers to share software, hardware and data through a communication medium between them. The computers connected in a network share files, folders, applications and resources like scanner, web-cams, printers etc.

- The best example of computer network is the Internet.

A computer network is an interconnection of various computers to share software, hardware, resources and data through a communication medium between them.

A computer networking is a set of autonomous computers that permits distributed processing of the information and data and increased Communication of resources.

Any Computer Networking communication need a sender, a receiver and a communication medium to transfer signal or Data from sender to the receiver. We need sender, receiver, communication channel, protocols and operating system to establish a computer networking.

A networks model describes the organization of various computers in a network for using resources.

Computer Network Properties

- Scope: A network architecture should solve so many general problems as possible.

- Scalability: A network must work well independently of the number of nodes that compose it.

- Robustness: The design of a network should allow it to function correctly, even though there are defective nodes.

- Self-configuration and Optimization: A network should have a minimal intervention of the administrator. In turn, you must have a series of parameters that allow the administrator to adjust them to obtain an optimal configuration for some and other networks according to their characteristics.

- Migration: If you decide to change networks, migration should not be affected in its properties and operation.

- Determinism: Under the same conditions, the network must always work the same.

Computer Network Model

A computer networks communication can be based on centralized, distributed or collaborative computing. Centralized computing involves many workstations or terminals, connected to one central mainframe or other powerful computer. Distributed computing interconnects one or more personal computers and allows various services like Data sharing, hardware sharing resources sharing or network sharing. The collaborative computing is the combination of centralized and distributed computing.

Centralized Computing

- It is also known as client-server computing.

- In this type of system, multiple computers are joined to one powerful mainframe computer.

- The server or mainframe computer has huge storage and processing capabilities.

- The computers that are connected to the mainframe or server are called Clients or Nodes.

- These nodes are not connected to each other; they are only connected to server.

Distributed Computing

- If one computer can forcibly start, stop or control another the computers are not autonomous. A system with one control unit and many slaves, or a large computer with remote printers and terminals is not called a computer network, it is called a Distributed System.

- Distributed computing means that the task is divided among multiple computers.

- Distributed computing interconnects one ore more personal computers or Workstations.

- In distributed computing, the nodes are capable of processing their own data and rely on network for services other than data processing.

- It allows various services like network sharing, hardware sharing and file sharing.

Collaborative Computing/Hybrid Computing

- It is the combination of centralized and distributed computing.

- In collaborative computing, the nodes are able to serve the basic needs of their users but they are dependent on some other computers for processing some specific request.

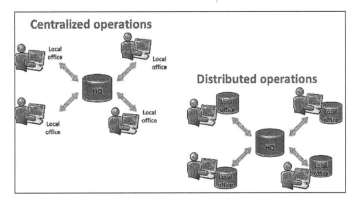

Computer Network Classification

The local area network communication can be constructed by using server based model or peer to peer model. In peer to peer networks, the individual clients share data and resources but no one computer is treated as server.

Networks can be classified into local area Networks, metropolitan area Networks and wide area networks. Local area network is the small network that cover a small area of Network. Metropolitan area networks are created by combining various local area networks. Wide area networks are the biggest networks that provide connectivity across the globe.

Networks provide the benefits of exchanging information or Data, sharing resources, reducing system costs, increased reliability and flexible working environment.

Network Packet

Computer communication links that do not support packets, such as traditional point-to-point telecommunication links, simply transmit data as a bit stream. However, the overwhelming majority of computer networks carry their data in *packets*. A network packet is a formatted unit of data (a list of bits or bytes, usually a few tens of bytes to a few kilobytes long) carried by a packet-switched network. Packets are sent through the network to their destination. Once the packets arrive they are reassembled into their original message.

Packets consist of two kinds of data: control information, and user data (payload). The control information provides data the network needs to deliver the user data, for example: source and destination network addresses, error detection codes, and sequencing information. Typically, control information is found in packet headers and trailers, with payload data in between.

With packets, the bandwidth of the transmission medium can be better shared among users than if the network were circuit switched. When one user is not sending packets, the link can be filled with packets from other users, and so the cost can be shared, with relatively little interference, provided the link isn't overused. Often the route a packet needs to take through a network is not immediately available. In that case the packet is queued and waits until a link is free.

Network Topology

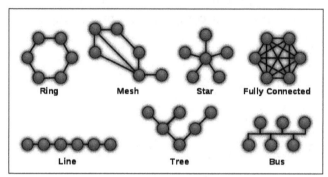

Common network topologies.

The physical layout of a network is usually less important than the topology that connects network nodes. Most diagrams that describe a physical network are therefore topological, rather than geographic. The symbols on these diagrams usually denote network links and network nodes.

Network topology is the layout or organizational hierarchy of interconnected nodes of a computer network. Different network topologies can affect throughput, but reliability is often more critical. With many technologies, such as bus networks, a single failure can cause the network to fail entirely. In general the more interconnections there are, the more robust the network is; but the more expensive it is to install.

Common layouts are:

- A bus network: All nodes are connected to a common medium along this medium. This was the layout used in the original Ethernet, called 10BASE5 and 10BASE2. This is still a common topology on the data link layer, although modern physical layer variants use point-to-point links instead.

- A star network: All nodes are connected to a special central node. This is the typical layout found in a Wireless LAN, where each wireless client connects to the central Wireless access point.

- A ring network: Each node is connected to its left and right neighbour node, such that all nodes are connected and that each node can reach each other node by traversing nodes left- or rightwards. The Fiber Distributed Data Interface (FDDI) made use of such a topology.

- A mesh network: Each node is connected to an arbitrary number of neighbours in such a way that there is at least one traversal from any node to any other.

- A fully connected network: Each node is connected to every other node in the network.

- A tree network: Nodes are arranged hierarchically.

The physical layout of the nodes in a network may not necessarily reflect the network topology. As an example, with FDDI, the network topology is a ring (actually two counter-rotating rings), but the physical topology is often a star, because all neighboring connections can be routed via a central physical location. Physical layout is not completely irrelevant, however, as common ducting and equipment locations can represent single points of failure due to issues like fires, power failures and flooding.

Overlay Network

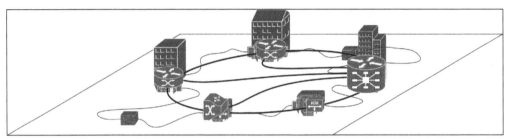

A sample overlay network.

An overlay network is a virtual computer network that is built on top of another network. Nodes in the overlay network are connected by virtual or logical links. Each link corresponds to a path, perhaps through many physical links, in the underlying network. The topology of the overlay network may (and often does) differ from that of the underlying one. For example, many peer-to-peer networks are overlay networks. They are organized as nodes of a virtual system of links that run on top of the Internet.

Overlay networks have been around since the invention of networking when computer systems were connected over telephone lines using modems, before any data network existed.

The most striking example of an overlay network is the Internet itself. The Internet itself was initially built as an overlay on the telephone network. Even today, each Internet node can communicate with virtually any other through an underlying mesh of sub-networks of wildly different topologies and technologies. Address resolution and routing are the means that allow mapping of a fully connected IP overlay network to its underlying network.

Another example of an overlay network is a distributed hash table, which maps keys to nodes in the network. In this case, the underlying network is an IP network, and the overlay network is a table (actually a map) indexed by keys.

Overlay networks have also been proposed as a way to improve Internet routing, such as through quality of service guarantees to achieve higher-quality streaming media. Previous proposals such as IntServ, DiffServ, and IP Multicast have not seen wide acceptance largely because they require modification of all routers in the network. On the other hand, an overlay network can be incrementally deployed on end-hosts running the overlay protocol software, without cooperation from

Internet service providers. The overlay network has no control over how packets are routed in the underlying network between two overlay nodes, but it can control, for example, the sequence of overlay nodes that a message traverses before it reaches its destination.

For example, Akamai Technologies manages an overlay network that provides reliable, efficient content delivery (a kind of multicast). Academic research includes end system multicast, resilient routing and quality of service studies, among others.

Network Links

The transmission media (often referred to in the literature as the *physical medium*) used to link devices to form a computer network include electrical cable, optical fiber, and radio waves. In the OSI model, these are defined at layers 1 and 2 — the physical layer and the data link layer.

A widely adopted *family* of transmission media used in local area network (LAN) technology is collectively known as Ethernet. The media and protocol standards that enable communication between networked devices over Ethernet are defined by IEEE 802.3. Ethernet transmits data over both copper and fiber cables. Wireless LAN standards use radio waves, others use infrared signals as a transmission medium. Power line communication uses a building's power cabling to transmit data.

Wired Technologies

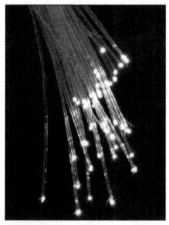

Fiber optic cables are used to transmit light from one computer/network node to another.

The following classes of wired technologies are used in computer networking:

- Coaxial cable is widely used for cable television systems, office buildings, and other worksites for local area networks. Transmission speed ranges from 200 million bits per second to more than 500 million bits per second.

- ITU-T G.hn technology uses existing home wiring (coaxial cable, phone lines and power lines) to create a high-speed local area network.

- Twisted pair cabling is used for wired Ethernet and other standards. It typically consists of 4 pairs of copper cabling that can be utilized for both voice and data transmission. The use of two wires twisted together helps to reduce crosstalk and electromagnetic induction. The transmission speed ranges from 2 Mbit/s to 10 Gbit/s. Twisted pair cabling comes in two forms: unshielded twisted pair (UTP) and shielded twisted-pair (STP). Each form comes in several category ratings, designed for use in various scenarios.

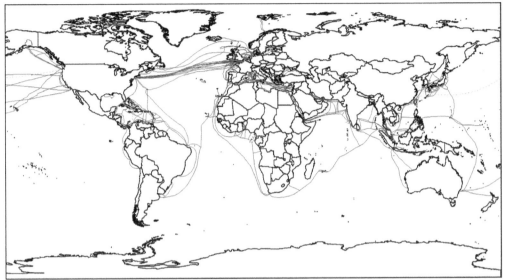

2007 map showing submarine optical fiber telecommunication cables around the world.

- An *optical fiber* is a glass fiber. It carries pulses of light that represent data. Some advantages of optical fibers over metal wires are very low transmission loss and immunity to electrical interference. Optical fibers can simultaneously carry multiple streams of data on different wavelengths of light, which greatly increases the rate that data can be sent to up to trillions of bits per second. Optic fibers can be used for long runs of cable carrying very high data rates, and are used for undersea cables to interconnect continents. There are two basic types of fiber optics, single-mode optical fiber (SMF) and multi-mode optical fiber (MMF). Single-mode fiber has the advantage of being able to sustain a coherent signal for dozens or even a hundred kilometers. Multimode fiber is cheaper to terminate but is limited to a few hundred or even only a few dozens of meters, depending on the data rate and cable grade.

Wireless Technologies

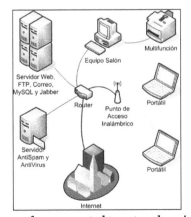

Computers are very often connected to networks using wireless links.

Network connections can be established wirelessly using radio or other electromagnetic means of communication.

- Terrestrial microwave: Terrestrial microwave communication uses Earth-based transmitters and receivers resembling satellite dishes. Terrestrial microwaves are in the low gigahertz range, which limits all communications to line-of-sight. Relay stations are spaced approximately 40 miles (64 km) apart.

- Communications satellites: Satellites communicate also communicate via microwave. The satellites are stationed in space, typically in geosynchronous orbit 35,400 km (22,000 mi) above the equator. These Earth-orbiting systems are capable of receiving and relaying voice, data, and TV signals.

- Cellular networks use several radio communications technologies. The systems divide the region covered into multiple geographic areas. Each area is served by a low-power transceiver.

- Radio and spread spectrum technologies: Wireless LANs use a high-frequency radio technology similar to digital cellular. Wireless LANs use spread spectrum technology to enable communication between multiple devices in a limited area. IEEE 802.11 defines a common flavor of open-standards wireless radio-wave technology known as Wi-Fi.

- Free-space optical communication uses visible or invisible light for communications. In most cases, line-of-sight propagation is used, which limits the physical positioning of communicating devices.

Exotic Technologies

There have been various attempts at transporting data over exotic media:

- IP over Avian Carriers was a humorous April fool's Request for Comments, issued as RFC 1149. It was implemented in real life in 2001.

- Extending the Internet to interplanetary dimensions via radio waves, the Interplanetary Internet.

Both cases have a large round-trip delay time, which gives slow two-way communication, but doesn't prevent sending large amounts of information.

Network Nodes

Apart from any physical transmission media there may be, networks comprise additional basic system building blocks, such as network interface controllers (NICs), repeaters, hubs, bridges, switches, routers, modems, and firewalls. Any particular piece of equipment will frequently contain multiple building blocks and perform multiple functions.

Network Interfaces

A network interface controller (NIC) is computer hardware that provides a computer with the ability to access the transmission media, and has the ability to process low-level network information. For example, the NIC may have a connector for accepting a cable, or an aerial for wireless transmission and reception, and the associated circuitry.

The NIC responds to traffic addressed to a network address for either the NIC or the computer as a whole.

An ATM network interface in the form of an accessory card. A lot of network interfaces are built-in.

In Ethernet networks, each network interface controller has a unique Media Access Control (MAC) address—usually stored in the controller's permanent memory. To avoid address conflicts between network devices, the Institute of Electrical and Electronics Engineers (IEEE) maintains and administers MAC address uniqueness. The size of an Ethernet MAC address is six octets. The three most significant octets are reserved to identify NIC manufacturers. These manufacturers, using only their assigned prefixes, uniquely assign the three least-significant octets of every Ethernet interface they produce.

Repeaters and Hubs

A repeater is an electronic device that receives a network signal, cleans it of unnecessary noise and regenerates it. The signal is retransmitted at a higher power level, or to the other side of an obstruction, so that the signal can cover longer distances without degradation. In most twisted pair Ethernet configurations, repeaters are required for cable that runs longer than 100 meters. With fiber optics, repeaters can be tens or even hundreds of kilometers apart.

A repeater with multiple ports is known as an Ethernet hub. Repeaters work on the physical layer of the OSI model. Repeaters require a small amount of time to regenerate the signal. This can cause a propagation delay that affects network performance and may affect proper function. As a result, many network architectures limit the number of repeaters that can be used in a row, e.g., the Ethernet 5-4-3 rule.

Hubs and repeaters in LANs have been mostly obsoleted by modern switches.

Bridges

A network bridge connects and filters traffic between two network segments at the data link layer (layer 2) of the OSI model to form a single network. This breaks the network's collision domain but maintains a unified broadcast domain. Network segmentation breaks down a large, congested network into an aggregation of smaller, more efficient networks.

Bridges come in three basic types:

- Local bridges: Directly connect LANs.
- Remote bridges: Can be used to create a wide area network (WAN) link between LANs. Remote bridges, where the connecting link is slower than the end networks, largely have been replaced with routers.

- Wireless bridges: Can be used to join LANs or connect remote devices to LANs.

Switches

A network switch is a device that forwards and filters OSI layer 2 datagrams (frames) between ports based on the destination MAC address in each frame. A switch is distinct from a hub in that it only forwards the frames to the physical ports involved in the communication rather than all ports connected. It can be thought of as a multi-port bridge. It learns to associate physical ports to MAC addresses by examining the source addresses of received frames. If an unknown destination is targeted, the switch broadcasts to all ports but the source. Switches normally have numerous ports, facilitating a star topology for devices, and cascading additional switches.

Routers

A typical home or small office router showing the
ADSL telephone line and Ethernet network cable connections.

A router is an internetworking device that forwards packets between networks by processing the routing information included in the packet or datagram (Internet protocol information from layer 3). The routing information is often processed in conjunction with the routing table (or forwarding table). A router uses its routing table to determine where to forward packets. A destination in a routing table can include a "null" interface, also known as the "black hole" interface because data can go into it, however, no further processing is done for said data, i.e. the packets are dropped.

Modems

Modems (MOdulator-DEModulator) are used to connect network nodes via wire not originally designed for digital network traffic, or for wireless. To do this one or more carrier signals are modulated by the digital signal to produce an analog signal that can be tailored to give the required properties for transmission. Modems are commonly used for telephone lines, using a digital subscriber line technology.

Firewalls

A firewall is a network device for controlling network security and access rules. Firewalls are typically configured to reject access requests from unrecognized sources while allowing actions from recognized ones. The vital role firewalls play in network security grows in parallel with the constant increase in cyber attacks.

Communication Protocols

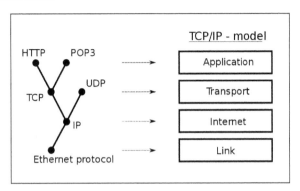

The TCP/IP model or Internet layering scheme and its relation to common protocols often layered on top of it.

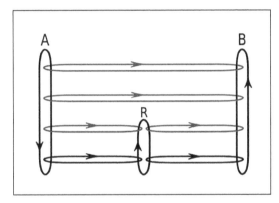

Message flows (A-B) in the presence of a router (R), red flows are effective communication paths, black paths are across the actual network links.

A communication protocol is a set of rules for exchanging information over a network. In a protocol stack, each protocol leverages the services of the protocol layer below it, until the lowest layer controls the hardware which sends information across the media. The use of protocol layering is today ubiquitous across the field of computer networking. An important example of a protocol stack is HTTP (the World Wide Web protocol) running over TCP over IP (the Internet protocols) over IEEE 802.11 (the Wi-Fi protocol). This stack is used between the wireless router and the home user's personal computer when the user is surfing the web.

Communication protocols have various characteristics. They may be connection-oriented or connectionless, they may use circuit mode or packet switching, and they may use hierarchical addressing or flat addressing.

There are many communication protocols, a few of which are described below:

IEEE 802

IEEE 802 is a family of IEEE standards dealing with local area networks and metropolitan area networks. The complete IEEE 802 protocol suite provides a diverse set of networking capabilities. The protocols have a flat addressing scheme. They operate mostly at levels 1 and 2 of the OSI model.

For example, MAC bridging (IEEE 802.1D) deals with the routing of Ethernet packets using a Spanning Tree Protocol. IEEE 802.1Q describes VLANs, and IEEE 802.1X defines a port-based Network Access Control protocol, which forms the basis for the authentication mechanisms used in VLANs (but it is also found in WLANs) – it is what the home user sees when the user has to enter a "wireless access key".

Ethernet

Ethernet, sometimes simply called *LAN*, is a family of protocols used in wired LANs, described by a set of standards together called IEEE 802.3 published by the Institute of Electrical and Electronics Engineers.

Wireless LAN

Wireless LAN, also widely known as WLAN or WiFi, is probably the most well-known member of the IEEE 802 protocol family for home users today. It is standardized by IEEE 802.11 and shares many properties with wired Ethernet.

Internet Protocol Suite

The Internet Protocol Suite, also called TCP/IP, is the foundation of all modern networking. It offers connection-less as well as connection-oriented services over an inherently unreliable network traversed by data-gram transmission at the Internet protocol (IP) level. At its core, the protocol suite defines the addressing, identification, and routing specifications for Internet Protocol Version 4 (IPv4) and for IPv6, the next generation of the protocol with a much enlarged addressing capability.

SONET/SDH

Synchronous optical networking (SONET) and Synchronous Digital Hierarchy (SDH) are standardized multiplexing protocols that transfer multiple digital bit streams over optical fiber using lasers. They were originally designed to transport circuit mode communications from a variety of different sources, primarily to support real-time, uncompressed, circuit-switched voice encoded in PCM (Pulse-Code Modulation) format. However, due to its protocol neutrality and transport-oriented features, SONET/SDH also was the obvious choice for transporting Asynchronous Transfer Mode (ATM) frames.

Asynchronous Transfer Mode

Asynchronous Transfer Mode (ATM) is a switching technique for telecommunication networks. It uses asynchronous time-division multiplexing and encodes data into small, fixed-sized cells. This differs from other protocols such as the Internet Protocol Suite or Ethernet that use variable sized packets or frames. ATM has similarity with both circuit and packet switched networking. This makes it a good choice for a network that must handle both traditional high-throughput data traffic, and real-time, low-latency content such as voice and video. ATM uses a connection-oriented model in which a virtual circuit must be established between two endpoints before the actual data exchange begins.

While the role of ATM is diminishing in favor of next-generation networks, it still plays a role in the last mile, which is the connection between an Internet service provider and the home user.

Cellular Standards

There are a number of different digital cellular standards, including: Global System for Mobile Communications (GSM), General Packet Radio Service (GPRS), cdmaOne, CDMA2000, Evolution-Data Optimized (EV-DO), Enhanced Data Rates for GSM Evolution (EDGE), Universal Mobile Telecommunications System (UMTS), Digital Enhanced Cordless Telecommunications (DECT), Digital AMPS (IS-136/TDMA), and Integrated Digital Enhanced Network (iDEN).

Organizational Scope

Networks are typically managed by the organizations that own them. Private enterprise networks may use a combination of intranets and extranets. They may also provide network access to the Internet, which has no single owner and permits virtually unlimited global connectivity.

Intranet

An intranet is a set of networks that are under the control of a single administrative entity. The intranet uses the IP protocol and IP-based tools such as web browsers and file transfer applications. The administrative entity limits use of the intranet to its authorized users. Most commonly, an intranet is the internal LAN of an organization. A large intranet typically has at least one web server to provide users with organizational information. An intranet is also anything behind the router on a local area network.

Extranet

An extranet is a network that is also under the administrative control of a single organization, but supports a limited connection to a specific external network. For example, an organization may provide access to some aspects of its intranet to share data with its business partners or customers. These other entities are not necessarily trusted from a security standpoint. Network connection to an extranet is often, but not always, implemented via WAN technology.

Internetwork

An internetwork is the connection of multiple computer networks via a common routing technology using routers.

Internet

The Internet is the largest example of an internetwork. It is a global system of interconnected governmental, academic, corporate, public, and private computer networks. It is based on the networking technologies of the Internet Protocol Suite. It is the successor of the Advanced Research Projects Agency Network (ARPANET) developed by DARPA of the United States Department of Defense. The Internet is also the communications backbone underlying the World Wide Web (WWW).

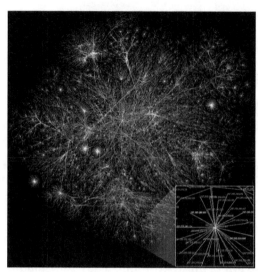

Partial map of the Internet based on the January 15, 2005. Each line is drawn between two nodes, representing two IP addresses. The length of the lines are indicative of the delay between those two nodes. This graph represents less than 30% of the Class C networks reachable.

Participants in the Internet use a diverse array of methods of several hundred documented, and often standardized, protocols compatible with the Internet Protocol Suite and an addressing system (IP addresses) administered by the Internet Assigned Numbers Authority and address registries. Service providers and large enterprises exchange information about the reachability of their address spaces through the Border Gateway Protocol (BGP), forming a redundant worldwide mesh of transmission paths.

Darknet

A darknet is an overlay network, typically running on the Internet, that is only accessible through specialized software. A darknet is an anonymizing network where connections are made only between trusted peers — sometimes called "friends" (F2F) — using non-standard protocols and ports.

Darknets are distinct from other distributed peer-to-peer networks as sharing is anonymous (that is, IP addresses are not publicly shared), and therefore users can communicate with little fear of governmental or corporate interference.

Routing

Routing is the process of selecting network paths to carry network traffic. Routing is performed for many kinds of networks, including circuit switching networks and packet switched networks.

In packet switched networks, routing directs packet forwarding (the transit of logically addressed network packets from their source toward their ultimate destination) through intermediate nodes. Intermediate nodes are typically network hardware devices such as routers, bridges, gateways, firewalls, or switches. General-purpose computers can also forward packets and perform routing, though they are not specialized hardware and may suffer from limited performance. The routing process usually directs forwarding on the basis of routing tables, which maintain a record of the routes to various network destinations. Thus, constructing routing tables, which are held in the router's memory, is very important for efficient routing.

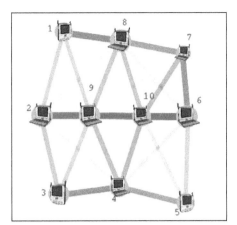

Routing calculates good paths through a network for information to take. For example, from node 1 to node 6 the best routes are likely to be 1-8-7-6 or 1-8-10-6, as this has the thickest routes.

There are usually multiple routes that can be taken, and to choose between them, different elements can be considered to decide which routes get installed into the routing table, such as (sorted by priority):

1. Prefix-Length: Where longer subnet masks are preferred (independent if it is within a routing protocol or over different routing protocol).

2. Metric: Where a lower metric/cost is preferred (only valid within one and the same routing protocol).

3. Administrative distance: Where a lower distance is preferred (only valid between different routing protocols).

Most routing algorithms use only one network path at a time. Multipath routing techniques enable the use of multiple alternative paths.

Routing, in a more narrow sense of the term, is often contrasted with bridging in its assumption that network addresses are structured and that similar addresses imply proximity within the network. Structured addresses allow a single routing table entry to represent the route to a group of devices. In large networks, structured addressing (routing, in the narrow sense) outperforms unstructured addressing (bridging). Routing has become the dominant form of addressing on the Internet. Bridging is still widely used within localized environments.

Network Service

Network services are applications hosted by servers on a computer network, to provide some functionality for members or users of the network, or to help the network itself to operate.

The World Wide Web, E-mail, printing and network file sharing are examples of well-known network services. Network services such as DNS (Domain Name System) give names for IP and MAC addresses (people remember names like "nm.lan" better than numbers like "210.121.67.18"), and DHCP to ensure that the equipment on the network has a valid IP address.

Services are usually based on a service protocol that defines the format and sequencing of messages between clients and servers of that network service.

Network Performance

Quality of Service

Depending on the installation requirements, network performance is usually measured by the quality of service of a telecommunications product. The parameters that affect this typically can include throughput, jitter, bit error rate and latency.

The following list gives examples of network performance measures for a circuit-switched network and one type of packet-switched network, viz. ATM:

- Circuit-switched networks: In circuit switched networks, network performance is synonymous with the grade of service. The number of rejected calls is a measure of how well the network is performing under heavy traffic loads. Other types of performance measures can include the level of noise and echo.

- ATM: In an Asynchronous Transfer Mode (ATM) network, performance can be measured by line rate, quality of service (QoS), data throughput, connect time, stability, technology, modulation technique and modem enhancements.

There are many ways to measure the performance of a network, as each network is different in nature and design. Performance can also be modelled instead of measured. For example, state transition diagrams are often used to model queuing performance in a circuit-switched network. The network planner uses these diagrams to analyze how the network performs in each state, ensuring that the network is optimally designed.

Network Congestion

Network congestion occurs when a link or node is subjected to a greater data load than it is rated for, resulting in a deterioration of its quality of service. Typical effects include queueing delay, packet loss or the blocking of new connections. A consequence of these latter two is that incremental increases in offered load lead either to only a small increase in network throughput, or to a reduction in network throughput.

Network protocols that use aggressive retransmissions to compensate for packet loss tend to keep systems in a state of network congestion—even after the initial load is reduced to a level that would not normally induce network congestion. Thus, networks using these protocols can exhibit two stable states under the same level of load. The stable state with low throughput is known as *congestive collapse.*

Modern networks use congestion control, congestion avoidance and traffic control techniques to try to avoid congestion collapse. These include: exponential backoff in protocols such as 802.11's CSMA/CA and the original Ethernet, window reduction in TCP, and fair queueing in devices such as routers. Another method to avoid the negative effects of network congestion is implementing priority schemes, so that some packets are transmitted with higher priority than others. Priority schemes do not solve network congestion by themselves, but they help to alleviate the effects of congestion for some services. An example of this is 802.1p. A third method to avoid network congestion is the explicit allocation of network resources to specific flows. One example of this is the use of Contention-Free Transmission Opportunities (CFTXOPs) in the ITU-T G.hn standard, which provides high-speed (up to 1 Gbit/s) Local area networking over existing home wires (power lines, phone lines and coaxial cables). For the Internet, RFC 2914 addresses the subject of congestion control in detail.

Network Resilience

Network resilience is "the ability to provide and maintain an acceptable level of service in the face of faults and challenges to normal operation."

Security

Network Security

Network security consists of provisions and policies adopted by the network administrator to prevent and monitor unauthorized access, misuse, modification, or denial of the computer network and its network-accessible resources. Network security is the authorization of access to data in a network, which is controlled by the network administrator. Users are assigned an ID and password that allows them access to information and programs within their authority. Network security is used on a variety of computer networks, both public and private, to secure daily transactions and communications among businesses, government agencies and individuals.

Network Surveillance

Network surveillance is the monitoring of data being transferred over computer networks such as the Internet. The monitoring is often done surreptitiously and may be done by or at the behest of governments, by corporations, criminal organizations, or individuals. It may or may not be legal and may or may not require authorization from a court or other independent agency.

Computer and network surveillance programs are widespread today, and almost all Internet traffic is or could potentially be monitored for clues to illegal activity.

Surveillance is very useful to governments and law enforcement to maintain social control, recognize and monitor threats, and prevent/investigate criminal activity. With the advent of programs such as the Total Information Awareness program, technologies such as high speed surveillance computers and biometrics software, and laws such as the Communications Assistance For Law Enforcement Act, governments now possess an unprecedented ability to monitor the activities of citizens.

However, many civil rights and privacy groups—such as Reporters Without Borders, the Electronic Frontier Foundation, and the American Civil Liberties Union—have expressed concern that increasing surveillance of citizens may lead to a mass surveillance society, with limited political and personal freedoms. Fears such as this have led to numerous lawsuits such as *Hepting v. AT&T*. The hacktivist group Anonymous has hacked into government websites in protest of what it considers "draconian surveillance".

End-to-End Encryption

End-to-end encryption (E2EE) is a digital communications paradigm of uninterrupted protection of data traveling between two communicating parties. It involves the originating party encrypting data so only the intended recipient can decrypt it, with no dependency on third parties. End-to-end encryption prevents intermediaries, such as Internet providers or application service providers, from discovering or tampering with communications. End-to-end encryption generally protects both confidentiality and integrity.

Examples of end-to-end encryption include HTTPS for web traffic, PGP for email, OTR for instant messaging, ZRTP for telephony, and TETRA for radio.

Typical server-based communications systems do not include end-to-end encryption. These systems can only guarantee protection of communications between clients and servers, not between the communicating parties themselves. Examples of non-E2EE systems are Google Talk, Yahoo Messenger, Facebook, and Dropbox. Some such systems, for example LavaBit and SecretInk, have even described themselves as offering "end-to-end" encryption when they do not. Some systems that normally offer end-to-end encryption have turned out to contain a back door that subverts negotiation of the encryption key between the communicating parties, for example Skype or Hushmail.

The end-to-end encryption paradigm does not directly address risks at the communications endpoints themselves, such as the technical exploitation of clients, poor quality random number generators, or key escrow. E2EE also does not address traffic analysis, which relates to things such as the identities of the end points and the times and quantities of messages that are sent.

SSL/TLS

The introduction and rapid growth of e-commerce on the World Wide Web in the mid-1990s made it obvious that some form of authentication and encryption was needed. Netscape took the first shot at a new standard. At the time, the dominant web browser was Netscape Navigator. Netscape created a standard called secure socket layer (SSL). SSL requires a server with a certificate. When a client requests access to an SSL-secured server, the server sends a copy of the certificate to the client. The SSL client checks this certificate (all web browsers come with an exhaustive list of CA root certificates preloaded), and if the certificate checks out, the server is authenticated and the client negotiates a symmetric-key cipher for use in the session. The session is now in a very secure encrypted tunnel between the SSL server and the SSL client.

Views of Networks

Users and network administrators typically have different views of their networks. Users can share printers and some servers from a workgroup, which usually means they are in the same geographic location and are on the same LAN, whereas a Network Administrator is responsible to keep that network up and running. A community of interest has less of a connection of being in a local area, and should be thought of as a set of arbitrarily located users who share a set of servers, and possibly also communicate via peer-to-peer technologies.

Network administrators can see networks from both physical and logical perspectives. The physical perspective involves geographic locations, physical cabling, and the network elements (e.g., routers, bridges and application layer gateways) that interconnect via the transmission media. Logical networks, called, in the TCP/IP architecture, subnets, map onto one or more transmission media. For example, a common practice in a campus of buildings is to make a set of LAN cables in each building appear to be a common subnet, using virtual LAN (VLAN) technology.

Both users and administrators are aware, to varying extents, of the trust and scope characteristics of a network. Again using TCP/IP architectural terminology, an intranet is a community of interest under private administration usually by an enterprise, and is only accessible by authorized users (e.g. employees). Intranets do not have to be connected to the Internet, but generally have a limited connection. An extranet is an extension of an intranet that allows secure communications to users outside of the intranet (e.g. business partners, customers).

Unofficially, the Internet is the set of users, enterprises, and content providers that are interconnected by Internet Service Providers (ISP). From an engineering viewpoint, the Internet is the set of subnets, and aggregates of subnets, which share the registered IP address space and exchange information about the reachability of those IP addresses using the Border Gateway Protocol. Typically, the human-readable names of servers are translated to IP addresses, transparently to users, via the directory function of the Domain Name System (DNS).

Over the Internet, there can be business-to-business (B2B), business-to-consumer (B2C) and consumer-to-consumer (C2C) communications. When money or sensitive information is exchanged, the communications are apt to be protected by some form of communications security mechanism. Intranets and extranets can be securely superimposed onto the Internet, without any access by general Internet users and administrators, using secure Virtual Private Network (VPN) technology.

LOCAL AREA NETWORK

A local area network (LAN) is a computer network that interconnects computers within a limited area such as a residence, school, laboratory, university campus or office building. By contrast, a wide area network (WAN) not only covers a larger geographic distance, but also generally involves leased telecommunication circuits.

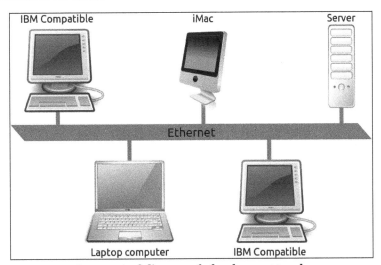

A conceptual diagram of a local area network.

Ethernet and Wi-Fi are the two most common technologies in use for local area networks. Historical technologies include ARCNET, Token ring, and AppleTalk.

Cabling

Early Ethernet (10BASE-5 and 10BASE-2) used coaxial cable. Shielded twisted pair was used in IBM's Token Ring LAN implementation. In 1984, StarLAN showed the potential of simple unshielded twisted pair by using Cat3 cable—the same cable used for telephone systems. This led to the development of 10BASE-T (and its successors) and structured cabling which is still the basis of most commercial LANs today. While optical fiber cable is common for links between network switches, use of fiber to the desktop is rare.

Wireless Media

In a wireless LAN, users have unrestricted movement within the coverage area. Wireless networks have become popular in residences and small businesses, because of their ease of installation. Most wireless LANs use Wi-Fi as it is built into smartphones, tablet computers and laptops. Guests are often offered Internet access via a hotspot service.

Technical Aspects

Network topology describes the layout of interconnections between devices and network segments. At the data link layer and physical layer, a wide variety of LAN topologies have been used, including ring, bus, mesh and star.

Simple LANs generally consist of cabling and one or more switches. A switch can be connected to a router, cable modem, or ADSL modem for Internet access. A LAN can include a wide variety of other network devices such as firewalls, load balancers, and network intrusion detection. Advanced LANs are characterized by their use of redundant links with switches using the spanning tree protocol to prevent loops, their ability to manage differing traffic types via quality of service (QoS), and their ability to segregate traffic with VLANs.

At the higher network layers, protocols such as NetBEUI, IPX/SPX, AppleTalk and others were once common, but the Internet Protocol Suite (TCP/IP) has prevailed as a standard of choice.

LANs can maintain connections with other LANs via leased lines, leased services, or across the Internet using virtual private network technologies. Depending on how the connections are established and secured, and the distance involved, such linked LANs may also be classified as a metropolitan area network (MAN) or a wide area network (WAN).

Various LAN Technologies

Ethernet

Ethernet is a widely deployed LAN technology.This technology was invented by Bob Metcalfe and D.R. Boggs in the year 1970. It was standardized in IEEE 802.3 in 1980.

Ethernet shares media. Network which uses shared media has high probability of data collision. Ethernet uses Carrier Sense Multi Access/Collision Detection (CSMA/CD) technology to detect collisions. On the occurrence of collision in Ethernet, all its hosts roll back, wait for some random amount of time, and then re-transmit the data.

Ethernet connector is,network interface card equipped with 48-bits MAC address. This helps other Ethernet devices to identify and communicate with remote devices in Ethernet.

Traditional Ethernet uses 10BASE-T specifications.The number 10 depicts 10MBPS speed, BASE stands for baseband, and T stands for Thick Ethernet. 10BASE-T Ethernet provides transmission speed up to 10MBPS and uses coaxial cable or Cat-5 twisted pair cable with RJ-45 connector. Ethernet follows star topology with segment length up to 100 meters. All devices are connected to a hub/switch in a star fashion.

Fast-Ethernet

To encompass need of fast emerging software and hardware technologies, Ethernet extends itself as Fast-Ethernet. It can run on UTP, Optical Fiber, and wirelessly too. It can provide speed up to 100 MBPS. This standard is named as 100BASE-T in IEEE 803.2 using Cat-5 twisted pair cable. It uses CSMA/CD technique for wired media sharing among the Ethernet hosts and CSMA/CA (CA stands for Collision Avoidance) technique for wireless Ethernet LAN.

Fast Ethernet on fiber is defined under 100BASE-FX standard which provides speed up to 100 MBPS on fiber. Ethernet over fiber can be extended up to 100 meters in half-duplex mode and can reach maximum of 2000 meters in full-duplex over multimode fibers.

Giga-Ethernet

After being introduced in 1995, Fast-Ethernet could enjoy its high speed status only for 3 years till Giga-Ethernet introduced. Giga-Ethernet provides speed up to 1000 mbits/seconds. IEEE802.3ab standardize Giga-Ethernet over UTP using Cat-5, Cat-5e and Cat-6 cables. IEEE802.3ah defines Giga-Ethernet over Fiber.

Virtual LAN

LAN uses Ethernet which in turn works on shared media. Shared media in Ethernet create one single Broadcast domain and one single Collision domain. Introduction of switches to Ethernet has removed single collision domain issue and each device connected to switch works in its separate collision domain. But even Switches cannot divide a network into separate Broadcast domains.

Virtual LAN is a solution to divide a single Broadcast domain into multiple Broadcast domains. Host in one VLAN cannot speak to a host in another. By default, all hosts are placed into the same VLAN.

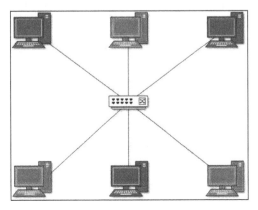

In this diagram, different VLANs are depicted in different color codes. Hosts in one VLAN, even if connected on the same Switch cannot see or speak to other hosts in different VLANs. VLAN is Layer-2 technology which works closely on Ethernet. To route packets between two different VLANs a Layer-3 device such as Router is required.

PERSONAL AREA NETWORK

The communication network established for the purpose of connecting computer devices of personal use is known as the personal area network PAN (Personal Area Network).when a network is established by connecting phone lines to personal digital devices or PDAs (personal digital assistants), this communication is known as PAN (Personal Area Network). Thomas Zimmerman was the first research scientist to introduce the idea of Personal Area Network (PAN).

PAN (Personal Area Network) Related Technologies

The basic purport of establishing PAN (Personal Area Network) is provide a communication channel to the individuals, who want to carry their own digital devices. However at the same they want to stay in contact with the network. PAN (Personal Area Network) networks often cover an area of 30 feet. Personal computer devices may include palm tops mobile phones, potable media players, play stations and net books. These devices help a person to browse internet while traveling, to write notes and to send instant messages. These personal digital devices assist a person to develop networks and communicate via intranet, internet or even extranet. There are many wireless technologies which are helpful in developing wireless personal area network. Personal area networks (PAN) are developed either using cables or wireless technologies. Wireless PAN (Personal Area Network) is connected to the wired PAN (Personal Area Network) system either using fire wire or USB.

Wireless Personal Area Network (WPAN)

PAN (Personal Area Network) are dependent on the Bluetooth or infrared technologies for the transmission of wireless signals. Blue tooth wireless PAN (Personal Area Network) is referred to as Pico nets. Pico nets are ad hoc networks. In this Pico nets network number of devices are connected by using Bluetooth technology. One key master device is further attached to seven or more than dynamic slave seven devices. Master device has a control and option to activate these devices at any time. Pico nets work over a range of 200metres and transmit data of about 2100 Kbit/sec. The main focus point of wireless PAN (Personal Area Network) is to facilitate individual workspace. The Bluetooth technology used in wireless PAN (Personal Area Network) connection is based on IEEE 802.15 standard.

Wireless Personal Area Network (WPAN) can perform really efficient operations if we connect them with specialized devices. For examples it can help surgeons to seek guidance from other surgeons or team members during a surgical operation. Wireless Personal Area Network (WPAN) is based on plug –in technology. When wireless equipment's come into contact with each other within the range of few kilometers, give an illusion if they are connected with a cable. Rapid development and improvement in this technology is needed in this area. This further development would help develop a seamless network between office and home devices. This development would help scientists, archeologists and people associated to other departments to transfer their findings to any database around them.

Purpose and uses of PAN (Personal Area Network)

The wearable and portable computer devices communicate with each other. These devices while communicating transfer digital signals and information, these signals are transferred using the electrical conductivity coming out of human body. This linkup information exchange can take place even between two people who are carrying digital assistance devices while they are shaking hands. In this process of hand shake, an electric field is generated around people, and they emit Pico amps. These emissions complete the circuit and hence an exchange of information takes place. This information exchange includes the transfer of personal data such as email address, phone numbers etc.

The purpose of PDAs is to make the use of electric field around human beings. Mobile phones (smart phones only), palmtops and even pagers serve this purpose. Wireless digital devices work twenty four hours a day and seven days a week. This enables you to stay in communication circle always. PAN (Personal Area Network) network has enabled the transfer of data within the small geographical areas with the help of many small and portable carrying devices.

Advantages of Personal Area Network

- No Extra Space Requires: Personal area network does not require extra wire or space. For connecting two devices you only need to enable Bluetooth in both devices to start sharing data among them. For example, connecting wireless keyboard and mouse with the tablet through Bluetooth.

- Connect to Many Devices at a Time: Many devices can be connected to one device at the same time in a personal area network. You can connect one mobile to many other mobiles or tablets to share files.

- Cost Effective: No extra wires are needed in this type of network. Also, no extra data charges are involved so PAN is an inexpensive way of communication.

- Easy to Use: It is easy to use. No advanced setup is required.

- Reliable: If you use this type of data connection within 10 meters then your network is stable and reliable.

- Secure: This network is secured because all the devices are authorized before data sharing. Third party injection and data hacking are not possible in PAN.

- Used in Office, Conference, and Meetings: Infrared is the technology used in TV remotes, AC remotes, and other devices. Bluetooth, infrared and other types of PAN is used to interconnect digital devices in offices, meetings, and conferences.

- Synchronize Data Between Different Devices: One person can synchronize several devices i.e. download, upload and exchanging data among devices.

- Portable: A person can move devices as it is a wireless network and data exchange is not affected. That mean PAN is portable as well.

Disadvantages of Personal Area Network

- Less Distance Range: Signal range is maximum 10 meters which makes limitation for long distance sharing.

- Interfere With Radio Signals: As personal area network also use infrared so it can interfere with radio signals and data can be dropped.

- Slow Data Transfer: Bluetooth and infrared have a slow data transfer rate as compared to another type of networks like LAN (local area network).

- Health Problem: In some cases, PAN uses microwave signals in some digital devices which have a bad effect on the human body like brain and heart problems may occur.

- Costly in Terms of Communication Devices: Personal area network is used in digital devices which are costly so it is another disadvantage of PAN. Examples are smartphones, PDA, laptops, and digital cameras.

- Infrared Signals Travel in a Straight Line: TV remote use infrared signals which have a problem that they travel in straight line. So this counts another disadvantage of PAN.

Examples of Personal Area Network

Some Examples of PAN are:

- Wireless keyboards,

- Wireless Mice,

- Smartphones,

- TV remotes,

- Wireless printers,

- Gaming consoles,

- Smartphone technologies include Infrared, Bluetooth, FireWire, ZigBee, Ultrawideband, Wibree, wireless USB.

WIDE AREA NETWORK

A wide area network (WAN) is a telecommunications network that extends over a large geographical area for the primary purpose of computer networking. Wide area networks are often established with leased telecommunication circuits.

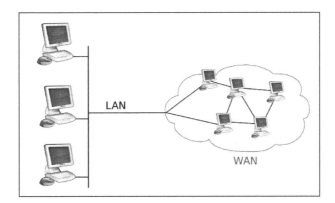

Business, as well as education and government entities use wide area networks to relay data to staff, students, clients, buyers and suppliers from various locations across the world. In essence, this mode of telecommunication allows a business to effectively carry out its daily function regardless of location. The Internet may be considered a WAN.

Similar types of networks are personal area networks (PANs), local area networks (LANs), campus area networks (CANs), or metropolitan area networks (MANs) which are usually limited to a room, building, campus or specific metropolitan area, respectively.

Design Options

The textbook definition of a WAN is a computer network spanning regions, countries, or even the world. However, in terms of the application of computer networking protocols and concepts, it may be best to view WANs as computer networking technologies used to transmit data over long distances, and between different LANs, MANs and other localised computer networking architectures. This distinction stems from the fact that common LAN technologies operating at lower layers of the OSI model (such as the forms of Ethernet or Wi-Fi) are often designed for physically proximal networks, and thus cannot transmit data over tens, hundreds, or even thousands of miles or kilometres.

WANs do not just necessarily connect physically disparate LANs. A CAN, for example, may have a localized backbone of a WAN technology, which connects different LANs within a campus. This could be to facilitate higher bandwidth applications or provide better functionality for users in the CAN.

WANs are used to connect LANs and other types of networks together so that users and computers in one location can communicate with users and computers in other locations. Many WANs are built for one particular organization and are private. Others, built by Internet service providers, provide connections from an organization's LAN to the Internet. WANs are often built using leased lines. At each end of the leased line, a router connects the LAN on one side with a second router within the LAN on the other. Leased lines can be very expensive. Instead of using leased lines, WANs can also be built using less costly circuit switching or packet switching methods. Network protocols including TCP/IP deliver transport and addressing functions. Protocols including Packet over SONET/SDH, Multiprotocol Label Switching (MPLS), Asynchronous Transfer Mode (ATM) and Frame Relay are often used by service providers to deliver the links that are used in WANs. X.25 was an important early WAN protocol, and is often considered to be the "grandfather" of Frame Relay as many of the underlying protocols and functions of X.25 are still in use today (with upgrades) by Frame Relay.

Academic research into wide area networks can be broken down into three areas: mathematical models, network emulation, and network simulation.

Performance improvements are sometimes delivered via wide area file services or WAN optimization.

Private Networks

Of the approximately four billion addresses defined in IPv4, about 18 million addresses in three ranges are reserved for use in private networks. Packets addresses in these ranges are not routable in the public Internet; they are ignored by all public routers. Therefore, private hosts cannot directly communicate with public networks, but require network address translation at a routing gateway for this purpose.

Reserved private IPv4 network ranges				
Name	CIDR block	Address range	Number of addresses	Classful description
24-bit block	10.0.0.0/8	10.0.0.0 – 10.255.255.255	16777216	Single Class A.
20-bit block	172.16.0.0/12	172.16.0.0 – 172.31.255.255	1048576	Contiguous range of 16 Class B blocks.
16-bit block	192.168.0.0/16	192.168.0.0 – 192.168.255.255	65536	Contiguous range of 256 Class C blocks.

Since two private networks, e.g., two branch offices, cannot directly interoperate via the public Internet, the two networks must be bridged across the Internet via a virtual private network (VPN) or an IP tunnel, which encapsulates packets, including their headers containing the private addresses, in a protocol layer during transmission across the public network. Additionally, encapsulated packets may be encrypted for the transmission across public networks to secure the data.

Connection Technology

Many technologies are available for wide area network links. Examples include circuit-switched telephone lines, radio wave transmission, and optical fiber. New developments in technologies have successively increased transmission rates. In ca. 1960, a 110 bit/s (bits per second) line was normal on the edge of the WAN, while core links of 56 kbit/s to 64 kbit/s were considered fast. As of 2014, households are connected to the Internet with Dial-Up, ADSL, Cable, Wimax, 4G or fiber. The speeds that people can currently use range from 28.8 kbit/s through a 28K modem over a telephone connection to speeds as high as 100 Gbit/s over an Ethernet 100GBaseY connection.

The following communication and networking technologies have been used to implement WANs:

- Asynchronous Transfer Mode,

- Cable modem,

- Dial-up internet,

- Digital subscriber line,

- Fiber-optic communication,

- Frame Relay,

- ISDN,

- Leased line,

- SD-WAN,

- Synchronous optical networking,

- X.25.

400 Gigabit Ethernet

AT&T conducted trials in 2017 for business use of 400 gigabit Ethernet. Researchers Robert Maher, Alex Alvarado, Domaniç Lavery, and Polina Bayvel of University College London were able to increase networking speeds to 1.125 terabits per second. Christos Santis, graduate student Scott Steger, Amnon Yariv, Martin and Eileen Summerfield developed a new laser that quadruples transfer speeds with fiber optics. If these two technologies were combined, then a transfer speed of up to 4.5 terabits per second could potentially be achieved.

METROPOLITAN AREA NETWORK

A metropolitan area network (MAN) is similar to a local area network (LAN) but spans an entire city or campus. MANs are formed by connecting multiple LANs. Thus, MANs are larger than LANs but smaller than wide area networks (WAN).

MANs are extremely efficient and provide fast communication via high-speed carriers, such as fiber optic cables.

A MAN is ideal for many kinds of network users because it is a medium-size network. MANs are used to build networks with high data connection speeds for cities and towns.

The working mechanism of a MAN is similar to an Internet Service Provider (ISP), but a MAN is not owned by a single organization. Like a WAN, a MAN provides shared network connections to its users. A MAN mostly works on the data link layer, which is Layer 2 of the Open Systems Interconnection (OSI) model.

Types of MAN (Metropolitan Area Network) Technologies

Most widely used technologies to develop a MAN (Metropolitan Area Network) network are FDDI (fiber distribution data interface), ATM (Asynchronous Transfer Mode) and SMDS (switched multi megabit data service). ATM (Asynchronous Transfer Mode) is the most frequently used of all. ATM (Asynchronous Transfer Mode) is a digital data transfer technology. It was developed in 1980 to improve the transportation of real time data over a single network. ATM (Asynchronous Transfer Mode) works just like cell relay system, where data is separated in the form of fixed equal sized packets and is transferred overtime. The purpose of ATM (Asynchronous Transfer Mode) was to access clear audio and video results during a video conferencing. The attributes of ATM has enabled it to become a base of wide area data networking.

ATM (Asynchronous Transfer Mode) combines the characteristics of circuit switching and packet switching, which allows it to transfer even the real time data. FDDI is a standard for data transfer over LAN, which can be extended to the range of approximately 200kms. FDDI can help support the data transmission of many thousand users. This is the reason why it is referred to as the MAN (Metropolitan Area Network) technology. FDDI uses optical fiber for its basic infrastructure that is why it is referred to as fiber distribution data interface. When data is transferred through a connectionless service we use the technology named as SMDS. Connectionless service implies that data is transferred by storing the information in the header and it reaches its destination independently through any network. When the data is transferred using the technology of SMDS, it also forms small data packets just like in ATM. However SMDS allows the transmission of data over large geographical areas in the form of datagrams (the data packets of an unreliable data service provider). Nowadays MAN (Metropolitan Area Network) links are established using infrared and microwave signals.

Working of Metropolitan Area Networks (MAN)

MAN (Metropolitan Area Network) usually falls between LAN and WAN. It is generally applied to connect geographically dispersed LANs. Therefore the goal of MAN is to develop a communication link between two independent LAN nodes. A MAN (Metropolitan Area Network) is usually established using optical fiber. The network is established using routers and switches. A switch is a port which is active in handling the filtration of data usually coming in the form of frames. Any switch acts as a dual port, at one end it is handling filtration of data and at the other end managing connections. Router is another device for facilitating the netwosrk connection. Router helps the data packets to identify the path to be taken. Hence in other words it keeps an eye on the data transfer. MAN (Metropolitan Area Network) is usually operated over an area of up to 50kms.

Advantages of a Metropolitan Area Network (MAN)

Below are some of the benefits of MAN:

Less Expensive

It is less expensive to attach MAN with WAN. MAN gives the good efficiency of data. In MAN data is easily managed in a centralized way.

Sending Local Emails

On MAN you can send local emails fast and free.

High Speed than WAN

MAN uses fiber optics so the speed of data can easily reach upon 1000 Mbps. Files and databases can be transferred fast.

Sharing of the Internet

In some installation of MANs, users can share their internet connection. So multiple users can get the same high-speed internet.

Conversion from LAN to MAN is Easy

MAN is a faster way to connect two fast LANs together. This is due to the fast configuration of links.

High Security

MAN has a high-security level than WAN.

Disadvantages of Metropolitan Area Network (MAN)

Difficult to Manage

If MAN becomes bigger then it becomes difficult to manage it. This is due to a security problem and other extra configuration.

Internet speed difference: MAN cannot work on traditional phone copper wires. If MAN is installed on copper wires then there will be very low speed. So it required the high cost to set up fiber optics for the first time.

Hackers Attack

In MAN there are high chances of attacking hackers on the network compared to LAN. So data may be leaked. Data can be secured but it needs high trained staff and security tools.

Technical people required to set up: To setup MAN it requires technical people that can correctly setup MAN. The technical people are network administrators and troubleshooters.

More Wires Required

In MAN additional cables are required to connect two LAN which is another problem.

Examples of Metropolitan Area Network (MAN)

Some of the examples of MAN are:

- Digital cable television,
- Used in government agencies,
- University campuses,
- Cable broadband,
- Used to connect several branches of the local school,
- In hospital (for communication between doctors, research offices, labs),

- A network of fire stations,

- In airports,

- Networking between community colleges within the country,

- Used in public libraries.

COMPUTER SECURITY

Computer security refers to the protection of computer systems and information from harm, theft, and unauthorized use. Computer hardware is typically protected by the same means used to protect other valuable or sensitive equipment, namely, serial numbers, doors and locks, and alarms. The protection of information and system access, on the other hand, is achieved through other tactics, some of them quite complex.

The security precautions related to computer information and access address four major threats: (1) theft of data, such as that of military secrets from government computers; (2) vandalism, including the destruction of data by a computer virus; (3) fraud, such as employees at a bank channeling funds into their own accounts; and (4) invasion of privacy, such as the illegal accessing of protected personal financial or medical data from a large database. The most basic means of protecting a computer system against theft, vandalism, invasion of privacy, and other irresponsible behaviours is to electronically track and record the access to, and activities of, the various users of a computer system. This is commonly done by assigning an individual password to each person who has access to a system. The computer system itself can then automatically track the use of these passwords, recording such data as which files were accessed under particular passwords and so on. Another security measure is to store a system's data on a separate device, or medium, such as magnetic tape or disks, that is normally inaccessible through the computer system. Finally, data is often encrypted so that it can be deciphered only by holders of a singular encryption key.

Computer security has become increasingly important since the late 1960s, when modems (devices that allow computers to communicate over telephone lines) were introduced. The proliferation of personal computers in the 1980s compounded the problem because they enabled hackers (irresponsible computerphiles) to illegally access major computer systems from the privacy of their homes. The development of advanced security techniques continues to diminish such threats, though concurrent refinements in the methods of computer crime pose ongoing hazards.

Vulnerabilities and Attacks

A vulnerability is a weakness in design, implementation, operation or internal control. Most of the vulnerabilities that have been discovered are documented in the Common Vulnerabilities and Exposures (CVE) database. An *exploitable* vulnerability is one for which at least one working attack or "exploit" exists. Vulnerabilities are often hunted or exploited with the aid of automated tools or manually using customized scripts. To secure a computer system, it is important to understand the attacks that can be made against it, and these threats can typically be classified into one of these categories below.

Backdoor

A backdoor in a computer system, a cryptosystem or an algorithm, is any secret method of bypassing normal authentication or security controls. They may exist for a number of reasons, including by original design or from poor configuration. They may have been added by an authorized party to allow some legitimate access, or by an attacker for malicious reasons; but regardless of the motives for their existence, they create a vulnerability.

Denial of Service Attack

Denial of service attacks (DoS) are designed to make a machine or network resource unavailable to its intended users. Attackers can deny service to individual victims, such as by deliberately entering a wrong password enough consecutive times to cause the victims account to be locked, or they may overload the capabilities of a machine or network and block all users at once. While a network attack from a single IP address can be blocked by adding a new firewall rule, many forms of Distributed denial of service (DDoS) attacks are possible, where the attack comes from a large number of points – and defending is much more difficult. Such attacks can originate from the zombie computers of a botnet, but a range of other techniques are possible including reflection and amplification attacks, where innocent systems are fooled into sending traffic to the victim.

Direct-access Attacks

An unauthorized user gaining physical access to a computer is most likely able to directly copy data from it. They may also compromise security by making operating system modifications, installing software worms, keyloggers, covert listening devices or using wireless mice. Even when the system is protected by standard security measures, these may be able to be by-passed by booting another operating system or tool from a CD-ROM or other bootable media. Disk encryption and Trusted Platform Module are designed to prevent these attacks.

Eavesdropping

Eavesdropping is the act of surreptitiously listening to a private computer "conversation" (communication), typically between hosts on a network. For instance, programs such as Carnivore and NarusInSight have been used by the FBI and NSA to eavesdrop on the systems of internet service providers. Even machines that operate as a closed system (i.e., with no contact to the outside world) can be eavesdropped upon via monitoring the faint electromagnetic transmissions generated by the hardware; TEMPEST is a specification by the NSA referring to these attacks.

Multi-vector and Polymorphic Attacks

Surfacing in 2017, a new class of multi-vector, polymorphic cyber threats surfaced that combined several types of attacks and changed form to avoid cyber security controls as they spread. These threats have been classified as fifth generation cyber attacks.

Privilege Escalation

Privilege escalation describes a situation where an attacker with some level of restricted access is able to, without authorization, elevate their privileges or access level. For example, a standard computer user may be able to exploit a vulnerability in the system to gain access to restricted data; or even become "root" and have full unrestricted access to a system.

Social Engineering

Social engineering aims to convince a user to disclose secrets such as passwords, card numbers, etc. by, for example, impersonating a bank, a contractor, or a customer.

A common scam involves fake CEO emails sent to accounting and finance departments. In early 2016, the FBI reported that the scam has cost US businesses more than $2bn in about two years.

In May 2016, the Milwaukee Bucks NBA team was the victim of this type of cyber scam with a perpetrator impersonating the team's president Peter Feigin, resulting in the handover of all the team's employees' 2015 W-2 tax forms.

Spoofing

Spoofing is the act of masquerading as a valid entity through falsification of data (such as an IP address or username), in order to gain access to information or resources that one is otherwise unauthorized to obtain. There are several types of spoofing, including:

- Email spoofing, where an attacker forges the sending (*From*, or source) address of an email.
- IP address spoofing, where an attacker alters the source IP address in a network packet to hide their identity or impersonate another computing system.
- MAC spoofing, where an attacker modifies the Media Access Control (MAC) address of their network interface to pose as a valid user on a network.
- Biometric spoofing, where an attacker produces a fake biometric sample to pose as another user.

Tampering

Tampering describes a malicious modification of products. So-called "Evil Maid" attacks and security services planting of surveillance capability into routers are examples.

Systems at Risk

The growth in the number of computer systems, and the increasing reliance upon them of individuals, businesses, industries and governments means that there are an increasing number of systems at risk.

Financial Systems

The computer systems of financial regulators and financial institutions like the U.S. Securities and Exchange Commission, SWIFT, investment banks, and commercial banks are prominent hacking targets for cyber criminals interested in manipulating markets and making illicit gains. Web sites and apps that accept or store credit card numbers, brokerage accounts, and bank account information are also prominent hacking targets, because of the potential for immediate financial gain from transferring money, making purchases, or selling the information on the black market. In-store payment systems and ATMs have also been tampered with in order to gather customer account data and PINs.

Utilities and Industrial Equipment

Computers control functions at many utilities, including coordination of telecommunications, the power grid, nuclear power plants, and valve opening and closing in water and gas networks. The Internet is a potential attack vector for such machines if connected, but the Stuxnet worm demonstrated that even equipment controlled by computers not connected to the Internet can be vulnerable. In 2014, the Computer Emergency Readiness Team, a division of the Department of Homeland Security, investigated 79 hacking incidents at energy companies. Vulnerabilities in smart meters (many of which use local radio or cellular communications) can cause problems with billing fraud.

Aviation

The aviation industry is very reliant on a series of complex systems which could be attacked. A simple power outage at one airport can cause repercussions worldwide, much of the system relies on radio transmissions which could be disrupted, and controlling aircraft over oceans is especially dangerous because radar surveillance only extends 175 to 225 miles offshore. There is also potential for attack from within an aircraft.

In Europe, with the (Pan-European Network Service) and NewPENS, and in the US with the Next-Gen program, air navigation service providers are moving to create their own dedicated networks.

The consequences of a successful attack range from loss of confidentiality to loss of system integrity, air traffic control outages, loss of aircraft, and even loss of life.

Consumer Devices

Desktop computers and laptops are commonly targeted to gather passwords or financial account information, or to construct a botnet to attack another target. Smartphones, tablet computers, smart watches, and other mobile devices such as quantified self devices like activity trackers have sensors such as cameras, microphones, GPS receivers, compasses, and accelerometers which could be exploited, and may collect personal information, including sensitive health information. WiFi, Bluetooth, and cell phone networks on any of these devices could be used as attack vectors, and sensors might be remotely activated after a successful breach.

The increasing number of home automation devices such as the Nest thermostat are also potential targets.

Large Corporations

Large corporations are common targets. In many cases attacks are aimed at financial gain through identity theft and involve data breaches. Examples include loss of millions of clients' credit card details by Home Depot, Staples, Target Corporation, and the most recent breach of Equifax.

Some cyberattacks are ordered by foreign governments, which engage in cyberwarfare with the intent to spread their propaganda, sabotage, or spy on their targets. Many people believe the Russian government played a major role in the US presidential election of 2016 by using Twitter and Facebook to affect the results of the election.

Medical records have been targeted in general identify theft, health insurance fraud, and impersonating patients to obtain prescription drugs for recreational purposes or resale. Although cyber threats continue to increase, 62% of all organizations did not increase security training for their business in 2015.

Not all attacks are financially motivated however; for example security firm HB Gary Federal suffered a serious series of attacks in 2011 from hacktivist group Anonymous in retaliation for the firm's CEO claiming to have infiltrated their group, and in the Sony Pictures attack of 2014 the motive appears to have been to embarrass with data leaks, and cripple the company by wiping workstations and servers.

Automobiles

Vehicles are increasingly computerized, with engine timing, cruise control, anti-lock brakes, seat belt tensioners, door locks, airbags and advanced driver-assistance systems on many models. Additionally, connected cars may use WiFi and Bluetooth to communicate with onboard consumer devices and the cell phone network. Self-driving cars are expected to be even more complex.

All of these systems carry some security risk, and such issues have gained wide attention. Simple examples of risk include a malicious compact disc being used as an attack vector, and the car's onboard microphones being used for eavesdropping. However, if access is gained to a car's internal controller area network, the danger is much greater – and in a widely publicized 2015 test, hackers remotely carjacked a vehicle from 10 miles away and drove it into a ditch.

Manufacturers are reacting in a number of ways, with Tesla in 2016 pushing out some security fixes "over the air" into its cars' computer systems.

In the area of autonomous vehicles, in September 2016 the United States Department of Transportation announced some initial safety standards, and called for states to come up with uniform policies.

Government

Government and military computer systems are commonly attacked by activists and foreign powers. Local and regional government infrastructure such as traffic light controls, police and intelligence agency communications, personnel records, student records, and financial systems are also potential targets as they are now all largely computerized. Passports and government ID cards that control access to facilities which use RFID can be vulnerable to cloning.

Internet of Things and Physical Vulnerabilities

The Internet of things (IoT) is the network of physical objects such as devices, vehicles, and buildings that are embedded with electronics, software, sensors, and network connectivity that enables them to collect and exchange data – and concerns have been raised that this is being developed without appropriate consideration of the security challenges involved.

While the IoT creates opportunities for more direct integration of the physical world into computer-based systems, it also provides opportunities for misuse. In particular, as the Internet of Things spreads widely, cyber attacks are likely to become an increasingly physical (rather than simply virtual) threat. If a front door's lock is connected to the Internet, and can be locked/unlocked from a phone, then a criminal could enter the home at the press of a button from a stolen or hacked phone. People could stand to lose much more than their credit card numbers in a world controlled by IoT-enabled devices. Thieves have also used electronic means to circumvent non-Internet-connected hotel door locks.

Medical Systems

Medical devices have either been successfully attacked or had potentially deadly vulnerabilities demonstrated, including both in-hospital diagnostic equipment and implanted devices including pacemakers and insulin pumps. There are many reports of hospitals and hospital organizations getting hacked, including ransomware attacks, Windows XP exploits, viruses, and data breaches of sensitive data stored on hospital servers. On 28 December 2016 the US Food and Drug Administration released its recommendations for how medical device manufacturers should maintain the security of Internet-connected devices – but no structure for enforcement.

Energy Sector

In distributed generation systems, the risk of a cyber attack is real, according to *Daily Energy Insider*. An attack could cause a loss of power in a large area for a long period of time, and such an attack could have just as severe consequences as a natural disaster. The District of Columbia is considering creating a Distributed Energy Resources (DER) Authority within the city, with the goal being for customers to have more insight into their own energy use and giving the local electric utility, Pepco, the chance to better estimate energy demand. The D.C. proposal, however, would "allow third-party vendors to create numerous points of energy distribution, which could potentially create more opportunities for cyber attackers to threaten the electric grid."

Impact of Security Breaches

Serious financial damage has been caused by security breaches, but because there is no standard model for estimating the cost of an incident, the only data available is that which is made public by the organizations involved. "Several computer security consulting firms produce estimates of total worldwide losses attributable to virus and worm attacks and to hostile digital acts in general. The 2003 loss estimates by these firms range from $13 billion (worms and viruses only) to $226 billion (for all forms of covert attacks). The reliability of these estimates is often challenged; the underlying methodology is basically anecdotal." Security breaches continue to cost businesses billions of dollars but a survey revealed that 66% of security staffs do not believe senior leadership takes cyber precautions as a strategic priority.

However, reasonable estimates of the financial cost of security breaches can actually help organizations make rational investment decisions. According to the classic Gordon-Loeb Model analyzing the optimal investment level in information security, one can conclude that the amount a firm spends to protect information should generally be only a small fraction of the expected loss (i.e., the expected value of the loss resulting from a cyber/information security breach).

Computer Protection (Countermeasures)

In computer security a countermeasure is an action, device, procedure, or technique that reduces a threat, a vulnerability, or an attack by eliminating or preventing it, by minimizing the harm it can cause, or by discovering and reporting it so that corrective action can be taken.

Some common countermeasures are listed in the following topics:

Security by Design

Security by design, or alternately secure by design, means that the software has been designed from the ground up to be secure. In this case, security is considered as a main feature.

Some of the techniques in this approach include:

- The principle of least privilege, where each part of the system has only the privileges that are needed for its function. That way even if an attacker gains access to that part, they have only limited access to the whole system.

- Automated theorem proving to prove the correctness of crucial software subsystems.

- Code reviews and unit testing, approaches to make modules more secure where formal correctness proofs are not possible.

- Defense in depth, where the design is such that more than one subsystem needs to be violated to compromise the integrity of the system and the information it holds.

- Default secure settings, and design to "fail secure" rather than "fail insecure". Ideally, a secure system should require a deliberate, conscious, knowledgeable and free decision on the part of legitimate authorities in order to make it insecure.

- Audit trails tracking system activity, so that when a security breach occurs, the mechanism and extent of the breach can be determined. Storing audit trails remotely, where they can only be appended to, can keep intruders from covering their tracks.

- Full disclosure of all vulnerabilities, to ensure that the "window of vulnerability" is kept as short as possible when bugs are discovered.

Security Architecture

The Open Security Architecture organization defines IT security architecture as "the design artifacts that describe how the security controls (security countermeasures) are positioned, and how they relate to the overall information technology architecture. These controls serve the purpose to maintain the system's quality attributes: confidentiality, integrity, availability, accountability and assurance services".

Techopedia defines security architecture as "a unified security design that addresses the necessities and potential risks involved in a certain scenario or environment. It also specifies when and where to apply security controls.

The design process is generally reproducible." The key attributes of security architecture are:

- The relationship of different components and how they depend on each other.
- The determination of controls based on risk assessment, good practice, finances, and legal matters.
- The standardization of controls.

Security Measures

A state of computer "security" is the conceptual ideal, attained by the use of the three processes: threat prevention, detection, and response. These processes are based on various policies and system components, which include the following:

- User account access controls and cryptography can protect systems files and data, respectively.
- Firewalls are by far the most common prevention systems from a network security perspective as they can (if properly configured) shield access to internal network services, and block certain kinds of attacks through packet filtering. Firewalls can be both hardware- or software-based.
- Intrusion Detection System (IDS) products are designed to detect network attacks in-progress and assist in post-attack forensics, while audit trails and logs serve a similar function for individual systems.
- "Response" is necessarily defined by the assessed security requirements of an individual system and may cover the range from simple upgrade of protections to notification of legal authorities, counter-attacks, and the like. In some special cases, a complete destruction of the compromised system is favored, as it may happen that not all the compromised resources are detected.

Today, computer security comprises mainly "preventive" measures, like firewalls or an exit procedure. A firewall can be defined as a way of filtering network data between a host or a network and another network, such as the Internet, and can be implemented as software running on the machine, hooking into the network stack (or, in the case of most UNIX-based operating systems such as Linux, built into the operating system kernel) to provide real-time filtering and blocking. Another implementation is a so-called "physical firewall", which consists of a separate machine filtering network traffic. Firewalls are common amongst machines that are permanently connected to the Internet.

Some organizations are turning to big data platforms, such as Apache Hadoop, to extend data accessibility and machine learning to detect advanced persistent threats.

However, relatively few organisations maintain computer systems with effective detection systems, and fewer still have organized response mechanisms in place. As a result, as Reuters points out: "Companies for the first time report they are losing more through electronic theft of data than physical stealing of assets". The primary obstacle to effective eradication of cyber crime could be traced to excessive reliance on firewalls and other automated "detection" systems. Yet it is basic evidence gathering by using packet capture appliances that puts criminals behind bars.

Vulnerability Management

Vulnerability management is the cycle of identifying, and remediating or mitigating vulnerabilities, especially in software and firmware. Vulnerability management is integral to computer security and network security.

Vulnerabilities can be discovered with a vulnerability scanner, which analyzes a computer system in search of known vulnerabilities, such as open ports, insecure software configuration, and susceptibility to malware.

Beyond vulnerability scanning, many organizations contract outside security auditors to run regular penetration tests against their systems to identify vulnerabilities. In some sectors, this is a contractual requirement.

Reducing Vulnerabilities

While formal verification of the correctness of computer systems is possible, it is not yet common. Operating systems formally verified include seL4, and SYSGO's PikeOS – but these make up a very small percentage of the market.

Two factor authentication is a method for mitigating unauthorized access to a system or sensitive information. It requires "something you know"; a password or PIN, and "something you have"; a card, dongle, cellphone, or other piece of hardware. This increases security as an unauthorized person needs both of these to gain access.

Social engineering and direct computer access (physical) attacks can only be prevented by non-computer means, which can be difficult to enforce, relative to the sensitivity of the information. Training is often involved to help mitigate this risk, but even in a highly disciplined environments (e.g. military organizations), social engineering attacks can still be difficult to foresee and prevent.

Enoculation, derived from inoculation theory, seeks to prevent social engineering and other fraudulent tricks or traps by instilling a resistance to persuasion attempts through exposure to similar or related attempts.

It is possible to reduce an attacker's chances by keeping systems up to date with security patches and updates, using a security scanner or/and hiring competent people responsible for security.(This statement is ambiguous. Even systems developed by "competent" people get penetrated) The effects of data loss/damage can be reduced by careful backing up and insurance.

Hardware Protection Mechanisms

While hardware may be a source of insecurity, such as with microchip vulnerabilities maliciously introduced during the manufacturing process, hardware-based or assisted computer security also offers an alternative to software-only computer security. Using devices and methods such as dongles, trusted platform modules, intrusion-aware cases, drive locks, disabling USB ports, and mobile-enabled access may be considered more secure due to the physical access (or sophisticated backdoor access) required in order to be compromised.

Each of these is covered in more detail below:

- USB dongles are typically used in software licensing schemes to unlock software capabilities, but they can also be seen as a way to prevent unauthorized access to a computer or other device's software. The dongle, or key, essentially creates a secure encrypted tunnel between the software application and the key. The principle is that an encryption scheme on the dongle, such as Advanced Encryption Standard (AES) provides a stronger measure of security, since it is harder to hack and replicate the dongle than to simply copy the native software to another machine and use it. Another security application for dongles is to use them for accessing web-based content such as cloud software or Virtual Private Networks (VPNs). In addition, a USB dongle can be configured to lock or unlock a computer.

- Trusted platform modules (TPMs) secure devices by integrating cryptographic capabilities onto access devices, through the use of microprocessors, or so-called computers-on-a-chip. TPMs used in conjunction with server-side software offer a way to detect and authenticate hardware devices, preventing unauthorized network and data access.

- Computer case intrusion detection refers to a device, typically a push-button switch, which detects when a computer case is opened. The firmware or BIOS is programmed to show an alert to the operator when the computer is booted up the next time.

- Drive locks are essentially software tools to encrypt hard drives, making them inaccessible to thieves. Tools exist specifically for encrypting external drives as well.

- Disabling USB ports is a security option for preventing unauthorized and malicious access to an otherwise secure computer. Infected USB dongles connected to a network from a computer inside the firewall are considered by the magazine Network World as the most common hardware threat facing computer networks.

- Disconnecting or disabling peripheral devices (like camera, GPS, removable storage etc.), that are not in use.

- Mobile-enabled access devices are growing in popularity due to the ubiquitous nature of cell phones. Built-in capabilities such as Bluetooth, the newer Bluetooth low energy (LE), Near field communication (NFC) on non-iOS devices and biometric validation such as thumb print readers, as well as QR code reader software designed for mobile devices, offer new, secure ways for mobile phones to connect to access control systems. These control systems provide computer security and can also be used for controlling access to secure buildings.

Secure Operating Systems

One use of the term "computer security" refers to technology that is used to implement secure operating systems. In the 1980s the United States Department of Defense (DoD) used the "Orange Book" standards, but the current international standard ISO/IEC 15408, "Common Criteria" defines a number of progressively more stringent Evaluation Assurance Levels. Many common operating systems meet the EAL4 standard of being "Methodically Designed, Tested and Reviewed", but the formal verification required for the highest levels means that they are uncommon. An example of an EAL6 ("Semiformally Verified Design and Tested") system is Integrity-178B, which is used in the Airbus A380 and several military jets.

Secure Coding

In software engineering, secure coding aims to guard against the accidental introduction of security vulnerabilities. It is also possible to create software designed from the ground up to be secure. Such systems are "secure by design". Beyond this, formal verification aims to prove the correctness of the algorithms underlying a system; important for cryptographic protocols for example.

Capabilities and Access Control Lists

Within computer systems, two of many security models capable of enforcing privilege separation are access control lists (ACLs) and capability-based security. Using ACLs to confine programs has been proven to be insecure in many situations, such as if the host computer can be tricked into indirectly allowing restricted file access, an issue known as the confused deputy problem. It has also been shown that the promise of ACLs of giving access to an object to only one person can never be guaranteed in practice. Both of these problems are resolved by capabilities. This does not mean practical flaws exist in all ACL-based systems, but only that the designers of certain utilities must take responsibility to ensure that they do not introduce flaws.

Capabilities have been mostly restricted to research operating systems, while commercial OSs still use ACLs. Capabilities can, however, also be implemented at the language level, leading to a style of programming that is essentially a refinement of standard object-oriented design. An open source project in the area is the E language.

End User Security Training

The end-user is widely recognized as the weakest link in the security chain and it is estimated that more than 90% of security incidents and breaches involve some kind of human error. Among the most commonly recorded forms of errors and misjudgment are poor password management, the inability to recognize misleading URLs and to identify fake websites and dangerous email attachments. A common mistake that users make is saving their userid/password in their browsers to make it easier to login to banking sites. This is a gift to attackers who have obtained access to a machine by some means. The risk may be mitigated by the use of two-factor authentication.

As the human component of cyber risk is particularly relevant in determining the global cyber risk an organization is facing, security awareness training, at all levels, not only provides formal compliance with regulatory and industry mandates but is considered essential in reducing cyber risk and protecting individuals and companies from the great majority of cyber threats.

The focus on the end-user represents a profound cultural change for many security practitioners, who have traditionally approached cybersecurity exclusively from a technical perspective, and moves along the lines suggested by major security centers to develop a culture of cyber awareness within the organization, recognizing that a security aware user provides an important line of defense against cyber attacks.

Response to Breaches

Responding forcefully to attempted security breaches (in the manner that one would for attempted physical security breaches) is often very difficult for a variety of reasons:

- Identifying attackers is difficult, as they are often in a different jurisdiction to the systems they attempt to breach, and operate through proxies, temporary anonymous dial-up accounts, wireless connections, and other anonymizing procedures which make back tracing difficult and are often located in yet another jurisdiction. If they successfully breach security, they are often able to delete logs to cover their tracks.

- The sheer number of attempted attacks is so large that organisations cannot spend time pursuing each attacker (a typical home user with a permanent (e.g., cable modem) connection will be attacked at least several times per day, so more attractive targets could be presumed). Note however, that most of the sheer bulk of these attacks are made by automated vulnerability scanners and computer worms.

- Law enforcement officers are often unfamiliar with information technology, and so lack the skills and interest in pursuing attackers. There are also budgetary constraints. It has been argued that the high cost of technology, such as DNA testing, and improved forensics mean less money for other kinds of law enforcement, so the overall rate of criminals not getting dealt with goes up as the cost of the technology increases. In addition, the identification of attackers across a network may require logs from various points in the network and in many countries, the release of these records to law enforcement (with the exception of being voluntarily surrendered by a network administrator or a system administrator) requires a search warrant and, depending on the circumstances, the legal proceedings required can be drawn out to the point where the records are either regularly destroyed, or the information is no longer relevant.

- The United States government spends the largest amount of money every year on cyber security. The United States has a yearly budget of 28 billion dollars. Canada has the 2nd highest annual budget at 1 billion dollars. Australia has the third highest budget with only 70 million dollars.

Types of Security and Privacy

- Access control
- Anti-keyloggers
- Anti-malware
- Anti-spyware
- Anti-subversion software
- Anti-tamper software
- Anti-theft
- Antivirus software

- Cryptographic software
- Computer-aided dispatch (CAD)
- Firewall
- Intrusion detection system (IDS)
- Intrusion prevention system (IPS)
- Log management software
- Parental control
- Records management

- Sandbox
- Security information management
- SIEM
- Software and operating system updating

Incident Response Planning

Incident response is an organized approach to addressing and managing the aftermath of a computer security incident or compromise with the goal of preventing a breach or thwarting a cyberattack. An incident that is not identified and managed at the time of intrusion, typically escalates to a more impactful event such as a data breach or system failure. The intended outcome of a computer security incident response plan is to limit damage and reduce recovery time and costs. Responding to compromises quickly can mitigate exploited vulnerabilities, restore services and processes and minimize impact and losses. Incident response planning allows an organization to establish a series of best practices to stop an intrusion before it causes damage. Typical incident response plans contain a set of written instructions that outline the organization's response to a cyberattack. Without a documented plan in place, an organization may not successfully detect an intrusion or compromise and stakeholders may not understand their roles, processes and procedures during an escalation, slowing the organizations response and resolution. There are four key components of a computer security incident response plan:

- Preparation: Preparing stakeholders on the procedures for handling computer security incidents or compromises.

- Detection & Analysis: Identifying and investigating suspicious activity to confirm a security incident, prioritizing the response based on impact and coordinating notification of the incident.

- Containment, Eradication & Recovery: Isolating affected systems to prevent escalation and limit impact, pinpointing the genesis of the incident, removing malware, affected systems and bad actors from the environment and restoring systems and data when a threat no longer remains.

- Post Incident Activity: Post mortem analysis of the incident, its root cause and the organization's response with the intent of improving the incident response plan and future response efforts.

Antivirus Software

Anti-virus software is a software utility that detects, prevents, and removes viruses, worms, and other malware from a computer. Most anti-virus programs include an auto-update feature that permits the program to download profiles, new viruses, enabling the system to check for new threats. Antivirus programs are essential utilities for any computer but the choice of which one is very important. One AV program might find a certain virus or worm while another cannot, or vice-versa.

Anti-virus software is also known as an anti-virus program or a vaccine.

Anti-virus software searches the hard drive and external media attached to a computer for any potential viruses or worms. Broadly speaking, the two main approaches to virus detection are:

- Dictionary Approach: The anti-virus software checks a file and automatically refers to a dictionary of known viruses. If there is a match, the file is deleted, quarantined or repaired.

- Suspicious Behavior Approach: The anti-virus software monitors the behavior of all programs and flags any suspicious behavior. For example, a program might be flagged if it tries to change settings to the operating system or write to a certain directory.

Identification Methods

One of the few solid theoretical results in the study of computer viruses is Frederick B. Cohen's 1987 demonstration that there is no algorithm that can perfectly detect all possible viruses. However, using different layers of defense, a good detection rate may be achieved.

There are several methods which antivirus engine can use to identify malware:

- Sandbox detection: A particular behavioural-based detection technique that, instead of detecting the behavioural fingerprint at run time, it executes the programs in a virtual environment, logging what actions the program performs. Depending on the actions logged, the antivirus engine can determine if the program is malicious or not. If not, then, the program is executed in the real environment. Albeit this technique has shown to be quite effective, given its heaviness and slowness, it is rarely used in end-user antivirus solutions.

- Data mining techniques: One of the latest approaches applied in malware detection. Data mining and machine learning algorithms are used to try to classify the behaviour of a file (as either malicious or benign) given a series of file features, that are extracted from the file itself.

Signature-based Detection

Traditional antivirus software relies heavily upon signatures to identify malware. Substantially, when a malware arrives in the hands of an antivirus firm, it is analysed by malware researchers or by dynamic analysis systems. Then, once it is determined to be a malware, a proper signature of the file is extracted and added to the signatures database of the antivirus software.

Although the signature-based approach can effectively contain malware outbreaks, malware authors have tried to stay a step ahead of such software by writing "oligomorphic", "polymorphic" and, more recently, "metamorphic" viruses, which encrypt parts of themselves or otherwise modify themselves as a method of disguise, so as to not match virus signatures in the dictionary.

Heuristics

Many viruses start as a single infection and through either mutation or refinements by other attackers, can grow into dozens of slightly different strains, called variants. Generic detection refers to the detection and removal of multiple threats using a single virus definition. For example, the Vundo trojan has several family members, depending on the antivirus vendor's classification. Symantec classifies members of the Vundo family into two distinct categories, *Trojan.Vundo* and *Trojan.Vundo.B*.

While it may be advantageous to identify a specific virus, it can be quicker to detect a virus family through a generic signature or through an inexact match to an existing signature. Virus researchers find common areas that all viruses in a family share uniquely and can thus create a single generic signature. These signatures often contain non-contiguous code, using wildcard characters where differences lie. These wildcards allow the scanner to detect viruses even if they are padded with extra, meaningless code. A detection that uses this method is said to be "heuristic detection."

Rootkit Detection

Anti-virus software can attempt to scan for rootkits. A rootkit is a type of malware designed to gain administrative-level control over a computer system without being detected. Rootkits can change how the operating system functions and in some cases can tamper with the anti-virus program and render it ineffective. Rootkits are also difficult to remove, in some cases requiring a complete re-installation of the operating system.

Real-time Protection

Real-time protection, on-access scanning, background guard, resident shield, autoprotect, and other synonyms refer to the automatic protection provided by most antivirus, anti-spyware, and other anti-malware programs. This monitors computer systems for suspicious activity such as computer viruses, spyware, adware, and other malicious objects in 'real-time', in other words while data loaded into the computer's active memory: when inserting a CD, opening an email, or browsing the web, or when a file already on the computer is opened or executed.

Issues of Concern

Unexpected Renewal Costs

Some commercial antivirus software end-user license agreements include a clause that the subscription will be automatically renewed, and the purchaser's credit card automatically billed, at the renewal time without explicit approval. For example, McAfee requires users to unsubscribe at least 60 days before the expiration of the present subscription while BitDefender sends notifications to unsubscribe 30 days before the renewal. Norton AntiVirus also renews subscriptions automatically by default.

Rogue Security Applications

Some apparent antivirus programs are actually malware masquerading as legitimate software, such as WinFixer, MS Antivirus, and Mac Defender.

Problems Caused by False Positives

A "false positive" or "false alarm" is when antivirus software identifies a non-malicious file as malware. When this happens, it can cause serious problems. For example, if an antivirus program is configured to immediately delete or quarantine infected files, as is common on Microsoft Windows antivirus applications, a false positive in an essential file can render the Windows operating system or some applications unusable. Recovering from such damage to critical software infrastructure incurs technical support costs and businesses can be forced to close whilst remedial action is undertaken. Examples of serious false-positives:

- May 2007: A faulty virus signature issued by Symantec mistakenly removed essential operating system files, leaving thousands of PCs unable to boot.

- May 2007: The executable file required by Pegasus Mail on Windows was falsely detected by Norton AntiVirus as being a Trojan and it was automatically removed, preventing Pegasus Mail from running. Norton AntiVirus had falsely identified three releases of Pegasus Mail as malware, and would delete the Pegasus Mail installer file when that happened.

- April 2010: McAfee VirusScan detected svchost.exe, a normal Windows binary, as a virus on machines running Windows XP with Service Pack 3, causing a reboot loop and loss of all network access.

- December 2010: A faulty update on the AVG anti-virus suite damaged 64-bit versions of Windows 7, rendering it unable to boot, due to an endless boot loop created.

- October 2011: Microsoft Security Essentials (MSE) removed the Google Chrome web browser, rival to Microsoft's own Internet Explorer. MSE flagged Chrome as a Zbot banking trojan.

- September 2012: Sophos' anti-virus suite identified various update-mechanisms, including its own, as malware. If it was configured to automatically delete detected files, Sophos Anti-virus could render itself unable to update, required manual intervention to fix the problem.

- September 2017: The Google Play Protect anti-virus started identifying Motorola's Moto G4 Bluetooth application as malware, causing Bluetooth functionality to become disabled.

System and Interoperability Related Issues

Running (the real-time protection of) multiple antivirus programs concurrently can degrade performance and create conflicts. However, using a concept called multiscanning, several companies (including G Data Software and Microsoft) have created applications which can run multiple engines concurrently.

It is sometimes necessary to temporarily disable virus protection when installing major updates such as Windows Service Packs or updating graphics card drivers. Active antivirus protection may partially or completely prevent the installation of a major update. Anti-virus software can cause problems during the installation of an operating system upgrade, e.g. when upgrading to a newer version of Windows "in place" — without erasing the previous version of Windows. Microsoft recommends that anti-virus software be disabled to avoid conflicts with the upgrade installation process. Active anti-virus software can also interfere with a firmware update process.

The functionality of a few computer programs can be hampered by active anti-virus software. For example, TrueCrypt, a disk encryption program, states on its troubleshooting page that anti-virus programs can conflict with TrueCrypt and cause it to malfunction or operate very slowly. Anti-virus software can impair the performance and stability of games running in the Steam platform.

Support issues also exist around antivirus application interoperability with common solutions like SSL VPN remote access and network access control products. These technology solutions often have policy assessment applications that require an up-to-date antivirus to be installed and running. If the antivirus application is not recognized by the policy assessment, whether because the antivirus application has been updated or because it is not part of the policy assessment library, the user will be unable to connect.

Effectiveness

Studies in December 2007 showed that the effectiveness of antivirus software had decreased in the previous year, particularly against unknown or zero day attacks. The computer magazine *c't* found that detection rates for these threats had dropped from 40–50% in 2006 to 20–30% in 2007.

At that time, the only exception was the NOD32 antivirus, which managed a detection rate of 68%. According to the *ZeuS tracker* website the average detection rate for all variants of the well-known ZeuS trojan is as low as 40%.

The problem is magnified by the changing intent of virus authors. Some years ago it was obvious when a virus infection was present. At the time, viruses were written by amateurs and exhibited destructive behavior or pop-ups. Modern viruses are often written by professionals, financed by criminal organizations.

In 2008, Eva Chen, CEO of Trend Micro, stated that the anti-virus industry has over-hyped how effective its products are — and so has been misleading customers — for years.

Independent testing on all the major virus scanners consistently shows that none provides 100% virus detection. The best ones provided as high as 99.9% detection for simulated real-world situations, while the lowest provided 91.1% in tests conducted in August 2013. Many virus scanners produce false positive results as well, identifying benign files as malware.

Although methods may differ, some notable independent quality testing agencies include AV-Comparatives, ICSA Labs, West Coast Labs, Virus Bulletin, AV-TEST and other members of the Anti-Malware Testing Standards Organization.

New Viruses

Anti-virus programs are not always effective against new viruses, even those that use non-signature-based methods that should detect new viruses. The reason for this is that the virus designers test their new viruses on the major anti-virus applications to make sure that they are not detected before releasing them into the wild.

Some new viruses, particularly ransomware, use polymorphic code to avoid detection by virus scanners.

A proof of concept virus has used the Graphics Processing Unit (GPU) to avoid detection from anti-virus software. The potential success of this involves bypassing the CPU in order to make it much harder for security researchers to analyse the inner workings of such malware.

Rootkits

Detecting rootkits is a major challenge for anti-virus programs. Rootkits have full administrative access to the computer and are invisible to users and hidden from the list of running processes in the task manager. Rootkits can modify the inner workings of the operating system and tamper with antivirus programs.

Damaged Files

If a file has been infected by a computer virus, anti-virus software will attempt to remove the virus code from the file during disinfection, but it is not always able to restore the file to its undamaged state. In such circumstances, damaged files can only be restored from existing backups or shadow copies (this is also true for ransomware); installed software that is damaged requires re-installation.

Firmware Infections

Any writeable firmware in the computer can be infected by malicious code. This is a major concern, as an infected BIOS could require the actual BIOS chip to be replaced to ensure the malicious code is completely removed. Anti-virus software is not effective at protecting firmware and the motherboard BIOS from infection. In 2014, security researchers discovered that USB devices contain writeable firmware which can be modified with malicious code (dubbed "BadUSB"), which anti-virus software cannot detect or prevent. The malicious code can run undetected on the computer and could even infect the operating system prior to it booting up.

Performance and other Drawbacks

Antivirus software has some drawbacks, first of which that it can impact a computer's performance.

Furthermore, inexperienced users can be lulled into a false sense of security when using the computer, considering their computers to be invulnerable, and may have problems understanding the prompts and decisions that antivirus software presents them with. An incorrect decision may lead to a security breach. If the antivirus software employs heuristic detection, it must be fine-tuned to minimize misidentifying harmless software as malicious (false positive).

Antivirus software itself usually runs at the highly trusted kernel level of the operating system to allow it access to all the potential malicious process and files, creating a potential avenue of attack. The US National Security Agency (NSA) and the UK Government Communications Headquarters (GCHQ) intelligence agencies, respectively, have been exploiting anti-virus software to spy on users. Anti-virus software has highly privileged and trusted access to the underlying operating system, which makes it a much more appealing target for remote attacks. Additionally anti-virus software is "years behind security-conscious client-side applications like browsers or document readers. It means that Acrobat Reader, Microsoft Word or Google Chrome are harder to exploit than 90 percent of the anti-virus products out there", according to Joxean Koret, a researcher with Coseinc, a Singapore-based information security consultancy.

Alternative Solutions

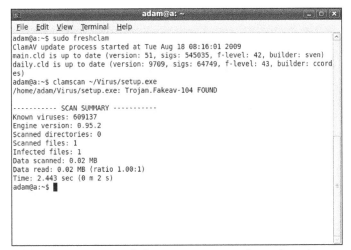

The command-line virus scanner of Clam AV 0.95.2 running a virus signature definition update, scanning a file, and identifying a Trojan.

Antivirus software running on individual computers is the most common method employed of guarding against malware, but it is not the only solution. Other solutions can also be employed by users, including Unified Threat Management (UTM), hardware and network firewalls, Cloud-based antivirus and online scanners.

Hardware and Network Firewall

Network firewalls prevent unknown programs and processes from accessing the system. However, they are not antivirus systems and make no attempt to identify or remove anything. They may protect against infection from outside the protected computer or network, and limit the activity of any malicious software which is present by blocking incoming or outgoing requests on certain TCP/IP ports. A firewall is designed to deal with broader system threats that come from network connections into the system and is not an alternative to a virus protection system.

Cloud Antivirus

Cloud antivirus is a technology that uses lightweight agent software on the protected computer, while offloading the majority of data analysis to the provider's infrastructure.

One approach to implementing cloud antivirus involves scanning suspicious files using multiple antivirus engines. This approach was proposed by an early implementation of the cloud antivirus concept called CloudAV. CloudAV was designed to send programs or documents to a network cloud where multiple antivirus and behavioral detection programs are used simultaneously in order to improve detection rates. Parallel scanning of files using potentially incompatible antivirus scanners is achieved by spawning a virtual machine per detection engine and therefore eliminating any possible issues. CloudAV can also perform "retrospective detection," whereby the cloud detection engine rescans all files in its file access history when a new threat is identified thus improving new threat detection speed. Finally, CloudAV is a solution for effective virus scanning on devices that lack the computing power to perform the scans themselves.

Some examples of cloud anti-virus products are Panda Cloud Antivirus, Crowdstrike, Cb Defense and Immunet. Comodo group has also produced cloud-based anti-virus.

Online Scanning

Some antivirus vendors maintain websites with free online scanning capability of the entire computer, critical areas only, local disks, folders or files. Periodic online scanning is a good idea for those that run antivirus applications on their computers because those applications are frequently slow to catch threats. One of the first things that malicious software does in an attack is disable any existing antivirus software and sometimes the only way to know of an attack is by turning to an online resource that is not installed on the infected computer.

Specialized Tools

Virus removal tools are available to help remove stubborn infections or certain types of infection. Examples include *Avast Free Anti- Malware, AVG Free Malware Removal Tools*, and *Avira AntiVir Removal Tool*. It is also worth noting that sometimes antivirus software can produce a false positive result, indicating an infection where there is none.

The command-line rkhunter scanner,
an engine to scan for Linux rootkits running on Ubuntu.

A rescue disk that is bootable, such as a CD or USB storage device, can be used to run antivirus software outside of the installed operating system, in order to remove infections while they are dormant. A bootable antivirus disk can be useful when, for example, the installed operating system is no longer bootable or has malware that is resisting all attempts to be removed by the installed antivirus software. Examples of some of these bootable disks include the *Bitdefender Rescue CD*, *Kaspersky Rescue Disk 2018*, and *Windows Defender Offline* (integrated into Windows 10 since the Anniversary Update). Most of the Rescue CD software can also be installed onto a USB storage device, that is bootable on newer computers.

Anti Malware

Anti-malware is any resource that protects computers and systems against malware, including viruses, spyware and other harmful programs.

Anti-malware resources are comprehensive solutions that maintain computer security and protect sensitive data that is transmitted by a network or stored on local devices. Anti-malware tools often include multiple components, including anti-spyware and phishing tools, as well as antivirus solutions for prominent viruses, which are isolated and identified by security resources.

Anti-malware tools may employ scanning, strategies, freeware or licensed tools to detect rootkits, worms, Trojans and other types of potentially damaging software. Each type of malware resource carries its own interface and system requirements, which impact user solutions for a given device or system.

Working of Anti Malware

Anti malware does its job using different techniques are:

Behavior Monitoring

Behavior Monitoring is a technique anti malware uses to identify malware based on its character and behavior. An anti malware program doesn't compare the file to any known threats anymore. If a file exhibits suspicious behaviors, anti malware will flag it as a threat.

Behavior monitoring technique is used to constantly monitor suspicious files that can be harmful to the computer. This feature makes malware detection more easily because an anti malware program doesn't have to scan a file anymore. By its behavior on the computer malware will be identified.

Sandboxing

Sandboxing is another efficient technique an anti malware program uses to isolate suspicious files. An anti malware holds the file in the sandbox to further analyze it. Threats will be instantly removed, while legitimate files will be allowed but it will be constantly monitored.

Sandboxing is a great way to prevent malware infection. An anti malware immediately separates malicious software from legitimate applications to prevent damage on the computer.

Malware Removal

Finally, once malware is identified, an anti malware removes it to prevent it from executing and infecting the computer. If the same type of file reaches the computer, it will automatically be eliminated. An anti malware will prevent it from installing.

Malware removal may sound like a lot of work but it's done within seconds. That's how fast an anti malware program works. In an instant malware is out of your computer and you're assured that your computer and personal information are safe.

Benefits of Anti Malware

An anti malware program has many benefits, particularly keeping your computer secure. But that's not all anti malware has to offer, you can benefit from anti malware in many ways.

- You're protected from hackers - Hackers gain access to your computer through malware. With the anti malware installed, you can browse the web safely.

- Your privacy is protected - Cyber criminals use your personal information to their advantage. An anti malware prevents any software that steal personal from installing.

- Your valuable files are secured - If malware and viruses are out of the computer, you can be assured that your data are protected.

- Your software are up-to-date - Nobody wants outdated software. An anti malware keeps your software updated. It will remind you if a new version or an update is available online.

- Your computer is free of junk - An antimalware notifies you if junks are consuming your computer memory, so you can free up some space. This eliminates useless files stored in your computer.

Need for Anti Malware

Besides the benefits of anti malware, you must install anti malware because hackers and cyber attacks are prevalent nowadays. You never know when hackers will access your computer. Your personal information will be at risk of getting stolen and be used without your knowledge.

In addition, with advanced hacking techniques, malware, viruses, and threats can easily install on your computer. Most of them remain undetected until they do a major damage on your computer. Don't leave your computer vulnerable.

Anti malware will prevent computer infections brought about by malware, as it is designed to protect your computer at all times. With anti malware installed, malware, worms, viruses don't have space on your computer.

Anti-spyware

Anti-spyware is a type of software that is designed to detect and remove unwanted spyware programs. Spyware is a type of malware that is installed on a computer without the user's knowledge in order to collect information about them. This can pose a security risk to the user, but more frequently spyware degrades system performance by taking up processing power, installing additional software, or redirecting users' browser activity.

Anti-spyware may also be called apyware on the Internet. Because "a" and "s" sit next to each other on the keyboard, many people accidentally type "apyware" when they try to search "spyware." Manufacturers and other interested parties capitalize on this by advertising "apyware."

Anti-spyware software detects spyware through rules-based methods or based on downloaded definition files that identify common spyware programs. Anti-spyware software can be used to find and remove spyware that has already been installed on the user's computer, or it can act much like an anti-virus program by providing real-time protection and preventing spyware from being downloaded in the first place.

Most modern-day security suites bundle anti-spyware functionality alongside anti-virus protection, personal firewalls, etc.

References

- Omura, Yasuhisa; Mallik, Abhijit; Matsuo, Naoto (2017). MOS Devices for Low-Voltage and Low-Energy Applications. John Wiley & Sons. P. 53. ISBN 9781119107354

- What-is-a-computer-network, computer-network, computernetworkingnotes: ecomputernotes.com, Retrieved 11 January, 2019

- "Inductee Details – Paul Baran". National Inventors Hall of Fame. Archived from the original on 6 September 2017. Retrieved 6 September 2017

- Personal-area-network-pan: freewimaxinfo.com, Retrieved 14 July, 2019

- Fossum, Jerry G.; Trivedi, Vishal P. (2013). Fundamentals of Ultra-Thin-Body mosfets and finfets. Cambridge University Press. P. Vii. ISBN 9781107434493

- Network-lan-technologies, data-communication-computer-network: tutorialspoint.com, Retrieved 29 June, 2019

- Metropolitan-area-network-man: techopedia.com, Retrieved 30 April, 2019

- Kim, Peter (2014). The Hacker Playbook: Practical Guide To Penetration Testing. Seattle: createspace Independent Publishing Platform. ISBN 978-1494932633

Information Science and Systems

The analysis, collection, retrieval, movement and protection of data and information falls under the field of information science. The information and communication technology that supports business processes by developing interaction between people and technology is termed as an information system. This chapter closely examines the important concepts of information science and systems such as information architecture and information management.

INFORMATION SCIENCE

Information science (also information studies) is an interdisciplinary science primarily concerned with the collection, classification, manipulation, storage, retrieval and dissemination of information. Information science studies the application and usage of knowledge in organizations, and the interaction between people, organizations and information systems. It is often (mistakenly) considered a branch of computer science. It is actually a broad, interdisciplinary field, incorporating not only aspects of computer science, but also library science, cognitive, and social sciences.

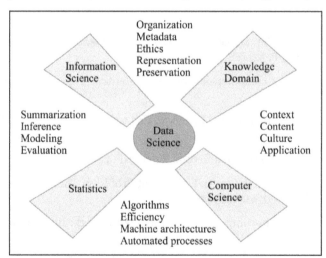

Information science focuses on understanding problems from the perspective of the stakeholders involved and then applying information (and other) technology as needed. In other words, it tackles systemic problems first rather than individual pieces of technology within that system. In this respect, information science can be seen as a response to technological determinism, the belief that technology "develops by its own laws, that it realizes its own potential, limited only by the material resources available, and must therefore be regarded as an autonomous system controlling and ultimately permeating all other subsystems of society." Within information science, attention has been given in recent years to human–computer interaction, groupware, the semantic web, value sensitive design, iterative design processes and to the ways people generate, use and find information.

Information science should not be confused with information theory, the study of a particular mathematical concept of information, or with library science, a field related to libraries which uses some of the principles of information science.

Information Science and Informatics

Some authors treat informatics as a synonym for information science. Because of the rapidly evolving, interdisciplinary nature of informatics, a precise meaning of the term "informatics" is presently difficult to pin down. Regional differences and international terminology complicate the problem. Some people note that much of what is called "Informatics" today was once called "Information Science" at least in fields such as Medical Informatics. However when library scientists began also to use the phrase "Information Science" to refer to their work, the term informatics emerged in the United States as a response by computer scientists to distinguish their work from that of library science, and in Britain as a term for a science of information that studies natural, as well as artificial or engineered, information-processing systems.

Aspects of Information Science

Data Modeling

Data modeling is the process of creating a data model by applying a data model theory to create a data model instance. A data model theory is a formal data model description.

When data modeling, one is structuring and organizing data. These data structures are then typically implemented in a database management system. In addition to defining and organizing the data, data modeling will impose (implicitly or explicitly) constraints or limitations on the data placed within the structure.

Managing large quantities of structured and unstructured data is a primary function of information systems. Data models describe structured data for storage in data management systems such as relational databases. They typically do not describe unstructured data, such as word processing documents, email messages, pictures, digital audio, and video.

Document Management

Document management and engineering is a computer system (or set of computer programs) used to track and store electronic documents and images of paper documents. Document management systems have some overlap with Content Management Systems, Enterprise Content Management Systems, Digital Asset Management, Document imaging, Workflow systems, and Records Management systems.

Groupware

Groupware is software designed to help people involved in a common task achieve their goals. Collaborative software is the basis for computer supported cooperative work.

Such software systems as email, calendaring, text chat, wiki belong in this category. It has been suggested that Metcalfe's law—the more people who use something, the more valuable it becomes—applies to such software.

The more general term social software applies to systems used outside the workplace, for example, online dating services and social networks like Friendster. The study of computer-supported collaboration includes the study of this software and social phenomena associated with it.

Human-computer Interaction

Human-computer interaction (HCI), alternatively man-machine interaction (MMI) or computer–human interaction (CHI), is the study of interaction between people (users) and computers. It is an interdisciplinary subject, relating computer science with many other fields of study and research. Interaction between users and computers occurs at the user interface (or simply interface), which includes both software and hardware, for example, general purpose computer peripherals and large-scale mechanical systems such as aircraft and power plants.

Information Ethics

Information ethics is the field that investigates the ethical issues arising from the development and application of information technologies. It provides a critical framework for considering moral issues concerning informational privacy, moral agency (for example, whether artificial agents may be moral), new environmental issues (especially how agents should one behave in the infosphere), problems arising from the life-cycle (creation, collection, recording, distribution, processing, and so on) of information (especially ownership and copyright, digital divide). Information Ethics is therefore strictly related to the fields of computer ethics and the philosophy of information.

Dilemmas regarding the life of information are becoming increasingly important in a society that is defined as "the information society." Information transmission and literacy are essential concerns in establishing an ethical foundation that promotes fair, equitable, and responsible practices. Information ethics broadly examines issues related to, among other things, ownership, access, privacy, security, and community.

Information technology affects fundamental rights involving copyright protection, intellectual freedom, accountability, and security.

Professional codes offer a basis for making ethical decisions and applying ethical solutions to situations involving information provision and use which reflect an organization's commitment to responsible information service. Evolving information formats and needs require continual reconsideration of ethical principles and how these codes are applied. Considerations regarding information ethics influence personal decisions, professional practice, and public policy.

Information Society

Information society is a society in which the creation, distribution, diffusion, use, and manipulation of information is a significant economic, political, and cultural activity. The knowledge economy is its economic counterpart whereby wealth is created through the economic exploitation of understanding.

Specific to this kind of society is the central position information technology has for production, economy, and society at large. Information society is seen as the successor to industrial society. Closely related concepts are the post-industrial society (Daniel Bell), post-fordism, post-modern society, knowledge society, Telematic Society, Information Revolution, and network society (Manuel Castells).

Intellectual Property

Intellectual property (IP) is a disputed umbrella term for various legal entitlements which attach to certain names, written and recorded media, and inventions. The holders of these legal entitlements are generally entitled to exercise various exclusive rights in relation to the subject matter of the IP. The term intellectual property links the idea that this subject matter is the product of the mind or the intellect together with the political and economical notion of property. The close linking of these two ideas is a matter of some controversy. It is criticized as "a fad" by Mark Lemley of Stanford Law School and by Richard Stallman of the Free Software Foundation as an "overgeneralization" and "at best a catch-all to lump together disparate laws."

Intellectual property laws and enforcement vary widely from jurisdiction to jurisdiction. There are inter-governmental efforts to harmonize them through international treaties such as the 1994 World Trade Organization (WTO) Agreement on Trade-Related Aspects of Intellectual Property Rights (TRIPs), while other treaties may facilitate registration in more than one jurisdiction at a time. Enforcement of copyright, disagreements over medical and software patents, and the dispute regarding the nature of "intellectual property" as a cohesive notion have so far prevented the emergence of a cohesive international system.

Knowledge Management

Knowledge management comprises a range of practices used by organizations to identify, create, represent, and distribute knowledge for reuse, awareness, and learning across the organizations.

Knowledge Management programs are typically tied to organizational objectives and are intended to lead to the achievement of specific outcomes, such as shared intelligence, improved performance, competitive advantage, or higher levels of innovation.

Knowledge transfer (one aspect of Knowledge Management) has always existed in one form or another. Examples include on-the-job peer discussions, formal apprenticeship, corporate libraries, professional training, and mentoring programs. However, since the late twentieth century, additional technology has been applied to this task.

Knowledge Engineering

Knowledge engineering (KE), often studied in conjunction with knowledge management, refers to the building, maintaining and development of knowledge-based systems. It has a great deal in common with software engineering, and is related to many computer science domains such as artificial intelligence, databases, data mining, expert systems, decision support systems and geographic information systems. Knowledge engineering is also related to mathematical logic, as well as strongly involved in cognitive science and socio-cognitive engineering where the knowledge is produced by socio-cognitive aggregates (mainly humans) and is structured according to our understanding of how human reasoning and logic works.

Semantic Web

Semantic Web is an evolving extension of the World Wide Web in which web content can be expressed not only in natural language, but also in a form that can be understood, interpreted and used by software agents, thus permitting them to find, share and integrate information more easily. It derives from W3C director Tim Berners-Lee's vision of the Web as a universal medium for data, information, and knowledge exchange.

At its core, the Semantic Web comprises a philosophy, a set of design principles, collaborative working groups, and a variety of enabling technologies. Some elements of the Semantic Web are expressed as prospective future possibilities that have yet to be implemented or realized. Other elements of the Semantic Web are expressed in formal specifications. Some of these include Resource Description Framework (RDF), a variety of data interchange formats (for example, RDF/XML, N3, Turtle, and notations such as RDF Schema (RDFS) and the Web Ontology Language (OWL). All of which are intended to formally describe concepts, terms, and relationships within a given problem domain.

Usability Engineering

Usability engineering is a subset of human factors that is specific to computer science and is concerned with the question of how to design software that is easy to use. It is closely related to the field of human-computer interaction and industrial design. The term "usability engineering" (UE) (in contrast to other names of the discipline, like interaction design or user experience design) tends to describe a pragmatic approach to user interface design which emphasizes empirical methods and operational definitions of user requirements for tools. Extending as far as International Standards Organization-approved definitions usability is considered a context-dependent agreement of the effectiveness, efficiency and satisfaction with which specific users should be able to perform tasks. Advocates of this approach engage in task analysis, then prototype interface designs and conduct usability tests. On the basis of such tests, the technology is (ideally) re-designed or (occasionally) the operational targets for user performance are revised.

User-centered Design

User-centered design is a design philosophy and a process in which the needs, wants, and limitations of the end user of an interface or document are given extensive attention at each stage of the design process. User-centered design can be characterized as a multi-stage problem solving process that not only requires designers to analyze and foresee how users are likely to use an interface, but to test the validity of their assumptions with regards to user behaviour in real world tests with actual users. Such testing is necessary as it is often very difficult for the designers of an interface to understand intuitively what a first-time user of their design experiences, and what each user's learning curve may look like.

The chief difference from other interface design philosophies is that user-centered design tries to optimize the user interface around how people can, want, or need to work, rather than forcing the users to change how they work to accommodate the system or function.

XML

XML is a W3C-recommended general-purpose markup language that supports a wide variety of applications. XML languages or "dialects" may be designed by anyone and may be processed by conforming software. XML is also designed to be reasonably human-legible, and to this end, terseness was not considered essential in its structure. XML is a simplified subset of Standard Generalized Markup Language (SGML). Its primary purpose is to facilitate the sharing of data across different information systems, particularly systems connected via the Internet Formally defined languages based on XML (such as RSS, MathML, GraphML, XHTML, Scalable Vector Graphics, MusicXML, and thousands of other examples) allow diverse software to reliably understand information formatted and passed in these languages.

INFORMATION ARCHITECTURE

Information architecture is the design and organization of content, pages and data into a structure that aids users understanding of a system. A more organised system enables users to more easily find the information they require and complete the intended tasks.

To create an effective information architecture you need to understand the relationship between the content and the interoperability of the system you are designing. A flow or hierarchy is often established with IA that allows users to understand where they are, and where they can go next.

Information Architecture is a discipline of it's own and can be performed by specialists or any other members of a design team. An Information architects output can be expressed visually through: site maps, wireframes, navigation, taxonomic designs, metadata and more.

Principles of Information Architecture

The Principle of Objects

This principle is founded on the idea that content should be perceived as an organic entity, with its own personality, weaknesses, and strengths. For instance, there is a clear difference between a blog and an online picture – they are different types of content, and they both have different functions.

The blog needs a title, paragraph breaks, subtitles, and maybe even a quote. If the image is part of a gallery, it may need to additional images, captions, titles, and subtitles too.

It is common to assume that text heavy pages are all part of the same content group, but within this category there is diversity as well.

If the example of a culinary recipe is employed, it is clear to see that this textual product contains measurements, lists, culinary techniques, pictures, and more. It may be an example of a textual product, but it is not necessarily the same as a blog.

WordPress is extremely popular with web designers. If you are familiar with it, think about dissimilarities between a page and a post. In lots of ways, they look like the same thing. However, on closer inspection, it is clear to see that they contain different types of content.

It is a good idea to clearly outline all of the content types which will be used when designing a website. These virtual categories are bound to all have their own needs and structural requirements.

According to the principle of objects, each new task must be defined by the identification of every content category due to be featured – at high and low levels.

For instance, an online store may feature content which describes a diverse selection of product types (low level), whilst also containing content within each of these classifications which lists data relating to individual products (high level).

This kind of website may also feature an introduction to the business, an FAQ page, a customer service promise, and more.

Therefore, organizing all of these very specific content categories, and the defining their interactions, is the initial phase in constructing a strategy to provide data to users in the most efficient way possible.

The Principle of Choices

It is important to produce pages which are valuable and relevant to users, but it is similarly important to restrict the options they offer to a clearly defined objective.

According to web design expert Barry Schwartz, too many choices can make it near impossible for users to make a selection.

The more choices, the more mental work involved in processing them, and increased work can lead to increased stress. Whilst human beings tend to claim that they enjoy a diverse range of options, in reality, studies have suggested that too many choices cause anxiety.

It is the case that business intranets are goldmines for extensive logs of content. The only problem is that enterprises release guidelines, all pertaining to a specific subject matter (benefits, for example), but they almost never put in the journalistic work required to keep logs relevant and easy to use.

The detriment to users is clear – they have to invest more time in finding what they need. As such, many will simply not use the logs and never locate what they require, or they will utilize other resources like direct telephone contact, which negate the function of the web.

In regards to constructing information hierarchies, it is useful to space things out. For instance, logs should be smaller and options fewer, if only at the highest rungs of the system.

The Principle of Disclosure

The best strategy is to reveal only as much data is needed to make sure that users know what kind of content categories to expect.

The principle of progressive disclosure is a popular design model which links with the notion that human beings can only take in a predefined amount of data in any one instant, but that they are able to utilize that data to predict what information will come after. According to design executive Jill Butler, data offered to a user who does not plan or is not able to utilize is meaningless.

The key way in which progressive disclosure can impact web designs is that it forces designers to consider content in the form of layers. A website offers varying layers of similar content, spread across each of its different component parts.

To return to the recipe analogy, a culinary website cannot publish this content on every single page, because it would look absurd.

Therefore, what is does is use categories to group and organize the content. The categories page provides less data than the page containing the full recipe, but it is the right and relevant data.

If a user were to browse a collection of seasonal summer recipes, it would be valuable for them to be provided with images and relevant recipe names, so that they can make a personal decision as to whether to find out more.

Principle of Exemplars

The strategy of outlining content contained within a data category is a good way to help users get to grips with what a website offers.

For instance, on the Amazon website, if a user searches through the product categories, examples of products which are contained within those categories are displayed. This makes it much simpler to automatically highlight the right one, particularly for users who are unsure about category names.

This principle can be tricky to implement in some cases, and its value is reliant on content type. However, it can still be very useful, and it is worth incorporating into a website design, as it potentially offers a significant increase in user happiness.

The Principle of Front Doors

At this point, web designers should be aware of the fact that a home page is not the only landing page. In fact, users can access a website via almost any page. In simple terms, this is like a building with lots and lots of open doors. The general rule of thumb is to presume that around 50% of all users will enter via a door which is not the home page.

The concept of front doors links to some useful advice, which states that every website page must be perceived as a potentially open door. As such, every page needs to solve two key issues – what is this website, and what will it allow me to achieve?

In some cases, users will arrive via a page, and it will provide them with all of the information that they need. However, each page still has to link to a number of other relevant pages, and it must outline what other information can be located across the website.

Plus, the front door model implies that the home page does not have to contain a vast wealth of data. Whilst your home page does have to inform users of the function of your website, and what it will allow them to achieve, it does not have to be connected to every content category featured.

In fact, a home page should be devoted to supporting users when it comes to grasping the purpose of the website, and to merely suggesting a number of other pages which might prove useful to them.

Principle of Multiple Classification

The principle of multiple classification refers to the fact that different visitors will need different approaches to navigating a website. In other, different users prefer different ways of browsing data.

For instance, some tend to move directly towards search tools, whilst others prefer to navigate information more fluidly.

A good example is an online store which sells fashion items. You could have one user who wishes to search through all of the handbags on the website, and you could have another who is trying to navigate through just the smaller garment sizes, or the items which are priced the lowest.

The ability to offer website visitors varying choices inevitably leads to greater customer satisfaction.

The Principle of Focused Navigation

This principle pertains to a simple rule – do not mix categories within a navigation framework.

It is common for designers to employ terminology such as 'international navigation,' 'left rail,' or 'right menu tab,' in order to describe resources which allow users to navigate content whilst its location is displayed on the page.

The construction of navigation resources equates to the implementation of an approach to locating content within a website. The approach can involve various different navigation tools, or features which allow users to utilize content in a range of ways. For a content driven platform, the following navigation tools could be employed:

- Subject Searching: The key navigation area, which is made up of the primary subjects.

- Timely Searching: A basic tool offering connections to valuable subtopics.

- Indicator Searching: A tool featured on interior pages, which shows how content is organized.

- Promotional Searching: A basic tool which offers direct links to available services.

Principle of Growth

For most websites, content is an organic and inconstant entity. The complexity or amount of content featured on a website this year is unlikely to stay the same next year.

This means that it is important to manage your content in a flexible manner. The search tools and overarching data framework that you implement should be inherently scalable, so that it can grow to assimilate large amounts of new content with little effort.

You need to take the time to think about the type of content which could feasibly incorporated in future years, and this needs to relate to completely new content categories, as well as expansions of the ones already featured on the website.

It is a good idea to consider how this new content will link with existing content, the ways in which they could complement one another, and the manner whereby they could be assimilated easily with no need for a site overhaul.

The IA principles outlined are essential when it comes to constructing successful data hierarchies.

Whilst some will undoubtedly be more useful than others, for specific tasks, the ability to think about and evaluate every one of them is something which will lead to more streamlined data approaches. As all designers should know, an improved data hierarchy is a good way to up user satisfaction.

INFORMATION MANAGEMENT

Information management (IM) concerns a cycle of organizational activity: the acquisition of information from one or more sources, the custodianship and the distribution of that information to those who need it, and its ultimate disposition through archiving or deletion.

This cycle of Organizational involvement with information involves a variety of stakeholders, including those who are responsible for assuring the quality, accessibility and utility of acquired information; those who are responsible for its safe storage and disposal; and those who need it for decision making. Stakeholders might have rights to originate, change, distribute or delete information according to Organizational information management policies.

Information management embraces all the generic concepts of management, including the planning, organizing, structuring, processing, controlling, evaluation and reporting of information activities, all of which is needed in order to meet the needs of those with Organizational roles or functions that depend on information. These generic concepts allow the information to be presented to the audience or the correct group of people. After individuals are able to put that information to use, it then gains more value.

Information management is closely related to, and overlaps with, the management of *data, systems, technology, processes* and – where the availability of information is critical to Organizational success – *strategy*. This broad view of the realm of information management contrasts with the earlier, more traditional view, that the life cycle of managing information is an operational matter that requires specific procedures, Organizational capabilities and standards that deal with information as a product or a service.

Behavioral and Organizational Theories

It is commonly believed that good information management is crucial to the smooth working of organizations, and although there is no commonly accepted theory of information management *per se*, Behavioral and Organizational theories help. Following the Behavioral science theory of management, mainly developed at Carnegie Mellon University and prominently supported by March and Simon, most of what goes on in modern organizations is actually information handling and decision making. One crucial factor in information handling and decision making is an individual's ability to process information and to make decisions under limitations that might derive from the context: a person's age, the situational complexity, or a lack of requisite quality in the information that is at hand – all of which is exacerbated by the rapid advance of technology and the new kinds of system that it enables, especially as the social web emerges as a phenomenon that business cannot ignore. And yet, well before there was any general recognition of the importance of information management in organizations, March and Simon argued that organizations have to be considered as cooperative systems, with a high level of information processing and a vast need for decision making at various levels. Instead of using the model of the "economic man", as advocated in classical theory they proposed "administrative man" as an alternative, based on their argumentation about the cognitive limits of rationality. Additionally they proposed the notion of satisficing, which entails searching through the available alternatives until an acceptability threshold is met - another idea that still has currency.

Economic Theory

In addition to the Organizational factors mentioned by March and Simon, there are other issues that stem from economic and environmental dynamics. There is the cost of collecting and evaluating the information needed to take a decision, including the time and effort required. The transaction cost associated with information processes can be high. In particular, established organizational rules and procedures can prevent the taking of the most appropriate decision, leading to sub-optimum outcomes . This is an issue that has been presented as a major problem with bureaucratic organizations that lose the economies of strategic change because of entrenched attitudes.

Strategic Information Management

According to the Carnegie Mellon School an organization's ability to process information is at the core of organizational and managerial competency, and an organization's strategies must be designed to improve information processing capability and as information systems that provide that capability became formalised and automated, competencies were severely tested at many levels. It was recognised that organizations needed to be able to learn and adapt in ways that were never so evident before and academics began to organise and publish definitive works concerning the strategic management of information, and information systems. Concurrently, the ideas of business process management and knowledge management although much of the optimistic early thinking about business process redesign has since been discredited in the information management literature. In the strategic studies field, it is considered of the highest priority the understanding of the information environment, conceived as the aggregate of individuals, organizations, and systems that collect, process, disseminate, or act on information. This environment consists of three interrelated dimensions which continuously interact with individuals, organizations, and systems. These dimensions are the physical, informational, and cognitive.

Aligning Technology and Business Strategy with Information Management

Venkatraman has provided a simple view of the requisite capabilities of an organization that wants to manage information well – the DIKAR model. He also worked with others to understand how technology and business strategies could be appropriately aligned in order to identify specific capabilities that are needed. This work was paralleled by other writers in the world of consulting, practice and academia.

A Contemporary Portfolio Model for Information

Byteway has collected and organised basic tools and techniques for information management in a single volume. At the heart of his view of information management is a portfolio model that takes account of the surging interest in external sources of information and the need to organise un-structured information external so as to make it useful.

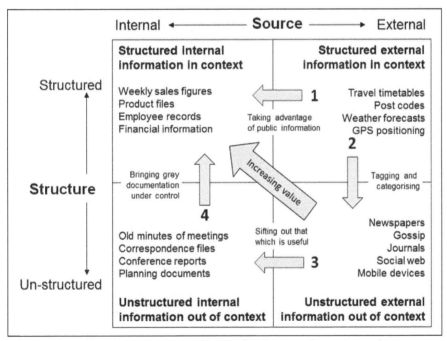

This portfolio model organizes issues of internal and external sourcing and management of information, that may be either structured or unstructured.

Such an information portfolio as this shows how information can be gathered and usefully organised, in four stages:

Stage 1: Taking advantage of public information: Recognise and adopt well-structured external schemes of reference data, such as post codes, weather data, GPS positioning data and travel timetables, exemplified in the personal computing press.

Stage 2: Tagging the noise on the world wide web: Use existing schemes such as post codes and GPS data or more typically by adding "tags", or construct a formal ontology that provides structure. Shirky provides an overview of these two approaches.

Stage 3: Sifting and analysing: In the wider world the generalised ontologies that are under development extend to hundreds of entities and hundreds of relations between them and provide the means to elicit meaning from large volumes of data. Structured data in databases works best when that structure reflects a higher-level information model – an ontology, or an entity-relationship model.

Stage 4: Structuring and archiving: With the large volume of data available from sources such as the social web and from the miniature telemetry systems used in personal health management, new ways to archive and then trawl data for meaningful information. Map-reduce methods, originating from functional programming, are a more recent way of eliciting information from large archival datasets that is becoming interesting to regular businesses that have very large data resources to work with, but it requires advanced multi-processor resources.

Competencies to Manage Information Well

The Information Management Body of Knowledge was made available on the world wide web in 2004 and sets out to show that the required management competencies to derive real benefits from an investment in information are complex and multi-layered. The framework model that is the basis for understanding competencies comprises six "knowledge" areas and four "process" areas.

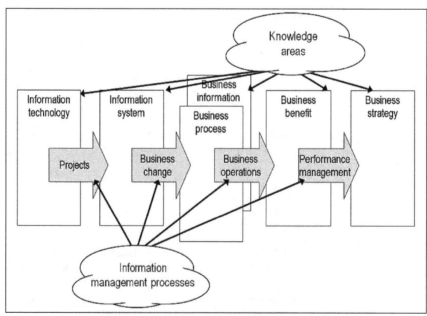

Information Management Body of Knowledge.

The Information Management Knowledge Areas

The IMBOK is based on the argument that there are six areas of required management competency, two of which ("business process management" and "business information management") are very closely related.

- Information technology: The pace of change of technology and the pressure to constantly acquire the newest technological products can undermine the stability of the infrastructure that supports systems, and thereby optimises business processes and delivers benefits. It is necessary to manage the "supply side" and recognise that technology is, increasingly, becoming a commodity.

- Information system: While historically information systems were developed in-house, over the years it has become possible to acquire most of the software systems that an organization needs from the software package industry. However, there is still the potential for competitive advantage from the implementation of new systems ideas that deliver to the strategic intentions of organizations.

- Business processes and Business information: Information systems are applied to business processes in order to improve them, and they bring data to the business that becomes useful as business information. Business process management is still seen as a relatively new idea because it is not universally adopted, and it has been difficult in many cases; business *information* management is even more of a challenge.

- Business benefit: What are the benefits that we are seeking? It is necessary not only to be brutally honest about what *can* be achieved, but also to ensure the active management and assessment of benefit delivery. Since the emergence and popularisation of the Balanced scorecard there has been huge interest in business performance management but not much serious effort has been made to relate business performance management to the benefits of information technology investments and the introduction of new information systems until the turn of the millennium.

- Business strategy: Although a long way from the workaday issues of managing information in organizations, strategy in most organizations simply has to be informed by information technology and information systems opportunities, whether to address poor performance or to improve differentiation and competitiveness. Strategic analysis tools such as the value chain and critical success factor analysis are directly dependent on proper attention to the information that is (or could be) managed.

The Information Management Processes

Even with full capability and competency within the six knowledge areas, it is argued that things can still go wrong. The problem lies in the migration of ideas and information management value from one area of competency to another. Summarising what Bytheway explains in some detail:

- Projects: Information technology is without value until it is engineered into information systems that meet the needs of the business by means of good project management.

- Business change: The best information systems succeed in delivering benefits through the achievement of change within the business systems, but people do not appreciate change that makes new demands upon their skills in the ways that new information systems often do. Contrary to common expectations, there is some evidence that the public sector has succeeded with information technology induced business change.

- Business operations: With new systems in place, with business processes and business information improved, and with staff finally ready and able to work with new processes, then the business can get to work, even when new systems extend far beyond the boundaries of a single business.

- Performance management: Investments are no longer solely about financial results, financial success must be balanced with internal efficiency, customer satisfaction, and with Organizational learning and development.

Operationalising Information Management

Managing Requisite Change

Organizations are often confronted with many information management challenges and issues at the operational level, especially when Organizational change is engendered. The novelty of new systems architectures and a lack of experience with new styles of information management requires a level of Organizational change management that is notoriously difficult to deliver. As a result of a general Organizational reluctance to change, to enable new forms of information management, there might be (for example): a shortfall in the requisite resources, a failure to acknowledge new classes of information and the new procedures that use them, a lack of support from senior management leading to a loss of strategic vision, and even political manoeuvring that undermines the operation of the whole organization. However, the implementation of new forms of information management should normally lead to operational benefits.

The Early Work of Galbraith

In early work, taking an information processing view of organization design, Jay Galbraith has identified five tactical areas to increase information processing capacity and reduce the need for information processing.

- Developing, implementing, and monitoring all aspects of the "environment" of an organization.

- Creation of slack resources so as to decrease the load on the overall hierarchy of resources and to reduce information processing relating to overload.

- Creation of self-contained tasks with defined boundaries and that can achieve proper closure, and with all the resources at hand required to perform the task.

- Recognition of lateral relations that cut across functional units, so as to move decision power to the process instead of fragmenting it within the hierarchy.

- Investment in vertical information systems that route information flows for a specific task (or set of tasks) in accordance to the applied business logic.

The Matrix Organization

The lateral relations concept leads to an organizational form that is different from the simple hierarchy, the "matrix organization". This brings together the vertical (hierarchical) view of an organization and the horizontal (product or project) view of the work that it does visible to the outside world. The creation of a matrix organization is one management response to a persistent fluidity of external demand, avoiding multifarious and spurious responses to episodic demands that tend to be dealt with individually.

DATABASE

```
dvdrental=# select title, release_year, length, replacement_cost from film
dvdrental-#   where length > 120 and replacement_cost > 29.50
dvdrental-#   order by title desc;
          title          | release_year | length | replacement_cost
-------------------------+--------------+--------+------------------
 West Lion               |         2006 |    159 |            29.99
 Virgin Daisy            |         2006 |    179 |            29.99
 Uncut Suicides          |         2006 |    172 |            29.99
 Tracy Cider             |         2006 |    142 |            29.99
 Song Hedwig             |         2006 |    165 |            29.99
 Slacker Liaisons        |         2006 |    179 |            29.99
 Sassy Packer            |         2006 |    154 |            29.99
 River Outlaw            |         2006 |    149 |            29.99
 Right Cranes            |         2006 |    153 |            29.99
 Quest Mussolini         |         2006 |    177 |            29.99
 Poseidon Forever        |         2006 |    159 |            29.99
 Loathing Legally        |         2006 |    140 |            29.99
 Lawless Vision          |         2006 |    181 |            29.99
 Jingle Sagebrush        |         2006 |    124 |            29.99
 Jericho Mulan           |         2006 |    171 |            29.99
 Japanese Run            |         2006 |    135 |            29.99
 Gilmore Boiled          |         2006 |    163 |            29.99
 Floats Garden           |         2006 |    145 |            29.99
 Fantasia Park           |         2006 |    131 |            29.99
 Extraordinary Conquerer |         2006 |    122 |            29.99
 Everyone Craft          |         2006 |    163 |            29.99
 Dirty Ace               |         2006 |    147 |            29.99
 Clyde Theory            |         2006 |    139 |            29.99
 Clockwork Paradise      |         2006 |    143 |            29.99
 Ballroom Mockingbird    |         2006 |    173 |            29.99
(25 rows)
```

An SQL select statement and its result.

A database is an organized collection of data, generally stored and accessed electronically from a computer system. Where databases are more complex they are often developed using formal design and modeling techniques.

The database management system (DBMS) is the software that interacts with end users, applications, and the database itself to capture and analyze the data. The DBMS software additionally encompasses the core facilities provided to administer the database. The sum total of the database, the DBMS and the associated applications can be referred to as a "database system". Often the term "database" is also used to loosely refer to any of the DBMS, the database system or an application associated with the database.

Computer scientists may classify database-management systems according to the database models that they support. Relational databases became dominant in the 1980s. These model data as rows and columns in a series of tables, and the vast majority use SQL for writing and querying data. In the 2000s, non-relational databases became popular, referred to as NoSQL because they use different query languages.

Formally, a "database" refers to a set of related data and the way it is organized. Access to this data is usually provided by a "database management system" (DBMS) consisting of an integrated set of computer software that allows users to interact with one or more databases and provides access to all of the data contained in the database (although restrictions may exist that limit access to particular data). The DBMS provides various functions that allow entry, storage and retrieval of large quantities of information and provides ways to manage how that information is organized.

Because of the close relationship between them, the term "database" is often used casually to refer to both a database and the DBMS used to manipulate it.

Outside the world of professional information technology, the term *database* is often used to refer to any collection of related data (such as a spreadsheet or a card index) as size and usage requirements typically necessitate use of a database management system.

Existing DBMSs provide various functions that allow management of a database and its data which can be classified into four main functional groups:

- Data definition – Creation, modification and removal of definitions that define the organization of the data.

- Update – Insertion, modification, and deletion of the actual data.

- Retrieval – Providing information in a form directly usable or for further processing by other applications. The retrieved data may be made available in a form basically the same as it is stored in the database or in a new form obtained by altering or combining existing data from the database.

- Administration – Registering and monitoring users, enforcing data security, monitoring performance, maintaining data integrity, dealing with concurrency control, and recovering information that has been corrupted by some event such as an unexpected system failure.

Both a database and its DBMS conform to the principles of a particular database model. "Database system" refers collectively to the database model, database management system, and database.

Physically, database servers are dedicated computers that hold the actual databases and run only the DBMS and related software. Database servers are usually multiprocessor computers, with generous memory and RAID disk arrays used for stable storage. RAID is used for recovery of data if any of the disks fail. Hardware database accelerators, connected to one or more servers via a high-speed channel, are also used in large volume transaction processing environments. DBMSs are found at the heart of most database applications. DBMSs may be built around a custom multitasking kernel with built-in networking support, but modern DBMSs typically rely on a standard operating system to provide these functions.

Since DBMSs comprise a significant market, computer and storage vendors often take into account DBMS requirements in their own development plans.

Databases and DBMSs can be categorized according to the database model that they support (such as relational or XML), the type of computer they run on (from a server cluster to a mobile phone), the query language used to access the database (such as SQL or XQuery), and their internal engineering, which affects performance, scalability, resilience, and security.

Use Cases

Databases are used to support internal operations of organizations and to underpin online interactions with customers and suppliers.

Databases are used to hold administrative information and more specialized data, such as engineering data or economic models. Examples include computerized library systems, flight reservation systems, computerized parts inventory systems, and many content management systems that store websites as collections of webpages in a database.

Classification

One way to classify databases involves the type of their contents, for example: bibliographic, document-text, statistical, or multimedia objects. Another way is by their application area, for example: accounting, music compositions, movies, banking, manufacturing, or insurance. A third way is by some technical aspect, such as the database structure or interface type. This section lists a few of the adjectives used to characterize different kinds of databases:

- An in-memory database is a database that primarily resides in main memory, but is typically backed-up by non-volatile computer data storage. Main memory databases are faster than disk databases, and so are often used where response time is critical, such as in telecommunications network equipment.

- An active database includes an event-driven architecture which can respond to conditions both inside and outside the database. Possible uses include security monitoring, alerting, statistics gathering and authorization. Many databases provide active database features in the form of database triggers.

- A cloud database relies on cloud technology. Both the database and most of its DBMS reside remotely, "in the cloud", while its applications are both developed by programmers and later maintained and used by end-users through a web browser and Open APIs.

- Data warehouses archive data from operational databases and often from external sources such as market research firms. The warehouse becomes the central source of data for use by managers and other end-users who may not have access to operational data. For example, sales data might be aggregated to weekly totals and converted from internal product codes to use UPCs so that they can be compared with ACNielsen data. Some basic and essential components of data warehousing include extracting, analyzing, and mining data, transforming, loading, and managing data so as to make them available for further use.

- A deductive database combines logic programming with a relational database.

- A distributed database is one in which both the data and the DBMS span multiple computers.

- A document-oriented database is designed for storing, retrieving, and managing document-oriented, or semi structured, information. Document-oriented databases are one of the main categories of NoSQL databases.

- An embedded database system is a DBMS which is tightly integrated with an application software that requires access to stored data in such a way that the DBMS is hidden from the application's end-users and requires little or no ongoing maintenance.

- End-user databases consist of data developed by individual end-users. Examples of these are collections of documents, spreadsheets, presentations, multimedia, and other files. Several products exist to support such databases. Some of them are much simpler than full-fledged DBMSs, with more elementary DBMS functionality.

- A federated database system comprises several distinct databases, each with its own DBMS. It is handled as a single database by a federated database management system (FDBMS), which transparently integrates multiple autonomous DBMSs, possibly of different types (in which case it would also be a heterogeneous database system), and provides them with an integrated conceptual view.

- Sometimes the term *multi-database* is used as a synonym to federated database, though it may refer to a less integrated (e.g., without an FDBMS and a managed integrated schema) group of databases that cooperate in a single application. In this case, typically middleware is used for distribution, which typically includes an atomic commit protocol (ACP), e.g., the two-phase commit protocol, to allow distributed (global) transactions across the participating databases.

- A graph database is a kind of NoSQL database that uses graph structures with nodes, edges, and properties to represent and store information. General graph databases that can store any graph are distinct from specialized graph databases such as triplestores and network databases.

- An array DBMS is a kind of NoSQL DBMS that allows modeling, storage, and retrieval of (usually large) multi-dimensional arrays such as satellite images and climate simulation output.

- In a hypertext or hypermedia database, any word or a piece of text representing an object, e.g., another piece of text, an article, a picture, or a film, can be hyperlinked to that object. Hypertext databases are particularly useful for organizing large amounts of disparate information. For example, they are useful for organizing online encyclopedias, where users can conveniently jump around the text. The World Wide Web is thus a large distributed hypertext database.

- A knowledge base (abbreviated KB, kb or Δ) is a special kind of database for knowledge management, providing the means for the computerized collection, organization, and retrieval of knowledge. Also a collection of data representing problems with their solutions and related experiences.

- A mobile database can be carried on or synchronized from a mobile computing device.

- Operational databases store detailed data about the operations of an organization. They typically process relatively high volumes of updates using transactions. Examples include customer databases that record contact, credit, and demographic information about a business's customers, personnel databases that hold information such as salary, benefits, skills data about employees, enterprise resource planning systems that record details about product components, parts inventory, and financial databases that keep track of the organization's money, accounting and financial dealings.

- A parallel database seeks to improve performance through parallelization for tasks such as loading data, building indexes and evaluating queries.

The major parallel DBMS architectures which are induced by the underlying hardware architecture are:

  ◦ Shared memory architecture, where multiple processors share the main memory space, as well as other data storage.

  ◦ Shared disk architecture, where each processing unit (typically consisting of multiple processors) has its own main memory, but all units share the other storage.

  ◦ Shared nothing architecture, where each processing unit has its own main memory and other storage.

- Probabilistic databases employ fuzzy logic to draw inferences from imprecise data.

- Real-time databases process transactions fast enough for the result to come back and be acted on right away.

- A spatial database can store the data with multidimensional features. The queries on such data include location-based queries, like "Where is the closest hotel in my area?".

- A temporal database has built-in time aspects, for example a temporal data model and a temporal version of SQL. More specifically the temporal aspects usually include valid-time and transaction-time.

- A terminology-oriented database builds upon an object-oriented database, often customized for a specific field.

- An unstructured data database is intended to store in a manageable and protected way diverse objects that do not fit naturally and conveniently in common databases. It may include email messages, documents, journals, multimedia objects, etc. The name may be misleading since some objects can be highly structured. However, the entire possible object collection does not fit into a predefined structured framework. Most established DBMSs now support unstructured data in various ways, and new dedicated DBMSs are emerging.

Database Interaction

Database Management System

Connolly and Begg define Database Management System (DBMS) as a "software system that enables users to define, create, maintain and control access to the database".

The DBMS acronym is sometime extended to indicated the underlying database model, with RDBMS for relational, OODBMS or ORDBMS for the object (orientated) model and ORDBMS for Object-Relational. Other extensions can indicate some other characteristic, such as DDBMS for a distributed database management systems.

The functionality provided by a DBMS can vary enormously. The core functionality is the storage, retrieval and update of data. Codd proposed the following functions and services a fully-fledged general purpose DBMS should provide:

- Data storage, retrieval and update.

- User accessible catalog or data dictionary describing the metadata.

- Support for transactions and concurrency.

- Facilities for recovering the database should it become damaged.

- Support for authorization of access and update of data.

- Access support from remote locations.

- Enforcing constraints to ensure data in the database abides by certain rules.

It is also generally to be expected the DBMS will provide a set of utilities for such purposes as may be necessary to administer the database effectively, including import, export, monitoring, defragmentation and analysis utilities. The core part of the DBMS interacting between the database and the application interface sometimes referred to as the database engine.

Often DBMSs will have configuration parameters that can be statically and dynamically tuned, for example the maximum amount of main memory on a server the database can use. The trend is to minimise the amount of manual configuration, and for cases such as embedded databases the need to target zero-administration is paramount.

The large major enterprise DBMSs have tended to increase in size and functionality and can have involved thousands of human years of development effort through their lifetime.

Early multi-user DBMS typically only allowed for the application to reside on the same computer with access via terminals or terminal emulation software. The client–server architecture was a development where the application resided on a client desktop and the database on a server allowing the processing to be distributed. This evolved into a multitier architecture incorporating application servers and web servers with the end user interface via a web browser with the database only directly connected to the adjacent tier.

A general-purpose DBMS will provide public application programming interfaces (API) and optionally a processor for database languages such as SQL to allow applications to be written to interact with the database. A special purpose DBMS may use a private API and be specifically customised and linked to a single application. For example, an email system performing many of the functions of a general-purpose DBMS such as message insertion, message deletion, attachment handling, blocklist lookup, associating messages an email address and so forth however these functions are limited to what is required to handle email.

Application

External interaction with the database will be via an application program that interfaces with the DBMS. This can range from a database tool that allows users to execute SQL queries textually or graphically, to a web site that happens to use a database to store and search information.

Application Program Interface

A programmer will code interactions to the database (sometimes referred to as a datasource) via an application program interface (API) or via a database language. The particular API or language chosen will need to be supported by DBMS, possible indirectly via a pre-processor or a bridging API. Some API's aim to be database independent, ODBC being a commonly known example. Other common API's include JDBC and ADO.NET.

Database Languages

Database languages are special-purpose languages, which allow one or more of the following tasks, sometimes distinguished as sublanguages:

- Data control language (DCL) – Controls access to data;

- Data definition language (DDL) – Defines data types such as creating, altering, or dropping tables and the relationships among them;

- Data manipulation language (DML) – Performs tasks such as inserting, updating, or deleting data occurrences;

- Data query language (DQL) – Allows searching for information and computing derived information.

Database languages are specific to a particular data model. Notable examples include:

- SQL combines the roles of data definition, data manipulation, and query in a single language. It was one of the first commercial languages for the relational model, although it departs in some respects from the relational model as described by Codd (for example, the rows and columns of a table can be ordered). SQL became a standard of the American National Standards Institute (ANSI) in 1986, and of the International Organization for Standardization (ISO) in 1987. The standards have been regularly enhanced since and is supported (with varying degrees of conformance) by all mainstream commercial relational DBMSs.

- OQL is an object model language standard (from the Object Data Management Group). It has influenced the design of some of the newer query languages like JDOQL and EJB QL.

- XQuery is a standard XML query language implemented by XML database systems such as MarkLogic and eXist, by relational databases with XML capability such as Oracle and DB2, and also by in-memory XML processors such as Saxon.

- SQL/XML combines XQuery with SQL.

A database language may also incorporate features like:

- DBMS-specific configuration and storage engine management.

- Computations to modify query results, like counting, summing, averaging, sorting, grouping, and cross-referencing.

- Constraint enforcement (e.g. in an automotive database, only allowing one engine type per car).

- Application programming interface version of the query language, for programmer convenience.

Storage

Database storage is the container of the physical materialization of a database. It comprises the *internal* (physical) *level* in the database architecture. It also contains all the information needed (e.g., metadata, "data about the data", and internal data structures) to reconstruct the *conceptual level* and *external level* from the internal level when needed. Putting data into permanent storage is generally the responsibility of the database engine a.k.a. "storage engine". Though typically accessed by a DBMS through the underlying operating system (and often using the operating systems' file systems as intermediates for storage layout), storage properties and configuration setting are extremely important for the efficient operation of the DBMS, and thus are closely maintained by database administrators. A DBMS, while in operation, always has its database residing in several types of storage (e.g., memory and external storage). The database data and the additional needed information, possibly in very large amounts, are coded into bits. Data typically reside in the storage in structures that look completely different from the way the data look in the conceptual and external levels, but in ways that attempt to optimize (the best possible) these levels' reconstruction when needed by users and programs, as well as for computing additional types of needed information from the data (e.g., when querying the database).

Some DBMSs support specifying which character encoding was used to store data, so multiple encodings can be used in the same database.

Various low-level database storage structures are used by the storage engine to serialize the data model so it can be written to the medium of choice. Techniques such as indexing may be used to improve performance. Conventional storage is row-oriented, but there are also column-oriented and correlation databases.

Materialized Views

Often storage redundancy is employed to increase performance. A common example is storing *materialized views*, which consist of frequently needed *external views* or query results. Storing such views saves the expensive computing of them each time they are needed. The downsides of materialized views are the overhead incurred when updating them to keep them synchronized with their original updated database data, and the cost of storage redundancy.

Replication

Occasionally a database employs storage redundancy by database objects replication (with one or more copies) to increase data availability (both to improve performance of simultaneous multiple end-user accesses to a same database object, and to provide resiliency in a case of partial failure of a distributed database). Updates of a replicated object need to be synchronized across the object copies. In many cases, the entire database is replicated.

Security

Database security deals with all various aspects of protecting the database content, its owners, and its users. It ranges from protection from intentional unauthorized database uses to unintentional database accesses by unauthorized entities (e.g., a person or a computer program).

Database access control deals with controlling who (a person or a certain computer program) is allowed to access what information in the database. The information may comprise specific database objects (e.g., record types, specific records, data structures), certain computations over certain objects (e.g., query types, or specific queries), or using specific access paths to the former (e.g., using specific indexes or other data structures to access information). Database access controls are set by special authorized (by the database owner) personnel that uses dedicated protected security DBMS interfaces.

This may be managed directly on an individual basis, or by the assignment of individuals and privileges to groups, or (in the most elaborate models) through the assignment of individuals and groups to roles which are then granted entitlements. Data security prevents unauthorized users from viewing or updating the database. Using passwords, users are allowed access to the entire database or subsets of it called "subschemas". For example, an employee database can contain all the data about an individual employee, but one group of users may be authorized to view only payroll data, while others are allowed access to only work history and medical data. If the DBMS provides a way to interactively enter and update the database, as well as interrogate it, this capability allows for managing personal databases.

Data security in general deals with protecting specific chunks of data, both physically (i.e., from corruption, or destruction, or removal; e.g.), or the interpretation of them, or parts of them to meaningful information (e.g., by looking at the strings of bits that they comprise, concluding specific valid credit-card numbers; e.g.).

Change and access logging records who accessed which attributes, what was changed, and when it was changed. Logging services allow for a forensic database audit later by keeping a record of access occurrences and changes. Sometimes application-level code is used to record changes rather than leaving this to the database. Monitoring can be set up to attempt to detect security breaches.

Transactions and Concurrency

Database transactions can be used to introduce some level of fault tolerance and data integrity after recovery from a crash. A database transaction is a unit of work, typically encapsulating a number of operations over a database (e.g., reading a database object, writing, acquiring lock, etc.), an abstraction supported in database and also other systems. Each transaction has well defined boundaries in terms of which program/code executions are included in that transaction (determined by the transaction's programmer via special transaction commands).

The acronym ACID describes some ideal properties of a database transaction: atomicity, consistency, isolation, and durability.

Migration

A database built with one DBMS is not portable to another DBMS (i.e., the other DBMS cannot run it). However, in some situations, it is desirable to migrate a database from one DBMS to another. The reasons are primarily economical (different DBMSs may have different total costs of ownership or TCOs), functional, and operational (different DBMSs may have different capabilities). The migration involves the database's transformation from one DBMS type to another. The transformation should maintain (if possible) the database related application (i.e., all related application programs) intact. Thus, the database's conceptual and external architectural levels should be maintained in the transformation. It may be desired that also some aspects of the architecture internal level are maintained. A complex or large database migration may be a complicated and costly (one-time) project by itself, which should be factored into the decision to migrate. This in spite of the fact that tools may exist to help migration between specific DBMSs. Typically, a DBMS vendor provides tools to help importing databases from other popular DBMSs.

Building, Maintaining and Tuning

After designing a database for an application, the next stage is building the database. Typically, an appropriate general-purpose DBMS can be selected to be used for this purpose. A DBMS provides the needed user interfaces to be used by database administrators to define the needed application's data structures within the DBMS's respective data model. Other user interfaces are used to select needed DBMS parameters (like security related, storage allocation parameters, etc.).

When the database is ready (all its data structures and other needed components are defined), it is typically populated with initial application's data (database initialization, which is typically a distinct project; in many cases using specialized DBMS interfaces that support bulk insertion) before making it operational. In some cases, the database becomes operational while empty of application data, and data are accumulated during its operation.

After the database is created, initialised and populated it needs to be maintained. Various database parameters may need changing and the database may need to be tuned (tuning) for better performance; application's data structures may be changed or added, new related application programs may be written to add to the application's functionality, etc.

Backup and Restore

Sometimes it is desired to bring a database back to a previous state (for many reasons, e.g., cases when the database is found corrupted due to a software error, or if it has been updated with erroneous data). To achieve this, a backup operation is done occasionally or continuously, where each desired database state (i.e., the values of its data and their embedding in database's data structures) is kept within dedicated backup files (many techniques exist to do this effectively). When it is decided by a database administrator to bring the database back to this state (e.g., by specifying this state by a desired point in time when the database was in this state), these files are used to restore that state.

Static Analysis

Static analysis techniques for software verification can be applied also in the scenario of query languages. In particular, the Abstract interpretation framework has been extended to the field of query languages for relational databases as a way to support sound approximation techniques. The semantics of query languages can be tuned according to suitable abstractions of the concrete domain of data. The abstraction of relational database system has many interesting applications, in particular, for security purposes, such as fine grained access control, watermarking, etc.

Miscellaneous Features

Other DBMS features might include:

- Database logs – This helps in keeping a history of the executed functions.
- Graphics component for producing graphs and charts, especially in a data warehouse system.
- Query optimizer – Performs query optimization on every query to choose an efficient *query plan* (a partial order (tree) of operations) to be executed to compute the query result. May be specific to a particular storage engine.
- Tools or hooks for database design, application programming, application program maintenance, database performance analysis and monitoring, database configuration monitoring, DBMS hardware configuration (a DBMS and related database may span computers, networks, and storage units) and related database mapping (especially for a distributed DBMS), storage allocation and database layout monitoring, storage migration, etc.

Increasingly, there are calls for a single system that incorporates all of these core functionalities into the same build, test, and deployment framework for database management and source control. Borrowing from other developments in the software industry, some market such offerings as "DevOps for database".

Design and Modeling

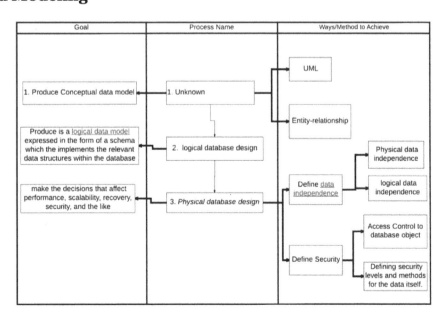

The first task of a database designer is to produce a conceptual data model that reflects the structure of the information to be held in the database. A common approach to this is to develop an entity-relationship model, often with the aid of drawing tools. Another popular approach is the Unified Modeling Language. A successful data model will accurately reflect the possible state of the external world being modeled: for example, if people can have more than one phone number, it will allow this information to be captured. Designing a good conceptual data model requires a good understanding of the application domain; it typically involves asking deep questions about the things of interest to an organization, like "can a customer also be a supplier?", or "if a product is sold with two different forms of packaging, are those the same product or different products?", or "if a plane flies from New York to Dubai via Frankfurt, is that one flight or two (or maybe even three)?". The answers to these questions establish definitions of the terminology used for entities (customers, products, flights, flight segments) and their relationships and attributes.

Producing the conceptual data model sometimes involves input from business processes, or the analysis of workflow in the organization. This can help to establish what information is needed in the database, and what can be left out. For example, it can help when deciding whether the database needs to hold historic data as well as current data.

Having produced a conceptual data model that users are happy with, the next stage is to translate this into a schema that implements the relevant data structures within the database. This process is often called logical database design, and the output is a logical data model expressed in the form of a schema. Whereas the conceptual data model is (in theory at least) independent of the choice of database technology, the logical data model will be expressed in terms of a particular database model supported by the chosen DBMS. (The terms *data model* and *database model* are often used interchangeably, but in this article we use *data model* for the design of a specific database, and *database model* for the modeling notation used to express that design).

The most popular database model for general-purpose databases is the relational model, or more precisely, the relational model as represented by the SQL language. The process of creating a logical database design using this model uses a methodical approach known as normalization. The goal of normalization is to ensure that each elementary "fact" is only recorded in one place, so that insertions, updates, and deletions automatically maintain consistency.

The final stage of database design is to make the decisions that affect performance, scalability, recovery, security, and the like, which depend on the particular DBMS. This is often called *physical database design*, and the output is the physical data model. A key goal during this stage is data independence, meaning that the decisions made for performance optimization purposes should be invisible to end-users and applications. There are two types of data independence: Physical data independence and logical data independence. Physical design is driven mainly by performance requirements, and requires a good knowledge of the expected workload and access patterns, and a deep understanding of the features offered by the chosen DBMS.

Another aspect of physical database design is security. It involves both defining access control to database objects as well as defining security levels and methods for the data itself.

Models

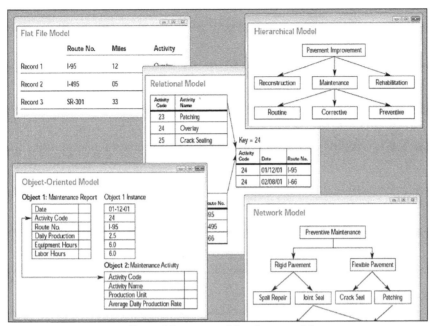

Collage of five types of database models.

A database model is a type of data model that determines the logical structure of a database and fundamentally determines in which manner data can be stored, organized, and manipulated. The most popular example of a database model is the relational model (or the SQL approximation of relational), which uses a table-based format.

Common logical data models for databases include:

- Navigational databases:
    - Hierarchical database model.
    - Network model.
    - Graph database.
- Relational model.
- Entity–relationship model:
    - Enhanced entity–relationship model.
- Object model.
- Document model.
- Entity–attribute–value model.
- Star schema.

An object-relational database combines the two related structures.

Physical data models include:

- Inverted index,

- Flat file.

Other models include:

- Associative model,

- Multidimensional model,

- Array model,

- Multivalue model.

Specialized models are optimized for particular types of data:

- XML database,

- Semantic model,

- Content store,

- Event store,

- Time series model.

External, Conceptual and Internal Views

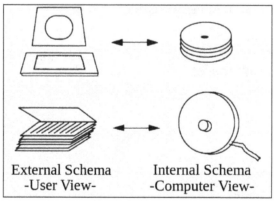

External Schema   Internal Schema
-User View-   -Computer View-

Traditional view of data.

A database management system provides three views of the database data:

- The external level defines how each group of end-users sees the organization of data in the database. A single database can have any number of views at the external level.

- The conceptual level unifies the various external views into a compatible global view. It provides the synthesis of all the external views. It is out of the scope of the various database end-users, and is rather of interest to database application developers and database administrators.

- The internal level (or *physical level*) is the internal organization of data inside a DBMS. It is concerned with cost, performance, scalability and other operational matters. It deals with storage layout of the data, using storage structures such as indexes to enhance performance. Occasionally it stores data of individual views (materialized views), computed from generic data, if performance justification exists for such redundancy. It balances all the external views' performance requirements, possibly conflicting, in an attempt to optimize overall performance across all activities.

While there is typically only one conceptual (or logical) and physical (or internal) view of the data, there can be any number of different external views. This allows users to see database information in a more business-related way rather than from a technical, processing viewpoint. For example, a financial department of a company needs the payment details of all employees as part of the company's expenses, but does not need details about employees that are the interest of the human resources department. Thus different departments need different *views* of the company's database.

The three-level database architecture relates to the concept of *data independence* which was one of the major initial driving forces of the relational model. The idea is that changes made at a certain level do not affect the view at a higher level. For example, changes in the internal level do not affect application programs written using conceptual level interfaces, which reduces the impact of making physical changes to improve performance.

The conceptual view provides a level of indirection between internal and external. On one hand it provides a common view of the database, independent of different external view structures, and on the other hand it abstracts away details of how the data are stored or managed (internal level). In principle every level, and even every external view, can be presented by a different data model. In practice usually a given DBMS uses the same data model for both the external and the conceptual levels (e.g., relational model). The internal level, which is hidden inside the DBMS and depends on its implementation, requires a different level of detail and uses its own types of data structure types.

Separating the *external*, *conceptual* and *internal* levels was a major feature of the relational database model implementations that dominate 21st century databases.

INFORMATION RETRIEVAL

Information retrieval refers to recovery of information, especially in a database stored in a computer. Two main approaches are matching words in the query against the database index (keyword searching) and traversing the database using hypertext or hypermedia links. Keyword searching has been the dominant approach to text retrieval since the early 1960s; hypertext has so far been confined largely to personal or corporate information-retrieval applications. Evolving information-retrieval techniques, exemplified by developments with modern Internet search engines, combine natural language, hyperlinks, and keyword searching. Other techniques that seek higher levels of retrieval precision are studied by researchers involved with artificial intelligence.

INFORMATION SYSTEM

Information system is an integrated set of components for collecting, storing, and processing data and for providing information, knowledge, and digital products. Business firms and other organizations rely on information systems to carry out and manage their operations, interact with their customers and suppliers, and compete in the marketplace. Information systems are used to run interorganizational supply chains and electronic markets. For instance, corporations use information systems to process financial accounts, to manage their human resources, and to reach their potential customers with online promotions. Many major companies are built entirely around information systems. These include eBay, a largely auction marketplace; Amazon, an expanding electronic mall and provider of cloud computing services; Alibaba, a business-to-business e-marketplace; and Google, a search engine company that derives most of its revenue from keyword advertising on Internet searches. Governments deploy information systems to provide services cost-effectively to citizens. Digital goods—such as electronic books, video products, and software—and online services, such as gaming and social networking, are delivered with information systems. Individuals rely on information systems, generally Internet-based, for conducting much of their personal lives: for socializing, study, shopping, banking, and entertainment.

As major new technologies for recording and processing information were invented over the millennia, new capabilities appeared, and people became empowered. The invention of the printing press by Johannes Gutenberg in the mid-15th century and the invention of a mechanical calculator by Blaise Pascal in the 17th century are but two examples. These inventions led to a profound revolution in the ability to record, process, disseminate, and reach for information and knowledge. This led, in turn, to even deeper changes in individual lives, business organization, and human governance.

The first large-scale mechanical information system was Herman Hollerith's census tabulator. Invented in time to process the 1890 U.S. census, Hollerith's machine represented a major step in automation, as well as an inspiration to develop computerized information systems.

One of the first computers used for such information processing was the UNIVAC I, installed at the U.S. Bureau of the Census in 1951 for administrative use and at General Electric in 1954 for commercial use. Beginning in the late 1970s, personal computers brought some of the advantages of information systems to small businesses and to individuals. Early in the same decade the Internet began its expansion as the global network of networks. In 1991 the World Wide Web, invented by Tim Berners-Lee as a means to access the interlinked information stored in the globally dispersed computers connected by the Internet, began operation and became the principal service delivered on the network. The global penetration of the Internet and the Web has enabled access to information and other resources and facilitated the forming of relationships among people and organizations on an unprecedented scale. The progress of electronic commerce over the Internet has resulted in a dramatic growth in digital interpersonal communications (via e-mail and social networks), distribution of products (software, music, e-books, and movies), and business transactions (buying, selling, and advertising on the Web). With the worldwide spread of smartphones, tablets, laptops, and other computer-based mobile devices, all of which are connected by wireless communication networks, information systems have been extended to support mobility as the natural human condition.

As information systems enabled more diverse human activities, they exerted a profound influence over society. These systems quickened the pace of daily activities, enabled people to develop and maintain new and often more-rewarding relationships, affected the structure and mix of organizations, changed the type of products bought, and influenced the nature of work. Information and knowledge became vital economic resources. Yet, along with new opportunities, the dependence on information systems brought new threats. Intensive industry innovation and academic research continually develop new opportunities while aiming to contain the threats.

Components of Information Systems

The main components of information systems are computer hardware and software, telecommunications, databases and data warehouses, human resources, and procedures. The hardware, software, and telecommunications constitute information technology (IT), which is now ingrained in the operations and management of organizations.

Computer Hardware

Today throughout the world even the smallest firms, as well as many households, own or lease computers. Individuals may own multiple computers in the form of smartphones, tablets, and other wearable devices. Large organizations typically employ distributed computer systems, from powerful parallel-processing servers located in data centres to widely dispersed personal computers and mobile devices, integrated into the organizational information systems. Sensors are becoming ever more widely distributed throughout the physical and biological environment to gather data and, in many cases, to effect control via devices known as actuators. Together with the peripheral equipment—such as magnetic or solid-state storage disks, input-output devices, and telecommunications gear—these constitute the hardware of information systems. The cost of hardware has steadily and rapidly decreased, while processing speed and storage capacity have increased vastly. This development has been occurring under Moore's law: the power of the microprocessors at the heart of computing devices has been doubling approximately every 18 to 24 months. However, hardware's use of electric power and its environmental impact are concerns being addressed by designers. Increasingly, computer and storage services are delivered from the cloud—from shared facilities accessed over telecommunications networks.

Computer Software

Computer software falls into two broad classes: system software and application software. The principal system software is the operating system. It manages the hardware, data and program files, and other system resources and provides means for the user to control the computer, generally via a graphical user interface (GUI). Application software is programs designed to handle specific tasks for users. Smartphone apps became a common way for individuals to access information systems. Other examples include general-purpose application suites with their spreadsheet and word-processing programs, as well as "vertical" applications that serve a specific industry segment—for instance, an application that schedules, routes, and tracks package deliveries for an overnight carrier. Larger firms use licensed applications developed and maintained by specialized software companies, customizing them to meet their specific needs, and develop other applications in-house or on an outsourced basis. Companies may also use applications delivered as software-as-a-service (SaaS) from the cloud over the Web. Proprietary software, available from and supported by its vendors, is being challenged by open-source software available on the Web for free use and modification under a license that protects its future availability.

Telecommunications

Telecommunications are used to connect, or network, computer systems and portable and wearable devices and to transmit information. Connections are established via wired or wireless media. Wired technologies include coaxial cable and fibre optics. Wireless technologies, predominantly based on the transmission of microwaves and radio waves, support mobile computing. Pervasive information systems have arisen with the computing devices embedded in many different physical objects. For example, sensors such as radio frequency identification devices (RFIDs) can be attached to products moving through the supply chain to enable the tracking of their location and the monitoring of their condition. Wireless sensor networks that are integrated into the Internet can produce massive amounts of data that can be used in seeking higher productivity or in monitoring the environment.

Various computer network configurations are possible, depending on the needs of an organization. Local area networks (LANs) join computers at a particular site, such as an office building or an academic campus. Metropolitan area networks (MANs) cover a limited densely populated area and are the electronic infrastructure of "smart cities." Wide area networks (WANs) connect widely distributed data centres, frequently run by different organizations. Peer-to-peer networks, without a centralized control, enable broad sharing of content. The Internet is a network of networks, connecting billions of computers located on every continent. Through networking, users gain access to information resources, such as large databases, and to other individuals, such as coworkers, clients, friends, or people who share their professional or private interests. Internet-type services can be provided within an organization and for its exclusive use by various intranets that are accessible through a browser; for example, an intranet may be deployed as an access portal to a shared corporate document base. To connect with business partners over the Internet in a private and secure manner, extranets are established as so-called virtual private networks (VPNs) by encrypting the messages.

A massive "Internet of things" has emerged, as sensors and actuators have been widely distributed in the physical environment and are supplying data, such as acidity of a square yard of soil, the speed of a driving vehicle, or the blood pressure of an individual. The availability of such information enables a rapid reaction when necessary as well as sustained decision making based on processing of the massive accumulated data.

Extensive networking infrastructure supports the growing move to cloud computing, with the information-system resources shared among multiple companies, leading to utilization efficiencies and freedom in localization of the data centres. Software-defined networking affords flexible control of telecommunications networks with algorithms that are responsive to real-time demands and resource availabilities.

Databases and Data Warehouses

Many information systems are primarily delivery vehicles for data stored in databases. A database is a collection of interrelated data organized so that individual records or groups of records can be retrieved to satisfy various criteria. Typical examples of databases include employee records and product catalogs. Databases support the operations and management functions of an enterprise. Data warehouses contain the archival data, collected over time, that can be mined for information in order to develop and market new products, serve the existing customers better, or reach out to potential new customers. Anyone who has ever purchased something with a credit card—in person, by mail order, or over the Web—is included within such data collections.

Massive collection and processing of the quantitative, or structured, data, as well as of the textual data often gathered on the Web, has developed into a broad initiative known as "big data." Many benefits can arise from decisions based on the facts reflected by big data. Examples include evidence-based medicine, economy of resources as a result of avoiding waste, and recommendations of new products (such as books or movies) based on a user's interests. Big data enables innovative business models. For example, a commercial firm collects the prices of goods by crowdsourcing (collecting from numerous independent individuals) via smartphones around the world. The aggregated data supplies early information on price movements, enabling more responsive decision making than was previously possible.

The processing of textual data—such as reviews and opinions articulated by individuals on social networks, blogs, and discussion boards—permits automated sentiment analysis for marketing, competitive intelligence, new product development, and other decision-making purposes.

Human Resources and Procedures

Qualified people are a vital component of any information system. Technical personnel include development and operations managers, business analysts, systems analysts and designers, database administrators, programmers, computer security specialists, and computer operators. In addition, all workers in an organization must be trained to utilize the capabilities of information systems as fully as possible. Billions of people around the world are learning about information systems as they use the Web.

Procedures for using, operating, and maintaining an information system are part of its documentation. For example, procedures need to be established to run a payroll program, including when to run it, who is authorized to run it, and who has access to the output. In the autonomous computing initiative, data centres are increasingly run automatically, with the procedures embedded in the software that controls those centres.

Types of Information Systems

Information systems support operations, knowledge work, and management in organizations. (The overall structure of organizational information systems is shown in the figure.) Functional information systems that support a specific organizational function, such as marketing or production, have been supplanted in many cases by cross-functional systems built to support complete business processes, such as order processing or employee management. Such systems can be more effective in the development and delivery of the firm's products and can be evaluated more closely with respect to the business outcomes. The information-system categories described here may be implemented with a great variety of application programs.

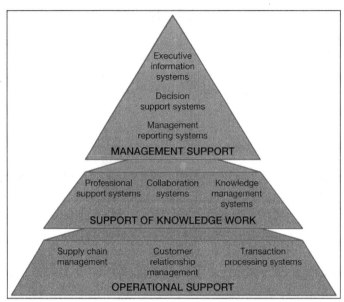

Structure of organizational information systems.

Information systems consist of three layers: operational support, support of knowledge work, and management support. Operational support forms the base of an information system and contains various transaction processing systems for designing, marketing, producing, and delivering products and services. Support of knowledge work forms the middle layer; it contains subsystems for sharing information within an organization. Management support, forming the top layer, contains subsystems for managing and evaluating an organization's resources and goals.

Operational Support and Enterprise Systems

Transaction processing systems support the operations through which products are designed, marketed, produced, and delivered. In larger organizations, transaction processing is frequently accomplished with large integrated systems known as enterprise systems. In this case, the information systems that support various functional units—sales and marketing, production, finance, and human resources—are integrated into an enterprise resource planning (ERP) system, the principal kind of enterprise system. ERP systems support the value chain—that is, the entire sequence of activities or processes through which a firm adds value to its products. For example, an individual or another business may submit a custom order over the Web that automatically initiates just-in-time production to the customer's specifications through an approach known as mass customization. This involves sending orders from the customers to the firm's warehouses and perhaps to suppliers to deliver input materials just in time for a batched custom production run. Financial accounts are updated accordingly, and delivery logistics and billing are initiated.

Along with helping to integrate a firm's own value chain, transaction processing systems can also serve to integrate the overall supply chain of which the organization is a part. This includes all firms involved in designing, producing, marketing, and delivering the goods and services—from raw materials to the final delivery of the product. A supply chain management (SCM) system manages the flow of products, data, money, and information throughout the entire supply chain, which starts with the suppliers of raw materials, runs through the intermediate tiers of the processing companies, and ends with the distributors and retailers. For example, purchasing an item at a major retail store generates more than a cash register receipt: it also automatically sends a restocking order to the appropriate supplier, which in turn may call for orders to the supplier's suppliers. With an SCM system, suppliers can also access a retailer's inventory database over the Web to schedule efficient and timely deliveries in appropriate quantities.

The third type of enterprise system, customer relationship management (CRM), supports dealing with the company's customers in marketing, sales, service, and new product development. A CRM system gives a business a unified view of each customer and its dealings with that customer, enabling a consistent and proactive relationship. In cocreation initiatives, the customers may be involved in the development of the company's new products.

Many transaction processing systems support electronic commerce over the Internet. Among these are systems for online shopping, banking, and securities trading. Other systems deliver information, educational services, and entertainment on demand. Yet other systems serve to support the search for products with desired attributes (for example, keyword search on search engines), price discovery (via an auction, for example), and delivery of digital products (such as software, music, movies, or greeting cards). Social network sites, such as Facebook and LinkedIn, are a powerful tool for supporting customer communities and individuals as they articulate opinions, evolve new ideas, and are exposed to promotional messages. A growing array of specialized services and information-based products are offered by various organizations on the Web, as an infrastructure for electronic commerce has emerged on a global scale.

Transaction processing systems accumulate the data in databases and data warehouses that are necessary for the higher-level information systems. Enterprise systems also provide software modules needed to perform many of these higher-level functions.

Support of Knowledge Work

A large proportion of work in an information society involves manipulating abstract information and knowledge (understood in this context as an organized and comprehensive structure of facts, relationships, theories, and insights) rather than directly processing, manufacturing, or delivering tangible materials. Such work is called knowledge work. Three general categories of information systems support such knowledge work: professional support systems, collaboration systems, and knowledge management systems.

Professional Support Systems

Professional support systems offer the facilities needed to perform tasks specific to a given profession. For example, automotive engineers use computer-aided engineering (CAE) software together with virtual reality systems to design and test new models as electronic prototypes for fuel efficiency, handling, and passenger protection before producing physical prototypes, and later they use CAE in the design and analysis of physical tests. Biochemists use specialized three-dimensional modeling software to visualize the molecular structure and probable effect of new drugs before investing in lengthy clinical tests. Investment bankers often employ financial software to calculate the expected rewards and potential risks of various investment strategies. Indeed, specialized support systems are now available for most professions.

Collaboration Systems

The main objectives of collaboration systems are to facilitate communication and teamwork among the members of an organization and across organizations. One type of collaboration system, known as a workflow system, is used to route relevant documents automatically to all appropriate individuals for their contributions.

Development, pricing, and approval of a commercial insurance policy is a process that can benefit from such a system. Another category of collaboration systems allows different individuals to work simultaneously on a shared project. Known as groupware, such systems accomplish this by allowing controlled shared access, often over an intranet, to the work objects, such as business proposals, new designs, or digital products in progress. The collaborators can be located anywhere in the world, and, in some multinational companies, work on a project continues 24 hours a day.

Other types of collaboration systems include enhanced e-mail and videoconferencing systems, sometimes with telepresence using avatars of the participants. Yet another type of collaboration software, enables multiple participants to add and edit content. (Some online encyclopaedias are produced on such platforms.) Collaboration systems can also be established on social network platforms or virtual life systems. In the open innovation initiative, members of the public, as well as existing and potential customers, can be drawn in, if desired, to enable the cocreation of new products or projection of future outcomes.

Knowledge Management Systems

Knowledge management systems provide a means to assemble and act on the knowledge accumulated throughout an organization. Such knowledge may include the texts and images contained in patents, design methods, best practices, competitor intelligence, and similar sources, with the elaboration and commentary included. Placing the organization's documents and communications in an indexed and cross-referenced form enables rich search capabilities. Numerous application programs, such as Microsoft's SharePoint, exist to facilitate the implementation of such systems. Organizational knowledge is often tacit, rather than explicit, so these systems must also direct users to members of the organization with special expertise.

Management Support

A large category of information systems comprises those designed to support the management of an organization. These systems rely on the data obtained by transaction processing systems, as well as on data and information acquired outside the organization (on the Web, for example) and provided by business partners, suppliers, and customers.

Management Reporting Systems

Information systems support all levels of management, from those in charge of short-term schedules and budgets for small work groups to those concerned with long-term plans and budgets for the entire organization. Management reporting systems provide routine, detailed, and voluminous information reports specific to each manager's areas of responsibility. These systems are typically used by first-level supervisors. Generally, such reports focus on past and present activities, rather than projecting future performance. To prevent information overload, reports may be automatically sent only under exceptional circumstances or at the specific request of a manager.

Decision Support Systems and Business Intelligence

All information systems support decision making, however indirectly, but decision support systems are expressly designed for this purpose. As these systems are increasingly being developed to analyze massive collections of data (known as big data), they are becoming known as business intelligence, or business analytics, applications. The two principal varieties of decision support systems are model-driven and data-driven.

In a model-driven decision support system, a preprogrammed model is applied to a relatively limited data set, such as a sales database for the present quarter. During a typical session, an analyst or sales manager will conduct a dialog with this decision support system by specifying a number of what-if scenarios. For example, in order to establish a selling price for a new product, the sales manager may use a marketing decision support system. It contains a model relating various factors—the price of the product, the cost of goods, and the promotion expense in various media—to the projected sales volume over the first five years on the market. By supplying different product prices to the model, the manager can compare predicted results and select the most profitable selling price.

The primary objective of data-driven business intelligence systems is to analyze large pools of data, accumulated over long periods of time in data warehouses, in a process known as data mining. Data mining aims to discover significant patterns, such as sequences (buying a new house, followed by a new dinner table), clusters, and correlations (large families and van sales), with which decisions can be made. Predictive analytics attempts to forecast future outcomes based on the discovered trends. Data-driven decision support systems include a variety of statistical models and may rely on various artificial intelligence techniques, such as expert systems, neural networks, and machine learning. In addition to mining numeric data, text mining is conducted on large aggregates of unstructured data, such as the contents of social media that include social networks, wikis, blogs, and microblogs. As used in electronic commerce, for example, text mining helps in finding buying trends, targeting advertisements, and detecting fraud.

An important variety of decision support systems enables a group of decision makers to work together without necessarily being in the same place at the same time. These group decision systems include software tools for brainstorming and reaching consensus.

Another category, geographic information systems, can help analyze and display data by using digitized maps. Digital mapping of various regions is a continuing activity of numerous business firms. Such data visualization supports rapid decision making. By looking at a geographic distribution of mortgage loans, for example, one can easily establish a pattern of discrimination.

Executive Information Systems

Executive information systems make a variety of critical information readily available in a highly summarized and convenient form, typically via a graphical digital dashboard. Senior managers characteristically employ many informal sources of information, however, so that formal, computerized information systems are only of partial assistance. Nevertheless, this assistance is important for the chief executive officer, senior and executive vice presidents, and the board of directors to monitor the performance of the company, assess the business environment, and develop strategic directions for the future. In particular, these executives need to compare their organization's performance with that of its competitors and investigate general economic trends in regions or countries. Often individualized and relying on multiple media formats, executive information systems give their users an opportunity to "drill down" from summary information to increasingly focused details.

Acquiring Information Systems and Services

Information systems are a major corporate asset, with respect both to the benefits they provide and to their high costs. Therefore, organizations have to plan for the long term when acquiring information systems and services that will support business initiatives. At the same time, firms have to be responsive to emerging opportunities. On the basis of long-term corporate plans and the requirements of various individuals from data workers to top management, essential applications are identified and project priorities are set. For example, certain projects may have to be carried out immediately to satisfy a new government reporting regulation or to interact with a new customer's information system. Other projects may be given a higher priority because of their strategic role or greater expected benefits.

Once the need for a specific information system has been established, the system has to be acquired. This is generally done in the context of the already existing information systems architecture of the firm. The acquisition of information systems can either involve external sourcing or rely on internal development or modification. With today's highly developed IT industry, companies tend to acquire information systems and services from specialized vendors. The principal tasks of information systems specialists involve modifying the applications for their employer's needs and integrating the applications to create a coherent systems architecture for the firm. Generally, only smaller applications are developed internally. Certain applications of a more personal nature may be developed by the end users themselves.

Acquisition from External Sources

There are several principal ways to acquire an information system from outside the organization. Many firms have resorted to outsourcing their information systems. Outsourcing entails transferring the major components of the firm's systems and operations—such as data centres, telecommunications, and software development and maintenance—to a specialized company that provides its services under long-term contracts specifying the service levels (that is, the scope and the quality of service to be provided). In some cases the outsourcing entails moving the services abroad—i.e., offshoring in pursuit of the cost or expertise advantages. Responsibility for the acquisition of new applications then falls to the outside company. In other cases the company may outsource just the development or maintenance of their information systems, with the outside company being a systems developer.

Cloud computing is increasingly being adopted as a source of information services. It offers on-demand access via the Internet to services furnished by a provider that runs data centres with the necessary software and other resources. The services can be provided at one of three levels: as the infrastructure for running existing applications, as the platform for developing new applications, or as software-as-a-service (SaaS) to be used by the firm over the network. In particular, SaaS has become a cost-effective way to use enterprise systems. Generally, cloud computing is provided by external vendors, although some firms implement their own private clouds in order to share resources that employees can access over the network from a variety of devices, often including smartphones. Scalability and avoidance of capital expenditures are notable advantages of public clouds; the partial loss of control is a drawback.

Companies may choose to acquire an application by leasing a proprietary package from a vendor under a license and having the software customized internally or externally by the vendor or another outside contractor. Enterprise systems are generally leased in this way. An alternative is to deploy an open-source application, whose program code is free and open for all to modify under a different type of license that enforces the openness of the application in perpetuity. Generally, the costs of the use of open-source software include the technical support from specialized vendors.

Internal Information Systems Development

When an information system is developed internally by an organization, one of two broad methods is used: life-cycle development or rapid application development (RAD).

The same methods are used by software vendors, which need to provide more general, customizable systems. Large organizational systems, such as enterprise systems, are generally developed and maintained through a systematic process, known as a system life cycle, which consists of six stages: feasibility study, system analysis, system design, programming and testing, installation, and operation and maintenance. The first five stages are system development proper, and the last stage is the long-term exploitation. Following a period of use (with maintenance as needed), the information system may be either phased out or upgraded. In the case of a major upgrade, the system enters another development life cycle.

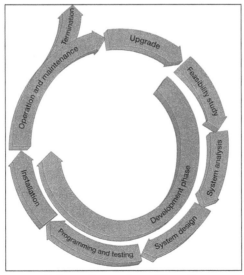

Information systems life cycle.

The development phase of the life cycle for an information system consists of a feasibility study, system analysis, system design, programming and testing, and installation. Following a period of operation and maintenance, typically 5 to 10 years, an evaluation is made of whether to terminate or upgrade the system.

The principal objective of a feasibility study is to determine whether the system is desirable on the basis of long-term plans, strategic initiatives, and a cost-benefit analysis. System analysis provides a detailed answer to the question, What will the new system do? The next stage, system design, results in an extensive blueprint for how the new system will be organized. During the programming and testing stage, the individual software modules of the system are developed, tested, and integrated into a coherent operational system. Further levels of testing ensure continuing quality control. Installation includes final testing of the system in the work environment and conversion of organizational operations to the new system, integrating it with other systems already in place. The later stages of development include such implementation activities as training users and modifying the organizational processes in which the system will be used.

Life-cycle development is frequently faulted for its long development times and voluminous documentation requirements—and, in some instances, for its failure to fulfill the user's requirements at the end of the long development road.

Increasingly, life-cycle development is being replaced by RAD. In various RAD methodologies a prototype—a preliminary working version of an application—is built quickly and inexpensively, albeit imperfectly. This prototype is turned over to the users, their reactions are collected, suggested modifications are incorporated, and successive prototype versions eventually evolve into the complete system. Formal processes for the collaboration between system developers and users, such as joint applications development (JAD), have been introduced by some firms. Sometimes RAD and life-cycle development are combined: a prototype is produced to determine user requirements during the initial system analysis stage, after which life-cycle development takes over. A version of RAD known as agile development aims to dispense with the notion of a prototype: an initial version of the system is built, released to users, and then subject to frequent modifications as needs arise.

Industrial methods of software production and reuse have been implemented in systems development. Thus, reusable software components are developed, tested, and catalogued to be deployed as parts of future information systems. A particularly important method of component-based development is the use of Web services, which are software objects that deliver a specific function (such as looking up a customer's order in a database) and can be stitched together into interorganizational information systems enabling business partners to cooperate.

After an installed system is handed over to its users and operations personnel, it will almost invariably be modified extensively over its useful life in a process known as system maintenance. A large system will typically be used and maintained for some 5 to 10 years or even longer. Most maintenance is to adjust the system to the organization's changing needs and to new equipment and other software, but inevitably some maintenance involves correcting design errors and exterminating software "bugs" as they are discovered.

Managing Information Systems

For an organization to use its information services to support its operations or to innovate by launching a new initiative, those services have to be part of a well-planned infrastructure of core resources. The specific systems ought to be configured into a coherent architecture to deliver the necessary information services. Many organizations rely on outside firms—that is, specialized IT companies—to deliver some, or even all, of their information services. If located in-house, the management of information systems can be decentralized to a certain degree to correspond to the organization's overall structure.

Information System Infrastructure and Architecture

A well-designed information system rests on a coherent foundation that supports responsive change—and, thus, the organization's agility—as new business or administrative initiatives arise. Known as the information system infrastructure, the foundation consists of core telecommunications networks, databases and data warehouses, software, hardware, and procedures managed by various specialists. With business globalization, an organization's infrastructure often crosses many national boundaries. Establishing and maintaining such a complex infrastructure requires extensive planning and consistent implementation to handle strategic corporate initiatives, transformations, mergers, and acquisitions. Information system infrastructure should be established in order to create meaningful options for future corporate development.

When organized into a coherent whole, the specific information systems that support operations, management, and knowledge work constitute the system architecture of an organization. Clearly, an organization's long-term general strategic plans must be considered when designing an information system infrastructure and architecture.

Organization of Information Services

Information services of an organization are delivered by an outside firm, by an internal unit, or by a combination of the two. Outsourcing of information services helps with such objectives as cost savings, access to superior personnel, and focusing on core competencies.

An information services unit is typically in charge of an organization's information systems. When the systems are largely outsourced, this unit is of a limited size and concentrates on aligning the systems with the corporate competitive strategy and on supervising the outside company's services. When information services are provided in-house and centralized, this unit is responsible for planning, acquiring, operating, and maintaining information systems for the entire organization. In decentralized structures, however, the central unit is responsible only for planning and maintaining the infrastructure, while business and administrative specialists supervise systems and services for their own units. A variety of intermediate organizational forms are possible.

In many organizations, information systems are headed by a chief information officer (CIO) or a chief technology officer (CTO). The activities of information services are usually supervised by a steering committee consisting of the executives representing various functional units of the organization. Steering committees set the priorities for the development of future systems. In the organizations where information systems play a strategic role, boards of directors need to be involved in their governance. A vital responsibility of an information services unit is to ensure uninterrupted service and integrity of the systems and information in the face of many security threats.

Information Systems Security and Control

With the opening of information systems to the global Internet and with their thorough infusion into the operation and management of business and government organizations and into the infrastructure of daily life across the world, information security issues have moved to the fore-front of concerns about global well-being.

Information Systems Security

Information systems security is responsible for the integrity and safety of system resources and activities. Most organizations in developed countries are dependent on the secure operation of their information systems. In fact, the very fabric of societies often depends on this security. Multiple infrastructural grids—including power, water supply, and health care—rely on it. Information systems are at the heart of intensive care units and air traffic control systems. Financial institutions could not survive a total failure of their information systems for longer than a day or two. Electronic funds transfer systems (EFTS) handle immense amounts of money that exist only as electronic signals sent over the networks or as spots on storage disks. Information systems are vulnerable to a number of threats and require strict controls, such as continuing countermeasures and regular audits to ensure that the system remains secure. (The relationship among security measures is shown in the figure).

The first step in creating a secure information system is to identify threats. Once potential problems are known, the second step, establishing controls, can be taken. Finally, the third step consists of audits to discover any breach of security.

Although instances of computer crime and abuse receive extensive media attention, human error is estimated to cause greater losses in information systems operation. Disasters such as earthquakes, floods, and fires are the particular concern of disaster recovery planning, which is a part of a corporate business continuity plan. A contingency scheme is also necessary to cover the failure of servers, telecommunications networks, or software.

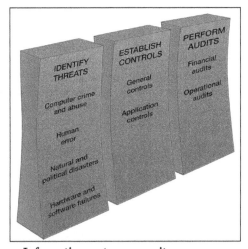

Information systems security measures.

Computer Crime and Abuse

Computer crime—illegal acts in which computers are the primary tool—costs the world economy many billions of dollars annually. Computer abuse does not rise to the level of crime, yet it involves unethical use of a computer. The objectives of the so-called hacking of information systems include vandalism, theft of consumer information, governmental and commercial espionage, sabotage, and cyberwar. Some of the more widespread means of computer crime include phishing and planting of malware, such as computer viruses and worms, Trojan horses, and logic bombs.

Phishing involves obtaining a legitimate user's login and other information by subterfuge via messages fraudulently claiming to originate with a legitimate entity, such as a bank or government office. A successful phishing raid to obtain a user's information may be followed by identity theft, an impersonation of the user to gain access to the user's resources.

Computer viruses are a particularly common form of attack. These are program instructions that are able not only to perform malicious acts but also to insert copies of themselves into other programs and thus spread to other computer systems. Similar to viruses, worms are complete computer programs that replicate and propagate through telecommunications networks. Because of their ability to spread rapidly and widely, viruses and worms can inflict immense damage. The damage can be in the form of tampering with system operation, theft of large volumes of data (e.g., credit card numbers), known as data breach, or denial of service by overloading systems with a barrage of spurious requests.

In a Trojan horse attack, the malefactor conceals unauthorized instructions within an authorized program. A logic bomb consists of hidden instructions, often introduced with the Trojan horse technique, that stay dormant until a specific event occurs, at which time the instructions are activated. In one well-known case, in 1985 a programmer at an insurance company in Fort Worth, Texas, placed a logic bomb in his company's human resources system; when he was fired and his name was deleted from the company's employee database, the entire database was erased.

Once a system connected to the Internet is invaded, it may be used to take over many others and organize them into so-called botnets that can launch massive attacks against other systems to steal information or sabotage their operation. There is a growing concern that, in the "Internet of things," computer-controlled devices such as refrigerators or TV sets may be deployed in botnets. The variety of devices makes them difficult to control against malware.

Information Systems Controls

To ensure secure and efficient operation of information systems, an organization institutes a set of procedures and technological measures called controls. Information systems are safeguarded through a combination of general and application controls.

General controls apply to information system activities throughout an organization. The most important general controls are the measures that control access to computer systems and the information stored there or transmitted over telecommunications networks. General controls include administrative measures that restrict employees' access to only those processes directly relevant to their duties. As a result, these controls limit the damage that any individual employee or employee impersonator can do. Fault-tolerant computer systems installed in critical environments, such as in hospital information systems or securities marketplaces, are designed to control and isolate problems so that the system can continue to function. Backup systems, often in remote locations, may be activated in the case of failure of the primary information system.

Application controls are specific to a given application and include such measures as validating input data, logging the accesses to the system, regularly archiving copies of various databases, and ensuring that information is disseminated only to authorized users.

Securing Information

Controlling access to information systems became profoundly more difficult with the spread of wide area networks (WANs) and, in particular, the Internet. Users, as well as interlopers, may access systems from any unattended computer within an organization or from virtually anywhere over the Internet. As a security measure, each legitimate user has a unique name and a regularly changed password. Another security measure is to require some form of physical authentication, such as an object (a physical token or a smart card) or a personal characteristic (fingerprint, retinal pattern, hand geometry, or signature). Many systems combine these types of measures—such as automatic teller machines, which rely on a combination of a personal identification number (PIN) and an identification card. Security measures placed between an organization's internal networks and the Internet are known as firewalls. These combinations of hardware and software continually filter the incoming, and often outgoing, data traffic.

A different way to prohibit access to information is via data encryption, which has gained particular importance in electronic commerce. Public key encryption is used widely in such commerce. To ensure confidentiality, only the intended addressee has the private key needed to decrypt messages that have been encrypted with the addressee's public key. Furthermore, authentication of both parties in an electronic transaction is possible through the digital certificates issued to both parties by a trusted third party and the use of digital signatures—an additional code attached to the message to verify its origin. A type of antitampering code can also be attached to a message to detect corruption. Similar means are available to ensure that parties to an electronic transaction cannot later repudiate their participation. Some messages require additional attributes. For example, a payment in electronic cash is a type of message, with encryption used to ensure the purchaser's anonymity, that acts like physical cash.

To continually monitor information systems, intrusion detection systems are used. They detect anomalous events and log the information necessary to produce reports and to establish the source and the nature of the possible intrusion. More active systems also attempt to prevent the intrusion upon detection in real time.

Information Systems Audit

The effectiveness of an information system's controls is evaluated through an information systems audit. An audit aims to establish whether information systems are safeguarding corporate assets, maintaining the integrity of stored and communicated data, supporting corporate objectives effectively, and operating efficiently. It is a part of a more general financial audit that verifies an organization's accounting records and financial statements. Information systems are designed so that every financial transaction can be traced. In other words, an audit trail must exist that can establish where each transaction originated and how it was processed. Aside from financial audits, operational audits are used to evaluate the effectiveness and efficiency of information systems operations, and technological audits verify that information technologies are appropriately chosen, configured, and implemented.

Impacts of Information Systems

Computerized information systems, particularly since the arrival of the Web and mobile computing, have had a profound effect on organizations, economies, and societies, as well as on individuals whose lives and activities are conducted in these social aggregates.

Organizational Impacts of Information Systems

Essential organizational capabilities are enabled or enhanced by information systems. These systems provide support for business operations; for individual and group decision making; for innovation through new product and process development; for relationships with customers, suppliers, and partners; for pursuit of competitive advantage; and, in some cases, for the business model itself (e.g., Google). Information systems bring new options to the way companies interact and compete, the way organizations are structured, and the way workplaces are designed. In general, use of Web-based information systems can significantly lower the costs of communication among workers and firms and cost-effectively enhance the coordination of supply chains or webs. This has led many organizations to concentrate on their core competencies and to outsource other parts of their value chain to specialized companies. The capability to communicate information efficiently within a firm has led to the deployment of flatter organizational structures with fewer hierarchical layers.

Nevertheless, information systems do not uniformly lead to higher profits. Success depends both on the skill with which information systems are deployed and on their use being combined with other resources of the firm, such as relationships with business partners or superior knowledge in the industrial segment.

The use of information systems has enabled new organizational structures. In particular, so-called virtual organizations have emerged that do not rely on physical offices and standard organizational charts. Two notable forms of virtual organizations are the network organization and the cluster organization.

In a network organization, long-term corporate partners supply goods and services through a central hub firm. Together, a network of relatively small companies can present the appearance of a large corporation. Indeed, at the core of such an organization may be nothing more than a single entrepreneur supported by only a few employees. Thus, network organization forms a flexible ecosystem of companies, whose formation and work is organized around Web-based information systems.

In a cluster organization, the principal work units are permanent and temporary teams of individuals with complementary skills. Team members, who are often widely dispersed around the globe, are greatly assisted in their work by the use of Web resources, corporate intranets, and collaboration systems. Global virtual teams are able to work around the clock, moving knowledge work electronically "to follow the sun." Information systems delivered over mobile platforms have enabled employees to work not just outside the corporate offices but virtually anywhere. "Work is the thing you do, not the place you go to" became the slogan of the emerging new workplace. Virtual workplaces include home offices, regional work centres, customers' premises, and mobile offices of people such as insurance adjusters. Employees who work in virtual workplaces outside their company's premises are known as teleworkers.

The role of consumers has changed, empowered by the Web. Instead of being just passive recipients of products, they can actively participate with the producers in the cocreation of value. By coordinating their collective work using information systems, individuals created such products as open-source software and online encyclopaedias. The value of virtual worlds and massively multiplayer online games has been created largely by the participants. The electronic word-of-mouth in the form of reviews and opinions expressed on the Web can make or break products.

In sponsored cocreation, companies attract their customers to generate and evaluate ideas, codevelop new products, and promote the existing goods and services. Virtual customer communities are created online for these purposes.

Information Systems in the Economy and Society

Along with the global transportation infrastructure, network-based information systems have been a factor in the growth of international business and corporations. A relationship between the deployment of information systems and higher productivity has been shown in a number of industries when these systems complement other corporate resources. Electronic commerce has moved many relationships and transactions among companies and individuals to the Internet and the Web, with the resulting expansion of possibilities and efficiencies. The development of the Internet-based ecosystem—accompanied by the low cost of hardware and telecommunications, the availability of open-source software, and the mass global access to mobile phones—has led to a flowering of entrepreneurial activity and the emergence to prominence and significant market value of numerous firms based on new business models. Among the examples are electronic auction firms, search engine firms, electronic malls, social network platforms, and online game companies. Because of the vast opportunities for moving work with data, information, and knowledge in electronic form to the most cost-effective venue, a global redistribution of work has been taking place.

As the use of information systems became pervasive in advanced economies and societies at large, several societal and ethical issues moved into the forefront. The most important are issues of individual privacy, property rights, universal access and free speech, information accuracy, and quality of life.

Individual privacy hinges on the right to control one's personal information. While invasion of privacy is generally perceived as an undesirable loss of autonomy, government and business organizations do need to collect data in order to facilitate administration and exploit sales and marketing opportunities. Electronic commerce presents a particular challenge to privacy, as personal information is routinely collected and potentially disseminated in a largely unregulated manner. The ownership of and control over the personal profiles, contacts, and communications in social networks are one example of a privacy issue that awaits resolution through a combination of market forces, industry self-regulation, and possibly government regulation. Preventing invasions of privacy is complicated by the lack of an international legal standard.

Intellectual property, such as software, books, music, and movies, is protected, albeit imperfectly, by patents, trade secrets, and copyrights. However, such intangible goods can be easily copied and transmitted electronically over the Web for unlawful reproduction and use. Combinations of legal statutes and technological safeguards, including antipiracy encryption and electronic watermarks, are in place, but much of the abuse prevention relies on the ethics of the user. The means of protection themselves, such as patents, play a great role in the information society. However, the protection of business methods (e.g., Amazon's patenting of one-click ordering) is being questioned, and the global enforcement of intellectual property protection encounters various challenges.

Access to information systems over the Web is necessary for full participation in modern society. In particular, it is desirable to avoid the emergence of digital divides between nations or regions and between social and ethnic groups. Open access to the Web as a medium for human communication and as a repository for shared knowledge is treasured. Indeed, many people consider free speech a universal human right and the Internet and Web the most widely accessible means to exercise that right. Yet, legitimate concerns arise about protecting children without resorting to censorship. Technological solutions, such as software that filters out pornography and inappropriate communications, are partially successful.

Of concern to everyone is the accuracy and security of information contained in databases and data warehouses—whether in health and insurance data, credit bureau records, or government files—as misinformation or privileged information released inappropriately can adversely affect personal safety, livelihood, and everyday life. Individuals must cooperate in reviewing and correcting their files, and organizations must ensure appropriate security, access to, and use of such files.

Information systems have affected the quality of personal and working lives. In the workplace, information systems can be deployed to eliminate tedious tasks and give workers greater autonomy, or they can be used to thoughtlessly eliminate jobs and subject the remaining workforce to pervasive electronic surveillance. Consumers can use the Web for shopping, networking, and entertainment—but at the risk of contending with spam (unsolicited e-mail), interception of credit card numbers, and attack by computer viruses.

Information systems can expand participation of ordinary citizens in government through electronic elections, referendums, and polls and also can provide electronic access to government services and information—permitting, for instance, electronic filing of taxes, direct deposit of government checks, and viewing of current and historical government documents. More transparent and beneficial government operations are possible by opening the data collected by and about governments to public scrutiny in a searchable and easy-to-use form. With the Web, the public sphere of deliberation and self-organization can expand and give voice to individuals. However, information systems have also conjured Orwellian images of government surveillance and business intrusion into private lives. It remains for society to harness the power of information systems by strengthening legal, social, and technological means.

With the exponentially growing power of computers, driven by Moore's law, and the development of ever more-sophisticated software—in particular, systems deploying the techniques of artificial intelligence (AI)—job markets and professions have been affected. Flexible and inexpensive robotics reduces some opportunities in the labour markets. Cognitive computing, with systems relying on AI techniques—such as computer learning, pattern recognition in multiple media, and massive amounts of stored information—emerged as a competitor to human professionals.

The emergence of the "on-demand economy," enabled by information system platforms, has raised concerns about the quality of jobs. Providing instant access to services, such as transportation, the platforms (for example, Uber and Lyft) connect the service suppliers, usually individuals, with those seeking the service. Although claimed to erode stable workplaces, such business models offer flexibility, a larger measure of independence to the suppliers, and convenience to the demanders.

References

- Information-Science, entry: newworldencyclopedia.org, Retrieved 29 March, 2019

- Information-retrieval, technology: britannica.com, Retrieved 16 January, 2019

- Information-architecture, definition: everyinteraction.com, Retrieved 25 February, 2019

- Graves, Steve. "COTS Databases For Embedded Systems" Archived 2007-11-14 at the Wayback Machine, Embedded Computing Design magazine, January 2007. Retrieved on August 13, 2008

- The-principles-of-information-architecture, inspiration: designyourway.net, Retrieved 5 February, 2019

5

Information Security: Threats and Protection

The process designed for the protection of private and confidential information from unauthorized access, misuse or disruption is referred to as information security. Some of the threats which are dealt within this field are malware, spyware, rootkit, ransomware, phishing, etc. This chapter discusses in detail these threats related to information security.

Information Security is not all about securing information from unauthorized access. Information Security is basically the practice of preventing unauthorized access, use, disclosure, disruption, modification, inspection, recording or destruction of information. Information can be physical or electrical one. Information can be anything like Your details or we can say your profile on social media, your data in mobile phone, your biometrics etc. Thus Information Security spans so many research areas like Cryptography, Mobile Computing, Cyber Forensics, Online Social Media etc.

During First World War, Multi-tier Classification System was developed keeping in mind sensitivity of information. With the beginning of Second World War formal alignment of Classification System was done. Alan Turing was the one who successfully decrypted Enigma Machine which was used by Germans to encrypt warfare data.

Information Security programs are build around 3 objectives, commonly known as CIA – Confidentiality, Integrity, Availability.

- Confidentiality – Means information is not disclosed to unauthorized individuals, entities and process. For example if we say you have a password for your Gmail account but someone saw while you were doing a login into Gmail account. In that case my password has been compromised and Confidentiality has been breached.

- Integrity – Means maintaining accuracy and completeness of data. This means data cannot be edited in an unauthorized way. For example if an employee leaves an organisation then in that case data for that employee in all departments like accounts, should be updated to reflect status to JOB LEFT so that data is complete and accurate and in addition to this only authorized person should be allowed to edit employee data.

- Availability – Means information must be available when needed. For example if one needs to access information of a particular employee to check whether employee has outstanded the number of leaves, in that case it requires collaboration from different organizational teams like network operations, development operations, incident response and policy/change management. Denial of service attack is one of the factor that can hamper the availability of information.

Apart from this there is one more principle that governs information security programs. This is Non repudiation.

- Non repudiation – Means one party cannot deny receiving a message or a transaction nor can the other party deny sending a message or a transaction. For example in cryptography it is sufficient to show that message matches the digital signature signed with sender's private key and that sender could have a sent a message and nobody else could have altered it in transit. Data Integrity and Authenticity are pre-requisites for Non repudiation.

- Authenticity – Means verifying that users are who they say they are and that each input arriving at destination is from a trusted source.This principle if followed guarantees the valid and genuine message received from a trusted source through a valid transmission. For example if take above example sender sends the message along with digital signature which was generated using the hash value of message and private key. Now at the receiver side this digital signature is decrypted using the public key generating a hash value and message is again hashed to generate the hash value. If the 2 value matches then it is known as valid transmission with the authentic or we say genuine message received at the recepient side.

- Accountability – Means that it should be possible to trace actions of an entity uniquely to that entity. Not every employee should be allowed to do changes in other employees data. For this there is a separate department in an organization that is responsible for making such changes and when they receive request for a change then that letter must be signed by higher authority for example Director of college and person that is allotted that change will be able to do change after verifying his bio metrics, thus timestamp with the user(doing changes) details get recorded. Thus we can say if a change goes like this then it will be possible to trace the actions uniquely to an entity.

At the core of Information Security is Information Assurance, which means the act of maintaining CIA of information, ensuring that information is not compromised in any way when critical issues arise. These issues are not limited to natural disasters, computer/server malfunctions etc.

Thus, the field of information security has grown and evolved significantly in recent years. It offers many areas for specialization, including securing networks and allied infrastructure, securing applications and databases, security testing, information systems auditing, business continuity planning etc.

IMPORTANCE OF INFORMATION SECURITY

Organizations have recognized the importance of having roadblocks to protect the private information from becoming public, especially when that information is privileged. The 2017 Cybersecurity Trends Report provided findings that express the need for skilled information security personnel based on current cyberattack predictions and concerns:

- Feeling confident about their organization's security level: When information security community members participated in the Cybersecurity Trends Report, they were asked how positive they felt about their security stance. 62% reported feeling only moderately to not at all confident; only 7% were extremely confident. "Cybersecurity professionals are most concerned about phishing attacks, malicious insiders and malware," the report stated.

- The need for skilled workers and allocation of funds for security within their budget: Companies are making the effort to allocate more funds in their budgets for security. As cyber-attack threats increase, information security experts are pushing for more focus on protecting the companies from losing time due to network defense disruptions.

- Disruptions in their day-to-day business: Time is money. Security disruptions that interfere with a company's essential functioning is a threat that can be fought against with skilled information security professionals stopping an infiltration that initially went undetected.

ADVANCED PERSISTENT THREAT

An Advanced Persistent Threat (APT) is a stealthy computer network threat actor, typically a nation state or state-sponsored group, which gains unauthorized access to a computer network and remains undetected for an extended period . In recent times, the term may also refer to non-state sponsored groups conducting large-scale targeted intrusions for specific goals.

Such threat actors motivations are typically political or economic. To date, every major business sector has recorded instances of attacks by advanced actors with specific goals seeking to steal, spy or disrupt. These include government, defense, financial services, legal services, industrial, telecoms, consumer goods and many more . Some groups utilize traditional espionage vectors, including social engineering, human intelligence and infiltration to gain access to a physical location to enable network attacks. The purpose of these attacks is to place custom malicious code on one or multiple computers for specific tasks .

The mean "dwell-time", the time an APT attack goes undetected, differs widely between regions. FireEye reports the mean dwell-time for 2018 in the Americas is 71 days, EMEA is 177 days and APAC is 204 days . This allows attackers a significant amount of time to go through the attack cycle, propagate and achieve their objective.

Definitions of precisely what an APT is can vary, but can be summarized by their named requirements below:

- Advanced – Operators behind the threat have a full spectrum of intelligence-gathering techniques at their disposal. These may include commercial and open source computer intrusion technologies and techniques, but may also extend to include the intelligence apparatus of a state. While individual components of the attack may not be considered particularly "advanced" (e.g. malware components generated from commonly available do-it-yourself malware construction kits, or the use of easily procured exploit materials), their operators can typically access and develop more advanced tools as required. They often combine multiple targeting methods, tools, and techniques in order to reach and compromise their target and maintain access to it. Operators may also demonstrate a deliberate focus on operational security that differentiates them from "less advanced" threats.

- Persistent – Operators give priority to a specific task, rather than opportunistically seeking information for financial or other gain. This distinction implies that the attackers are guided by external entities. The targeting is conducted through continuous monitoring and interaction in order to achieve the defined objectives. It does not mean a barrage of constant attacks and malware updates. In fact, a "low-and-slow" approach is usually more successful. If the operator loses access to their target they usually will reattempt access, and most often, successfully. One of the operator's goals is to maintain long-term access to the target, in contrast to threats who only need access to execute a specific task.

- Threat – APTs are a threat because they have both capability and intent. APT attacks are executed by coordinated human actions, rather than by mindless and automated pieces of code. The operators have a specific objective and are skilled, motivated, organized and well funded. Note that actors are not limited to state sponsored groups.

Characteristics

Bodmer, Kilger, Carpenter and Jones defined the following APT criteria:

- Objectives – The end goal of the threat, your adversary.
- Timeliness – The time spent probing and accessing your system.
- Resources – The level of knowledge and tools used in the event (skills and methods will weigh on this point).
- Risk tolerance – The extent the threat will go to in order to remain undetected.
- Skills and methods – The tools and techniques used throughout the event.
- Actions – The precise actions of a threat or numerous threats.
- Attack origination points – The number of points where the event originated.
- Numbers involved in the attack – How many internal and external systems were involved in the event, and how many people's systems have different influence/importance weights.
- Knowledge source – The ability to discern any information regarding any of the specific threats through online information gathering (you might be surprised by what you can find by being a little proactive).

Life Cycle

Actors behind advanced persistent threats create a growing and changing risk to organizations' financial assets, intellectual property, and reputation by following a continuous process or kill chain:

- Target specific organizations for a singular objective.
- Attempt to gain a foothold in the environment (common tactics include spear phishing emails).

- Use the compromised systems as access into the target network.

- Deploy additional tools that help fulfill the attack objective.

- Cover tracks to maintain access for future initiatives.

The global landscape of APTs from all sources is sometimes referred to in the singular as "the" APT, as are references to the actor behind a specific incident or series of incidents, but the definition of APT includes both actor and method.

In 2013, Mandiant presented results of their research on alleged Chinese attacks using APT method between 2004 and 2013 that followed similar lifecycle:

- Initial compromise – Performed by use of social engineering and spear phishing, over email, using zero-day viruses. Another popular infection method was planting malware on a website that the victim's employees will be likely to visit.

- Establish Foothold – Plant remote administration software in victim's network, create net backdoors and tunnels allowing stealth access to its infrastructure.

- Escalate privileges – Use exploits and password cracking to acquire administrator privileges over victim's computer and possibly expand it to Windows domain administrator accounts.

- Internal reconnaissance – Collect information on surrounding infrastructure, trust relationships, Windows domain structure.

- Move laterally – Expand control to other workstations, servers and infrastructure elements and perform data harvesting on them.

- Maintain presence – Ensure continued control over access channels and credentials acquired in previous steps.

- Complete mission – Exfiltrate stolen data from victim's network.

In incidents analysed by Mandiant, the average period over which the attackers controlled the victim's network was one year, with longest – almost five years. The infiltrations were allegedly performed by Shanghai-based Unit 61398 of People's Liberation Army. Chinese officials have denied any involvement in these attacks.

Mitigation Strategies

There are hundreds of malware variations, which makes it extremely challenging to protect organizations from APT. While APT activities are stealthy and hard to detect, the command and control network traffic associated with APT can be detected at the network layer level with sophisticated methods. Deep log analyses and log correlation from various sources is of limited usefulness in detecting APT activities. It is challenging to separate noises from legitimate traffic. Traditional security technology and methods have been ineffective in detecting or mitigating APTs. Active cyber defence has yielded greater efficacy in detecting and prosecuting APTs (find, fix, finish) when applying cyber threat intelligence to hunt and adversary pursuit activities.

MALWARE

Malware is any software intentionally designed to cause damage to a computer, server, client, or computer network (by contrast, software that causes unintentional harm due to some deficiency is typically described as a software bug). A wide variety of types of malware exist, including computer viruses, worms, Trojan horses, ransomware, spyware, adware, and scareware.

Programs are also considered malware if they secretly act against the interests of the computer user. For example, at one point Sony music Compact discs silently installed a rootkit on purchasers' computers with the intention of preventing illicit copying, but which also reported on users' listening habits, and unintentionally created extra security vulnerabilities.

A range of antivirus software, firewalls and other strategies are used to help protect against the introduction of malware, to help detect it if it is already present, and to recover from malware-associated malicious activity and attacks.

Purposes

This pie chart shows that in 2011, 70% of malware infections were by Trojan horses, 17% were from viruses, 8% from worms, with the remaining percentages divided among adware, backdoor, spyware, and other exploits.

Many early infectious programs, including the first Internet Worm, were written as experiments or pranks. Today, malware is used by both black hat hackers and governments, to steal personal, financial, or business information.

Malware is sometimes used broadly against government or corporate websites to gather guarded information, or to disrupt their operation in general. However, malware can be used against individuals to gain information such as personal identification numbers or details, bank or credit card numbers, and passwords.

Since the rise of widespread broadband Internet access, malicious software has more frequently been designed for profit. Since 2003, the majority of widespread viruses and worms have been designed to take control of users' computers for illicit purposes. Infected "zombie computers" can be used to send email spam, to host contraband data such as child pornography, or to engage in distributed denial-of-service attacks as a form of extortion.

Programs designed to monitor users' web browsing, display unsolicited advertisements, or redirect affiliate marketing revenues are called spyware. Spyware programs do not spread like viruses; instead they are generally installed by exploiting security holes. They can also be hidden and packaged together with unrelated user-installed software. The Sony BMG rootkit was intended to preventing illicit copying; but also reported on users' listening habits, and unintentionally created extra security vulnerabilities.

Ransomware affects an infected computer system in some way, and demands payment to bring it back to its normal state. There are two variations of ransomware, being crypto ransomware and locker ransomware. With the locker ransomware just locking down a computer system without encrypting its contents. Whereas the traditional ransomware is one that locks down your system and encrypts the contents of the system. For example, programs such as CryptoLocker encrypt files securely, and only decrypt them on payment of a substantial sum of money.

Some malware is used to generate money by click fraud, making it appear that the computer user has clicked an advertising link on a site, generating a payment from the advertiser. It was estimated in 2012 that about 60 to 70% of all active malware used some kind of click fraud, and 22% of all ad-clicks were fraudulent.

In addition to criminal money-making, malware can be used for sabotage, often for political motives. Stuxnet, for example, was designed to disrupt very specific industrial equipment. There have been politically motivated attacks that have spread over and shut down large computer networks, including massive deletion of files and corruption of master boot records, described as "computer killing." Such attacks were made on Sony Pictures Entertainment (25 November 2014, using malware known as Shamoon or W32.Disttrack) and Saudi Aramco.

Infectious Malware

The best-known types of malware, viruses and worms, are known for the manner in which they spread, rather than any specific types of behavior. A computer virus is software that embeds itself in some other executable software (including the operating system itself) on the target system without the user's knowledge and consent and when it is run, the virus is spread to other executables. On the other hand, a worm is a stand-alone malware software that actively transmits itself over a network to infect other computers. These definitions lead to the observation that a virus requires the user to run an infected software or operating system for the virus to spread, whereas a worm spreads itself.

Concealment

These categories are not mutually exclusive, so malware may use multiple techniques. This section only applies to malware designed to operate undetected, not sabotage and ransomware.

Viruses

A computer virus is software usually hidden within another seemingly innocuous program that can produce copies of itself and insert them into other programs or files, and that usually performs a harmful action (such as destroying data). An example of this is a PE infection, a technique, usually used to spread malware, that inserts extra data or executable code into PE files.

Screen-locking Ransomware

'Lock-screens', or screen lockers is a type of "cyber police" ransomware that blocks screens on Windows or Android devices with a false accusation in harvesting illegal content, trying to scare the victims into paying up a fee. Jisut and SLocker impact Android devices more than other lock-screens, with Jisut making up nearly 60 percent of all Android ransomware detections.

Trojan Horses

A Trojan horse is a harmful program that misrepresents itself to masquerade as a regular, benign program or utility in order to persuade a victim to install it. A Trojan horse usually carries a hidden destructive function that is activated when the application is started. The term is derived from the Ancient Greek story of the Trojan horse used to invade the city of Troy by stealth.

Trojan horses are generally spread by some form of social engineering, for example, where a user is duped into executing an e-mail attachment disguised to be unsuspicious, (e.g., a routine form to be filled in), or by drive-by download. Although their payload can be anything, many modern forms act as a backdoor, contacting a controller which can then have unauthorized access to the affected computer. While Trojan horses and backdoors are not easily detectable by themselves, computers may appear to run slower due to heavy processor or network usage. Unlike computer viruses and worms, Trojan horses generally do not attempt to inject themselves into other files or otherwise propagate themselves.

In spring 2017 Mac users were hit by the new version of Proton Remote Access Trojan (RAT) trained to extract password data from various sources, such as browser auto-fill data, the Mac-OS keychain, and password vaults.

Rootkits

Once malicious software is installed on a system, it is essential that it stays concealed, to avoid detection. Software packages known as rootkits allow this concealment, by modifying the host's operating system so that the malware is hidden from the user. Rootkits can prevent a harmful process from being visible in the system's list of processes, or keep its files from being read.

Some types of harmful software contain routines to evade identification and/or removal attempts, not merely to hide themselves. An early example of this behavior is recorded in the Jargon File tale of a pair of programs infesting a Xerox CP-V time sharing system:

> "Each ghost-job would detect the fact that the other had been killed, and would start a new copy of the recently stopped program within a few milliseconds. The only way to kill both ghosts was to kill them simultaneously (very difficult) or to deliberately crash the system."

Backdoors

A backdoor is a method of bypassing normal authentication procedures, usually over a connection to a network such as the Internet. Once a system has been compromised, one or more backdoors may be installed in order to allow access in the future, invisibly to the user.

The idea has often been suggested that computer manufacturers preinstall backdoors on their systems to provide technical support for customers, but this has never been reliably verified. It was reported in 2014 that US government agencies had been diverting computers purchased by those considered "targets" to secret workshops where software or hardware permitting remote access by the agency was installed, considered to be among the most productive operations to obtain access to networks around the world. Backdoors may be installed by Trojan horses, worms, implants, or other methods.

Evasion

Since the beginning of 2015, a sizable portion of malware utilizes a combination of many techniques designed to avoid detection and analysis. From the more common, to the least common:

*   Evasion of analysis and detection by fingerprinting the environment when executed.

*   Confusing automated tools' detection methods. This allows malware to avoid detection by technologies such as signature-based antivirus software by changing the server used by the malware.

*   Timing-based evasion: This is when malware runs at certain times or following certain actions taken by the user, so it executes during certain vulnerable periods, such as during the boot process, while remaining dormant the rest of the time.

*   Obfuscating internal data so that automated tools do not detect the malware.

An increasingly common technique is adware that uses stolen certificates to disable anti-malware and virus protection; technical remedies are available to deal with the adware.

Nowadays, one of the most sophisticated and stealthy ways of evasion is to use information hiding techniques, namely stegomalware. A survey on stegomalware was published by Cabaj et al. in 2018.

Vulnerability

*   In this context, and throughout, what is called the "system" under attack may be anything from a single application, through a complete computer and operating system, to a large network.

*   Various factors make a system more vulnerable to malware.

Security Defects in Software

Malware exploits security defects (security bugs or vulnerabilities) in the design of the operating system, in applications (such as browsers, e.g. older versions of Microsoft Internet

Explorer supported by Windows XP), or in vulnerable versions of browser plugins such as Adobe Flash Player, Adobe Acrobat or Reader, or Java SE. Sometimes even installing new versions of such plugins does not automatically uninstall old versions. Security advisories from plug-in providers announce security-related updates. Common vulnerabilities are assigned CVE IDs and listed in the US National Vulnerability Database. Secunia PSI is an example of software, free for personal use, that will check a PC for vulnerable out-of-date software, and attempt to update it.

Malware authors target bugs, or loopholes, to exploit. A common method is exploitation of a buffer overrun vulnerability, where software designed to store data in a specified region of memory does not prevent more data than the buffer can accommodate being supplied. Malware may provide data that overflows the buffer, with malicious executable code or data after the end; when this payload is accessed it does what the attacker, not the legitimate software, determines.

Insecure Design or User Error

Early PCs had to be booted from floppy disks. When built-in hard drives became common, the operating system was normally started from them, but it was possible to boot from another boot device if available, such as a floppy disk, CD-ROM, DVD-ROM, USB flash drive or network. It was common to configure the computer to boot from one of these devices when available. Normally none would be available; the user would intentionally insert, say, a CD into the optical drive to boot the computer in some special way, for example, to install an operating system. Even without booting, computers can be configured to execute software on some media as soon as they become available, e.g. to autorun a CD or USB device when inserted.

Malware distributors would trick the user into booting or running from an infected device or medium. For example, a virus could make an infected computer add autorunnable code to any USB stick plugged into it. Anyone who then attached the stick to another computer set to autorun from USB would in turn become infected, and also pass on the infection in the same way. More generally, any device that plugs into a USB port - even lights, fans, speakers, toys, or peripherals such as a digital microscope - can be used to spread malware. Devices can be infected during manufacturing or supply if quality control is inadequate.

This form of infection can largely be avoided by setting up computers by default to boot from the internal hard drive, if available, and not to autorun from devices. Intentional booting from another device is always possible by pressing certain keys during boot.

Older email software would automatically open HTML email containing potentially malicious JavaScript code. Users may also execute disguised malicious email attachments. The 2018 Data Breach Investigations Report by Verizon, cited by CSO Online, states that emails are the primary method of malware delivery, accounting for 92% of malware delivery around the world.

Over-privileged Users and Over-privileged Code

In computing, privilege refers to how much a user or program is allowed to modify a system. In poorly designed computer systems, both users and programs can be assigned more privileges than they should have, and malware can take advantage of this. The two ways that malware does this is through overprivileged users and overprivileged code.

Some systems allow all users to modify their internal structures, and such users today would be considered over-privileged users. This was the standard operating procedure for early microcomputer and home computer systems, where there was no distinction between an administrator or root, and a regular user of the system. In some systems, non-administrator users are over-privileged by design, in the sense that they are allowed to modify internal structures of the system. In some environments, users are over-privileged because they have been inappropriately granted administrator or equivalent status.

Some systems allow code executed by a user to access all rights of that user, which is known as over-privileged code. This was also standard operating procedure for early microcomputer and home computer systems. Malware, running as over-privileged code, can use this privilege to subvert the system. Almost all currently popular operating systems, and also many scripting applications allow code too many privileges, usually in the sense that when a user executes code, the system allows that code all rights of that user. This makes users vulnerable to malware in the form of e-mail attachments, which may or may not be disguised.

Use of the same Operating System

Homogeneity can be a vulnerability. For example, when all computers in a network run the same operating system, upon exploiting one, one worm can exploit them all. In particular, Microsoft Windows or Mac OS X have such a large share of the market that an exploited vulnerability concentrating on either operating system could subvert a large number of systems. Introducing diversity purely for the sake of robustness, such as adding Linux computers, could increase short-term costs for training and maintenance. However, as long as all the nodes are not part of the same directory service for authentication, having a few diverse nodes could deter total shutdown of the network and allow those nodes to help with recovery of the infected nodes. Such separate, functional redundancy could avoid the cost of a total shutdown, at the cost of increased complexity and reduced usability in terms of single sign-on authentication.

Anti-malware Strategies

As malware attacks become more frequent, attention has begun to shift from viruses and spyware protection, to malware protection, and programs that have been specifically developed to combat malware. .

Anti-virus and Anti-malware Software

A specific component of anti-virus and anti-malware software, commonly referred to as an on-access or real-time scanner, hooks deep into the operating system's core or kernel and functions in a manner similar to how certain malware itself would attempt to operate, though with the user's informed permission for protecting the system. Any time the operating system accesses a file, the on-access scanner checks if the file is a 'legitimate' file or not. If the file is identified as malware by the scanner, the access operation will be stopped, the file will be dealt with by the scanner in a pre-defined way (how the anti-virus program was configured during/post installation), and the user will be notified. This may have a considerable performance impact on the operating system, though the degree of impact is dependent on how well the scanner was programmed. The goal is to stop any operations the malware may attempt on the system before they occur, including activities which might exploit bugs or trigger unexpected operating system behavior.

Anti-malware programs can combat malware in two ways:

1. They can provide real time protection against the installation of malware software on a computer. This type of malware protection works the same way as that of antivirus protection in that the anti-malware software scans all incoming network data for malware and blocks any threats it comes across.

2. Anti-malware software programs can be used solely for detection and removal of malware software that has already been installed onto a computer. This type of anti-malware software scans the contents of the Windows registry, operating system files, and installed programs on a computer and will provide a list of any threats found, allowing the user to choose which files to delete or keep, or to compare this list to a list of known malware components, removing files that match.

Real-time protection from malware works identically to real-time antivirus protection: the software scans disk files at download time, and blocks the activity of components known to represent malware. In some cases, it may also intercept attempts to install start-up items or to modify browser settings. Because many malware components are installed as a result of browser exploits or user error, using security software (some of which are anti-malware, though many are not) to "sandbox" browsers (essentially isolate the browser from the computer and hence any malware induced change) can also be effective in helping to restrict any damage done.

Examples of Microsoft Windows antivirus and anti-malware software include the optional Microsoft Security Essentials (for Windows XP, Vista, and Windows 7) for real-time protection, the Windows Malicious Software Removal Tool (now included with Windows (Security) Updates on "Patch Tuesday", the second Tuesday of each month), and Windows Defender (an optional download in the case of Windows XP, incorporating MSE functionality in the case of Windows 8 and later). Additionally, several capable antivirus software programs are available for free download from the Internet (usually restricted to non-commercial use). Tests found some free programs to be competitive with commercial ones. Microsoft's System File Checker can be used to check for and repair corrupted system files.

Some viruses disable System Restore and other important Windows tools such as Task Manager and Command Prompt. Many such viruses can be removed by rebooting the computer, entering Windows safe mode with networking, and then using system tools or Microsoft Safety Scanner.

Hardware implants can be of any type, so there can be no general way to detect them.

Website Security Scans

As malware also harms the compromised websites (by breaking reputation, blacklisting in search engines, etc.), some websites offer vulnerability scanning. Such scans check the website, detect malware, may note outdated software, and may report known security issues.

Air Gap Isolation or Parallel Network

As a last resort, computers can be protected from malware, and infected computers can be prevented from disseminating trusted information, by imposing an "air gap" (i.e. completely disconnecting them from all other networks). However, malware can still cross the air gap in some situations. For example, removable media can carry malware across the gap.

"AirHopper", "BitWhisper", "GSMem" and "Fansmitter" are four techniques introduced by researchers that can leak data from air-gapped computers using electromagnetic, thermal and acoustic emissions.

Grayware

Grayware is a term applied to unwanted applications or files that are not classified as malware, but can worsen the performance of computers and may cause security risks.

It describes applications that behave in an annoying or undesirable manner, and yet are less serious or troublesome than malware. Grayware encompasses spyware, adware, fraudulent dialers, joke programs, remote access tools and other unwanted programs that may harm the performance of computers or cause inconvenience. The term came into use around 2004.

Another term, potentially unwanted program (PUP) or potentially unwanted application (PUA), refers to applications that would be considered unwanted despite often having been downloaded by the user, possibly after failing to read a download agreement. PUPs include spyware, adware, and fraudulent dialers. Many security products classify unauthorised key generators as grayware, although they frequently carry true malware in addition to their ostensible purpose.

Software maker Malwarebytes lists several criteria for classifying a program as a PUP. Some types of adware (using stolen certificates) turn off anti-malware and virus protection; technical remedies are available.

SPYWARE

Spyware is software that aims to gather information about a person or organization, sometimes without their knowledge, that may send such information to another entity without the consumer's consent, that asserts control over a device without the consumer's knowledge, or it may send such information to another entity with the consumer's consent, through cookies.

"Spyware" is mostly classified into four types: adware, system monitors, tracking cookies, and trojans; examples of other notorious types include digital rights management capabilities that "phone home", keyloggers, rootkits, and web beacons.

Spyware is mostly used for the stealing information and storing Internet users' movements on the Web and serving up pop-up ads to Internet users. Whenever spyware is used for malicious purposes, its presence is typically hidden from the user and can be difficult to detect. Some spyware, such as keyloggers, may be installed by the owner of a shared, corporate, or public computer intentionally in order to monitor users.

While the term *spyware* suggests software that monitors a user's computing, the functions of spyware can extend beyond simple monitoring. Spyware can collect almost any type of data, including personal information like internet surfing habits, user logins, and bank or credit account information. Spyware can also interfere with a user's control of a computer by installing additional software or redirecting web browsers. Some spyware can change computer settings, which can result in slow Internet connection speeds, un-authorized changes in browser settings, or changes to software settings.

Sometimes, spyware is included along with genuine software, and may come from a malicious website or may have been added to the intentional functionality of genuine software. In response to the emergence of spyware, a small industry has sprung up dealing in anti-spyware software. Running anti-spyware software has become a widely recognized element of computer security practices, especially for computers running Microsoft Windows. A number of jurisdictions have passed anti-spyware laws, which usually target any software that is surreptitiously installed to control a user's computer.

In German-speaking countries, spyware used or made by the government is called *govware* by computer experts (in common parlance: *Regierungstrojaner*, literally "Government Trojan"). Govware is typically a trojan horse software used to intercept communications from the target computer. Some countries, like Switzerland and Germany, have a legal framework governing the use of such software. In the US, the term "policeware" has been used for similar purposes.

Use of the term "spyware" has eventually declined as the practice of tracking users has been pushed ever further into the mainstream by major websites and data mining companies; these generally break no known laws and compel users to be tracked, not by fraudulent practices *per se*, but by the default settings created for users and the language of terms-of-service agreements. In one documented example, on CBS/CNet News reported, on March 7, 2011, on a *Wall Street Journal* analysis revealing the practice of Facebook and other websites of tracking users' browsing activity, linked to their identity, far beyond users' visits and activity within the Facebook site itself. The report stated: "Here's how it works. You go to Facebook, you log in, you spend some time there, and then you move on without logging out. Let's say the next site you go to is *New York Times*. Those buttons, without you clicking on them, have just reported back to Facebook and Twitter that you went there and also your identity within those accounts. Let's say you moved on to something like a site about depression. This one also has a tweet button, a Google widget, and those, too, can report back who you are and that you went there." The *WSJ* analysis was researched by Brian Kennish, founder of Disconnect, Inc.

Routes of Infection

Spyware does not necessarily spread in the same way as a virus or worm because infected systems generally do not attempt to transmit or copy the software to other computers. Instead, spyware installs itself on a system by deceiving the user or by exploiting software vulnerabilities.

Most spyware is installed without knowledge, or by using deceptive tactics. Spyware may try to deceive users by bundling itself with desirable software. Other common tactics are using a Trojan horse, spy gadgets that look like normal devices but turn out to be something else, such as a USB Keylogger. These devices actually are connected to the device as memory units but are capable of recording each stroke made on the keyboard. Some spyware authors infect a system through security holes in the Web browser or in other software. When the user navigates to a Web page controlled by the spyware author, the page contains code which attacks the browser and forces the download and installation of spyware.

The installation of spyware frequently involves Internet Explorer. Its popularity and history of security issues have made it a frequent target. Its deep integration with the Windows environment make it susceptible to attack into the Windows operating system. Internet Explorer also serves as a point of attachment for spyware in the form of Browser Helper Objects, which modify the browser's behavior.

Effects and Behaviors

A spyware rarely operates alone on a computer; an affected machine usually has multiple infections. Users frequently notice unwanted behavior and degradation of system performance. A spyware infestation can create significant unwanted CPU activity, disk usage, and network traffic. Stability issues, such as applications freezing, failure to boot, and system-wide crashes are also common. Spyware, which interferes with networking software commonly causes difficulty connecting to the Internet.

In some infections, the spyware is not even evident. Users assume in those situations that the performance issues relate to faulty hardware, Windows installation problems, or another malware infection. Some owners of badly infected systems resort to contacting technical support experts, or even buying a new computer because the existing system "has become too slow". Badly infected systems may require a clean reinstallation of all their software in order to return to full functionality.

Moreover, some types of spyware disable software firewalls and antivirus software, and reduce browser security settings, which opens the system to further opportunistic infections. Some spyware disables or even removes competing spyware programs, on the grounds that more spyware-related annoyances increase the likelihood that users will take action to remove the programs.

Keyloggers are sometimes part of malware packages downloaded onto computers without the owners' knowledge. Some keylogger software is freely available on the internet, while others are commercial or private applications. Most keyloggers allow not only keyboard keystrokes to be captured, they also are often capable of collecting screen captures from the computer.

A typical Windows user has administrative privileges, mostly for convenience. Because of this, any program the user runs has unrestricted access to the system. As with other operating systems, Windows users are able to follow the principle of least privilege and use non-administrator accounts. Alternatively, they can reduce the privileges of specific vulnerable Internet-facing processes, such as Internet Explorer.

Since Windows Vista is, by default, a computer administrator that runs everything under limited user privileges, when a program requires administrative privileges, a User Account Control popup will prompt the user to allow or deny the action. This improves on the design used by previous versions of Windows.

Remedies and Prevention

As the spyware threat has evolved, a number of techniques have emerged to counteract it. These include programs designed to remove or block spyware, as well as various user practices which reduce the chance of getting spyware on a system.

Nonetheless, spyware remains a costly problem. When a large number of pieces of spyware have infected a Windows computer, the only remedy may involve backing up user data, and fully reinstalling the operating system. For instance, some spyware cannot be completely removed by Symantec, Microsoft, PC Tools.

Anti-spyware Programs

Many programmers and some commercial firms have released products dedicated to remove or block spyware. Programs such as PC Tools' Spyware Doctor, Lavasoft's *Ad-Aware SE* and Patrick Kolla's *Spybot - Search & Destroy* rapidly gained popularity as tools to remove, and in some cases intercept, spyware programs. On December 16, 2004, Microsoft acquired the *GIANT AntiSpyware* software, rebranding it as *Windows AntiSpyware beta* and releasing it as a free download for Genuine Windows XP and Windows 2003 users. (In 2006 it was renamed Windows Defender).

Major anti-virus firms such as Symantec, PC Tools, McAfee and Sophos have also added anti-spyware features to their existing anti-virus products. Early on, anti-virus firms expressed reluctance to add anti-spyware functions, citing lawsuits brought by spyware authors against the authors of web sites and programs which described their products as "spyware". However, recent versions of these major firms home and business anti-virus products do include anti-spyware functions, albeit treated differently from viruses. Symantec Anti-Virus, for instance, categorizes spyware programs as "extended threats" and now offers real-time protection against these threats.

How Anti-spyware Software Works

Anti-spyware programs can combat spyware in two ways:

1. They can provide real-time protection in a manner similar to that of anti-virus protection: they scan all incoming network data for spyware and blocks any threats it detects.

2. Anti-spyware software programs can be used solely for detection and removal of spyware software that has already been installed into the computer. This kind of anti-spyware can often be set to scan on a regular schedule.

Such programs inspect the contents of the Windows registry, operating system files, and installed programs, and remove files and entries which match a list of known spyware. Real-time protection from spyware works identically to real-time anti-virus protection: the software scans disk files at download time, and blocks the activity of components known to represent spyware. In some cases, it may also intercept attempts to install start-up items or to modify browser settings. Earlier versions of anti-spyware programs focused chiefly on detection and removal. Javacool Software's SpywareBlaster, one of the first to offer real-time protection, blocked the installation of ActiveX-based spyware.

Like most anti-virus software, many anti-spyware/adware tools require a frequently updated database of threats. As new spyware programs are released, anti-spyware developers discover and evaluate them, adding to the list of known spyware, which allows the software to detect and remove new spyware. As a result, anti-spyware software is of limited usefulness without regular updates. Updates may be installed automatically or manually.

A popular generic spyware removal tool used by those that requires a certain degree of expertise is HijackThis, which scans certain areas of the Windows OS where spyware often resides and presents a list with items to delete manually. As most of the items are legitimate windows files/registry entries it is advised for those who are less knowledgeable on this subject to post a HijackThis log on the numerous antispyware sites and let the experts decide what to delete.

If a spyware program is not blocked and manages to get itself installed, it may resist attempts to terminate or uninstall it. Some programs work in pairs: when an anti-spyware scanner (or the user) terminates one running process, the other one respawns the killed program. Likewise, some spyware will detect attempts to remove registry keys and immediately add them again. Usually, booting the infected computer in safe mode allows an anti-spyware program a better chance of removing persistent spyware. Killing the process tree may also work.

Security Practices

To detect spyware, computer users have found several practices useful in addition to installing anti-spyware programs. Many users have installed a web browser other than Internet Explorer, such as Mozilla Firefox or Google Chrome. Though no browser is completely safe, Internet Explorer was once at a greater risk for spyware infection due to its large user base as well as vulnerabilities such as ActiveX but these three major browsers are now close to equivalent when it comes to security.

Some ISPs—particularly colleges and universities—have taken a different approach to blocking spyware: they use their network firewalls and web proxies to block access to Web sites known to install spyware. On March 31, 2005, Cornell University's Information Technology department released a report detailing the behavior of one particular piece of proxy-based spyware, *Marketscore*, and the steps the university took to intercept it. Many other educational institutions have taken similar steps.

Individual users can also install firewalls from a variety of companies. These monitor the flow of information going to and from a networked computer and provide protection against spyware and malware. Some users install a large hosts file which prevents the user's computer from connecting to known spyware-related web addresses. Spyware may get installed via certain shareware programs offered for download. Downloading programs only from reputable sources can provide some protection from this source of attack.

Individual users can use cellphone/computer with physical (electric) switch, or isolated electronic switch that disconnects microphone, camera without bypass and keep it in disconnected position where not in use, that limits information that spyware can collect. .

Applications

Stealware and Affiliate Fraud

A few spyware vendors, notably 180 Solutions, have written what the *New York Times* has dubbed "stealware", and what spyware researcher Ben Edelman terms *affiliate fraud*, a form of click fraud. Stealware diverts the payment of affiliate marketing revenues from the legitimate affiliate to the spyware vendor.

Spyware which attacks affiliate networks places the spyware operator's affiliate tag on the user's activity – replacing any other tag, if there is one. The spyware operator is the only party that gains from this. The user has their choices thwarted, a legitimate affiliate loses revenue, networks' reputations are injured, and vendors are harmed by having to pay out affiliate revenues to an "affiliate" who is not party to a contract. Affiliate fraud is a violation of the terms of service of most affiliate marketing networks. As a result, spyware operators such as 180 Solutions have been terminated from affiliate networks including LinkShare and ShareSale. Mobile devices can also be vulnerable to chargeware, which manipulates users into illegitimate mobile charges.

Identity Theft and Fraud

In one case, spyware has been closely associated with identity theft. In August 2005, researchers from security software firm Sunbelt Software suspected the creators of the common CoolWebSearch spyware had used it to transmit "chat sessions, user names, passwords, bank information, etc."; however it turned out that "it actually (was) its own sophisticated criminal little trojan that's independent of CWS." This case is currently under investigation by the FBI.

The Federal Trade Commission estimates that 27.3 million Americans have been victims of identity theft, and that financial losses from identity theft totaled nearly $48 billion for businesses and financial institutions and at least $5 billion in out-of-pocket expenses for individuals.

Digital Rights Management

Some copy-protection technologies have borrowed from spyware. In 2005, Sony BMG Music Entertainment was found to be using rootkits in its XCP digital rights management technology Like spyware, not only was it difficult to detect and uninstall, it was so poorly written that most efforts to remove it could have rendered computers unable to function. Texas Attorney General Greg Abbott filed suit, and three separate class-action suits were filed. Sony BMG later provided a workaround on its website to help users remove it.

Beginning on April 25, 2006, Microsoft's Windows Genuine Advantage Notifications application was installed on most Windows PCs as a "critical security update". While the main purpose of this deliberately uninstallable application is to ensure the copy of Windows on the machine was lawfully purchased and installed, it also installs software that has been accused of "phoning home" on a daily basis, like spyware. It can be removed with the RemoveWGA tool.

Personal Relationships

Spyware has been used to monitor electronic activities of partners in intimate relationships. At least one software package, Loverspy, was specifically marketed for this purpose. Depending on local laws regarding communal/marital property, observing a partner's online activity without their consent may be illegal; the author of Loverspy and several users of the product were indicted in California in 2005 on charges of wiretapping and various computer crimes.

Browser Cookies

Anti-spyware programs often report Web advertisers' HTTP cookies, the small text files that track browsing activity, as spyware. While they are not always inherently malicious, many users object to third parties using space on their personal computers for their business purposes, and many anti-spyware programs offer to remove them.

Examples:

These common spyware programs illustrate the diversity of behaviors found in these attacks. Note that as with computer viruses, researchers give names to spyware programs which may not be used by their creators. Programs may be grouped into "families" based not on shared program code, but on common behaviors, or by "following the money" of apparent financial or business connections. For instance, a number of the spyware programs distributed by Claria are collectively known as "Gator". Likewise, programs that are frequently installed together may be described as parts of the same spyware package, even if they function separately.

- CoolWebSearch, a group of programs, takes advantage of Internet Explorer vulnerabilities. The package directs traffic to advertisements on Web sites including *coolwebsearch.com*. It displays pop-up ads, rewrites search engine results, and alters the infected computer's hosts file to direct DNS lookups to these sites.

- FinFisher, sometimes called FinSpy is a high-end surveillance suite sold to law enforcement and intelligence agencies. Support services such as training and technology updates are part of the package.

- GO Keyboard virtual Android keyboard apps (GO Keyboard - Emoji keyboard and GO Keyboard - Emoticon keyboard) transmit personal information to its remote servers without explicit users' consent. This information includes user's Google account email, language, IMSI, location, network type, Android version and build, and device's model and screen size. The apps also download and execute a code from a remote server, breaching the Malicious Behavior section of the Google Play privacy policies. Some of these plugins are detected as Adware or PUP by many Anti-Virus engines, while the developer, a Chinese company GOMO Dev Team, claims in the apps' description that they will never collect personal data including credit card information. The apps with about 2 million users in total were caught spying in September 2017 by security researchers from AdGuard who then reported their findings to Google.

- HuntBar, aka WinTools or Adware.Websearch, was installed by an ActiveX drive-by download at affiliate Web sites, or by advertisements displayed by other spyware programs—an example of how spyware can install more spyware. These programs add toolbars to IE, track aggregate browsing behavior, redirect affiliate references, and display advertisements.

- Internet Optimizer, also known as DyFuCa, redirects Internet Explorer error pages to advertising. When users follow a broken link or enter an erroneous URL, they see a page of advertisements. However, because password-protected Web sites (HTTP Basic authentication) use the same mechanism as HTTP errors, Internet Optimizer makes it impossible for the user to access password-protected sites.

- Spyware such as Look2Me hides inside system-critical processes and start up even in safe mode. With no process to terminate they are harder to detect and remove, which is a combination of both spyware and a rootkit. Rootkit technology is also seeing increasing use, as newer spyware programs also have specific countermeasures against well known anti-malware products and may prevent them from running or being installed, or even uninstall them.

- Movieland, also known as Moviepass.tv and Popcorn.net, is a movie download service that has been the subject of thousands of complaints to the Federal Trade Commission (FTC), the Washington State Attorney General's Office, the Better Business Bureau, and other agencies. Consumers complained they were held hostage by a cycle of oversized pop-up windows demanding payment of at least $29.95, claiming that they had signed up for a three-day free trial but had not cancelled before the trial period was over, and were thus obligated to pay. The FTC filed a complaint, since settled, against Movieland and eleven other defendants charging them with having "engaged in a nationwide scheme to use deception and coercion to extract payments from consumers".

- Onavo Protect is used by Facebook to monetize usage habits within a privacy-focused environment, and was criticized because the app listing did not contain a prominent disclosure of Facebook's ownership. The app was removed from the Apple iOS App Store Apple deemed it a violation of guidelines barring apps from harvesting data from other apps on a user's device.

- Zango (formerly 180 Solutions) transmits detailed information to advertisers about the Web sites which users visit. It also alters HTTP requests for affiliate advertisements linked from a Web site, so that the advertisements make unearned profit for the 180 Solutions company. It opens pop-up ads that cover over the Web sites of competing companies.

- Zlob trojan, or just Zlob, downloads itself to a computer via an ActiveX codec and reports information back to Control Server. Some information can be the search-history, the Websites visited, and even keystrokes. More recently, Zlob has been known to hijack routers set to defaults.

- Zwangi redirects URLs typed into the browser's address bar to a search page at www.zwangi.com, and may also take screenshots without permission.

ROOTKIT

A rootkit is a collection of computer software, typically malicious, designed to enable access to a computer or an area of its software that is not otherwise allowed (for example, to an unauthorized user) and often masks its existence or the existence of other software. The term *rootkit* is a concatenation of "root" (the traditional name of the privileged account on Unix-like operating systems) and the word "kit" (which refers to the software components that implement the tool). The term "rootkit" has negative connotations through its association with malware.

Rootkit installation can be automated, or an attacker can install it after having obtained root or Administrator access. Obtaining this access is a result of direct attack on a system, i.e. exploiting a known vulnerability (such as privilege escalation) or a password (obtained by cracking or social engineering tactics like "phishing"). Once installed, it becomes possible to hide the intrusion as well as to maintain privileged access. The key is the root or administrator access. Full control over a system means that existing software can be modified, including software that might otherwise be used to detect or circumvent it.

Rootkit detection is difficult because a rootkit may be able to subvert the software that is intended to find it. Detection methods include using an alternative and trusted operating system, behavioral-based methods, signature scanning, difference scanning, and memory dump analysis. Removal can be complicated or practically impossible, especially in cases where the rootkit resides in the kernel; reinstallation of the operating system may be the only available solution to the problem. When dealing with firmware rootkits, removal may require hardware replacement, or specialized equipment.

Uses

Modern rootkits do not elevate access, but rather are used to make another software payload undetectable by adding stealth capabilities. Most rootkits are classified as malware, because the payloads they are bundled with are malicious. For example, a payload might covertly steal user passwords, credit card information, computing resources, or conduct other unauthorized activities. A small number of rootkits may be considered utility applications by their users: for example, a rootkit might cloak a CD-ROM-emulation driver, allowing video game users to defeat anti-piracy measures that require insertion of the original installation media into a physical optical drive to verify that the software was legitimately purchased.

Rootkits and their payloads have many uses:

- Provide an attacker with full access via a backdoor, permitting unauthorized access to, for example, steal or falsify documents. One of the ways to carry this out is to subvert the login mechanism, such as the/bin/login program on Unix-like systems or GINA on Windows. The replacement appears to function normally, but also accepts a secret login combination that allows an attacker direct access to the system with administrative privileges, bypassing standard authentication and authorization mechanisms.

- Conceal other malware, notably password-stealing key loggers and computer viruses.

- Appropriate the compromised machine as a zombie computer for attacks on other computers. (The attack originates from the compromised system or network, instead of the attacker's system). "Zombie" computers are typically members of large botnets that can launch denial-of-service attacks, distribute e-mail spam, conduct click fraud, etc.

- Enforcement of digital rights management (DRM).

In some instances, rootkits provide desired functionality, and may be installed intentionally on behalf of the computer user:

- Conceal cheating in online games from software like Warden.

- Detect attacks, for example, in a honeypot.

- Enhance emulation software and security software. Alcohol 120% and Daemon Tools are commercial examples of non-hostile rootkits used to defeat copy-protection mechanisms such as SafeDisc and SecuROM. Kaspersky antivirus software also uses techniques resembling rootkits to protect itself from malicious actions. It loads its own drivers to intercept system activity, and then prevents other processes from doing harm to itself. Its processes are not hidden, but cannot be terminated by standard methods.

- Anti-theft protection: Laptops may have BIOS-based rootkit software that will periodically report to a central authority, allowing the laptop to be monitored, disabled or wiped of information in the event that it is stolen.

- Bypassing Microsoft Product Activation.

Types

There are at least five types of rootkit, ranging from those at the lowest level in firmware (with the highest privileges), through to the least privileged user-based variants that operate in Ring 3. Hybrid combinations of these may occur spanning, for example, user mode and kernel mode.

User Mode

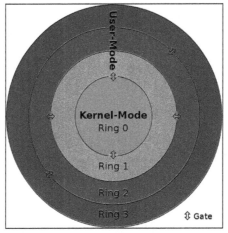

Computer security rings (Note that Ring 1 is not shown).

User-mode rootkits run in Ring 3, along with other applications as user, rather than low-level system processes. They have a number of possible installation vectors to intercept and modify the standard behavior of application programming interfaces (APIs). Some inject a dynamically linked library (such as a .DLL file on Windows, or a .dylib file on Mac OS X) into other processes, and are thereby able to execute inside any target process to spoof it; others with sufficient privileges simply overwrite the memory of a target application. Injection mechanisms include:

- Use of vendor-supplied application extensions. For example, Windows Explorer has public interfaces that allow third parties to extend its functionality.

- Interception of messages.

- Debuggers.

- Exploitation of security vulnerabilities.

- Function hooking or patching of commonly used APIs, for example, to hide a running process or file that resides on a filesystem.

Since user mode applications all run in their own memory space, the rootkit needs to perform this patching in the memory space of every running application. In addition, the rootkit needs to monitor the system for any new applications that execute and patch those programs' memory space before they fully execute.

Kernel Mode

Kernel-mode rootkits run with the highest operating system privileges (Ring 0) by adding code or replacing portions of the core operating system, including both the kernel and associated device drivers. Most operating systems support kernel-mode device drivers, which execute with the same privileges as the operating system itself. As such, many kernel-mode rootkits are developed as device drivers or loadable modules, such as loadable kernel modules in Linux or device drivers in Microsoft Windows. This class of rootkit has unrestricted security access, but is more difficult to write. The complexity makes bugs common, and any bugs in code operating at the kernel level may seriously impact system stability, leading to discovery of the rootkit. One of the first widely known kernel rootkits was developed for Windows NT 4.0 and released in Phrack magazine in 1999 by Greg Hoglund. Kernel rootkits can be especially difficult to detect and remove because they operate at the same security level as the operating system itself, and are thus able to intercept or subvert the most trusted operating system operations. Any software, such as antivirus software, running on the compromised system is equally vulnerable. In this situation, no part of the system can be trusted.

A rootkit can modify data structures in the Windows kernel using a method known as *direct kernel object manipulation* (DKOM). This method can be used to hide processes. A kernel mode rootkit can also hook the System Service Descriptor Table (SSDT), or modify the gates between user mode and kernel mode, in order to cloak itself. Similarly for the Linux operating system, a rootkit can modify the *system call table* to subvert kernel functionality. It is common that a rootkit creates a hidden, encrypted filesystem in which it can hide other malware or original copies of files it has infected. Operating systems are evolving to counter the threat of kernel-mode rootkits. For example, 64-bit editions of Microsoft Windows now implement mandatory signing of all kernel-level drivers in order to make it more difficult for untrusted code to execute with the highest privileges in a system.

Bootkits

A kernel-mode rootkit variant called a bootkit can infect startup code like the Master Boot Record (MBR), Volume Boot Record (VBR), or boot sector, and in this way can be used to attack full disk encryption systems.

An example of such an attack on disk encryption is the "evil maid attack", in which an attacker installs a bootkit on an unattended computer. The envisioned scenario is a maid sneaking into the hotel room where the victims left their hardware. The bootkit replaces the legitimate boot loader with one under their control. Typically the malware loader persists through the transition to protected mode when the kernel has loaded, and is thus able to subvert the kernel. For example, the "Stoned Bootkit" subverts the system by using a compromised boot loader to intercept encryption keys and passwords. More recently, the Alureon rootkit has successfully subverted the requirement for 64-bit kernel-mode driver signing in Windows 7, by modifying the master boot record. Although not malware in the sense of doing something the user doesn't want, certain "Vista Loader" or "Windows Loader" software work in a similar way by injecting an ACPI SLIC (System Licensed Internal Code) table in the RAM-cached version of the BIOS during boot, in order to defeat the Windows Vista and Windows 7 activation process. This vector of attack was rendered useless in the (non-server) versions of Windows 8, which use a unique, machine-specific key for each system, that can only be used by that one machine. Many antivirus companies provide free utilities and programs to remove bootkits.

Hypervisor Level

Rootkits have been created as Type II Hypervisors in academia as proofs of concept. By exploiting hardware virtualization features such as Intel VT or AMD-V, this type of rootkit runs in Ring -1 and hosts the target operating system as a virtual machine, thereby enabling the rootkit to intercept hardware calls made by the original operating system. Unlike normal hypervisors, they do not have to load before the operating system, but can load into an operating system before promoting it into a virtual machine. A hypervisor rootkit does not have to make any modifications to the kernel of the target to subvert it; however, that does not mean that it cannot be detected by the guest operating system. For example, timing differences may be detectable in CPU instructions. The "SubVirt" laboratory rootkit, developed jointly by Microsoft and University of Michigan researchers, is an academic example of a virtual machine–based rootkit (VMBR), while Blue Pill software is another. In 2009, researchers from Microsoft and North Carolina State University demonstrated a hypervisor-layer anti-rootkit called Hooksafe, which provides generic protection against kernel-mode rootkits. Windows 10 introduced a new feature called "Device Guard", that takes advantage of virtualization to provide independent external protection of an operating system against rootkit-type malware.

Firmware and Hardware

A firmware rootkit uses device or platform firmware to create a persistent malware image in hardware, such as a router, network card, hard drive, or the system BIOS. The rootkit hides in firmware, because firmware is not usually inspected for code integrity. John Heasman demonstrated the viability of firmware rootkits in both ACPI firmware routines and in a PCI expansion card ROM. In October 2008, criminals tampered with European credit card-reading machines before they were installed. The devices intercepted and transmitted credit card details via a mobile phone network. In March 2009, researchers Alfredo Ortega and Anibal Sacco published details of a BIOS-level Windows rootkit that was able to survive disk replacement and operating system re-installation. A few months later they learned that some laptops are sold with a legitimate rootkit, known as Absolute CompuTrace or Absolute LoJack for Laptops, preinstalled in many BIOS images. This is an anti-theft technology system that researchers showed can be turned to malicious purposes.

Intel Active Management Technology, part of Intel vPro, implements out-of-band management, giving administrators remote administration, remote management, and remote control of PCs with no involvement of the host processor or BIOS, even when the system is powered off. Remote administration includes remote power-up and power-down, remote reset, redirected boot, console redirection, pre-boot access to BIOS settings, programmable filtering for inbound and outbound network traffic, agent presence checking, out-of-band policy-based alerting, access to system information, such as hardware asset information, persistent event logs, and other information that is stored in dedicated memory (not on the hard drive) where it is accessible even if the OS is down or the PC is powered off. Some of these functions require the deepest level of rootkit, a second non-removable spy computer built around the main computer. Sandy Bridge and future chipsets have "the ability to remotely kill and restore a lost or stolen PC via 3G". Hardware rootkits built into the chipset can help recover stolen computers, remove data, or render them useless, but they also present privacy and security concerns of undetectable spying and redirection by management or hackers who might gain control.

Installation and Cloaking

Rootkits employ a variety of techniques to gain control of a system; the type of rootkit influences the choice of attack vector. The most common technique leverages security vulnerabilities to achieve surreptitious privilege escalation. Another approach is to use a Trojan horse, deceiving a computer user into trusting the rootkit's installation program as benign—in this case, social engineering convinces a user that the rootkit is beneficial. The installation task is made easier if the principle of least privilege is not applied, since the rootkit then does not have to explicitly request elevated (administrator-level) privileges. Other classes of rootkits can be installed only by someone with physical access to the target system. Some rootkits may also be installed intentionally by the owner of the system or somebody authorized by the owner, e.g. for the purpose of employee monitoring, rendering such subversive techniques unnecessary. Some malicious rootkit installations are commercially driven, with a pay-per-install (PPI) compensation method typical for distribution.

Once installed, a rootkit takes active measures to obscure its presence within the host system through subversion or evasion of standard operating system security tools and application programming interface (APIs) used for diagnosis, scanning, and monitoring. Rootkits achieve this by modifying the behavior of core parts of an operating system through loading code into other processes, the installation or modification of drivers, or kernel modules. Obfuscation techniques include concealing running processes from system-monitoring mechanisms and hiding system files and other configuration data. It is not uncommon for a rootkit to disable the event logging capacity of an operating system, in an attempt to hide evidence of an attack. Rootkits can, in theory, subvert *any* operating system activities. The "perfect rootkit" can be thought of as similar to a "perfect crime": one that nobody realizes has taken place. Rootkits also take a number of measures to ensure their survival against detection and "cleaning" by antivirus software in addition to commonly installing into Ring 0 (kernel-mode), where they have complete access to a system. These include polymorphism (changing so their "signature" is hard to detect), stealth techniques, regeneration, disabling or turning off anti-malware software, and not installing on virtual machines where it may be easier for researchers to discover and analyze them.

Detection

The fundamental problem with rootkit detection is that if the operating system has been subverted, particularly by a kernel-level rootkit, it cannot be trusted to find unauthorized modifications to itself or its components. Actions such as requesting a list of running processes, or a list of files in a directory, cannot be trusted to behave as expected. In other words, rootkit detectors that work while running on infected systems are only effective against rootkits that have some defect in their camouflage, or that run with lower user-mode privileges than the detection software in the kernel. As with computer viruses, the detection and elimination of rootkits is an ongoing struggle between both sides of this conflict. Detection can take a number of different approaches, including looking for virus "signatures" (e.g. antivirus software), integrity checking (e.g. digital signatures), difference-based detection (comparison of expected vs. actual results), and behavioral detection (e.g. monitoring CPU usage or network traffic).

For kernel-mode rootkits, detection is considerably more complex, requiring careful scrutiny of the System Call table to look for hooked functions where the malware may be subverting system behavior, as well as forensic scanning of memory for patterns that indicate hidden processes. Unix rootkit detection offerings include Zeppoo, chkrootkit, rkhunter and OSSEC. For Windows, detection tools include Microsoft Sysinternals RootkitRevealer, Avast Antivirus, Sophos Anti-Rootkit, F-Secure, Radix, GMER, and WindowsSCOPE. Any rootkit detectors that prove effective ultimately contribute to their own ineffectiveness, as malware authors adapt and test their code to escape detection by well-used tools. Detection by examining storage while the suspect operating system is not operational can miss rootkits not recognised by the checking software, as the rootkit is not active and suspicious behavior is suppressed; conventional anti-malware software running with the rootkit operational may fail if the rootkit hides itself effectively.

Alternative Trusted Medium

The best and most reliable method for operating-system-level rootkit detection is to shut down the computer suspected of infection, and then to check its storage by booting from an alternative trusted medium (e.g. a "rescue" CD-ROM or USB flash drive). The technique is effective because a rootkit cannot actively hide its presence if it is not running.

Behavioral-based

The behavioral-based approach to detecting rootkits attempts to infer the presence of a rootkit by looking for rootkit-like behavior. For example, by profiling a system, differences in the timing and frequency of API calls or in overall CPU utilization can be attributed to a rootkit. The method is complex and is hampered by a high incidence of false positives. Defective rootkits can sometimes introduce very obvious changes to a system: the Alureon rootkit crashed Windows systems after a security update exposed a design flaw in its code. Logs from a packet analyzer, firewall, or intrusion prevention system may present evidence of rootkit behaviour in a networked environment.

Signature-based

Antivirus products rarely catch all viruses in public tests (depending on what is used and to what extent), even though security software vendors incorporate rootkit detection into their products. Should a rootkit attempt to hide during an antivirus scan, a stealth detector may notice; if the rootkit attempts to temporarily unload itself from the system, signature detection (or "fingerprinting") can still find it. This combined approach forces attackers to implement counterattack mechanisms, or "retro" routines, that attempt to terminate antivirus programs. Signature-based detection methods can be effective against well-published rootkits, but less so against specially crafted, custom-root rootkits.

Difference-based

Another method that can detect rootkits compares "trusted" raw data with "tainted" content returned by an API. For example, binaries present on disk can be compared with their copies within operating memory (in some operating systems, the in-memory image should be identical to the on-disk image), or the results returned from file system or Windows Registry APIs can be checked against raw structures on the underlying physical disks—however, in the case of the former, some valid differences can be introduced by operating system mechanisms like memory relocation or shimming. A rootkit may detect the presence of such a difference-based scanner or virtual machine (the latter being commonly used to perform forensic analysis), and adjust its behaviour so that no differences can be detected. Difference-based detection was used by Russinovich's *RootkitRevealer* tool to find the Sony DRM rootkit.

Integrity Checking

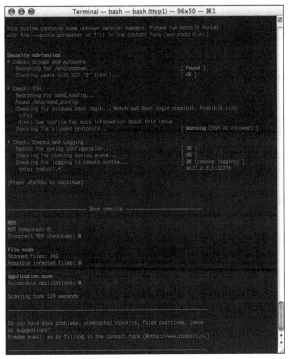

The rkhunter utility uses SHA-1 hashes to verify the integrity of system files.

Code signing uses public-key infrastructure to check if a file has been modified since being digitally signed by its publisher. Alternatively, a system owner or administrator can use a cryptographic hash function to compute a "fingerprint" at installation time that can help to detect subsequent unauthorized changes to on-disk code libraries. However, unsophisticated schemes check only whether the code has been modified since installation time; subversion prior to that time is not detectable. The fingerprint must be re-established each time changes are made to the system: for example, after installing security updates or a service pack. The hash function creates a *message digest*, a relatively short code calculated from each bit in the file using an algorithm that creates large changes in the message digest with even smaller changes to the original file. By recalculating and comparing the message digest of the installed files at regular intervals against a trusted list of message digests, changes in the system can be detected and monitored—as long as the original baseline was created before the malware was added.

More-sophisticated rootkits are able to subvert the verification process by presenting an unmodified copy of the file for inspection, or by making code modifications only in memory, reconfiguration registers, which are later compared to a white list of expected values. The code that performs hash, compare, or extend operations must also be protected—in this context, the notion of an *immutable root-of-trust* holds that the very first code to measure security properties of a system must itself be trusted to ensure that a rootkit or bootkit does not compromise the system at its most fundamental level.

Memory Dumps

Forcing a complete dump of virtual memory will capture an active rootkit (or a kernel dump in the case of a kernel-mode rootkit), allowing offline forensic analysis to be performed with a debugger against the resulting dump file, without the rootkit being able to take any measures to cloak itself. This technique is highly specialized, and may require access to non-public source code or debugging symbols. Memory dumps initiated by the operating system cannot always be used to detect a hypervisor-based rootkit, which is able to intercept and subvert the lowest-level attempts to read memory—a hardware device, such as one that implements a non-maskable interrupt, may be required to dump memory in this scenario. Virtual machines also make it easier to analyze the memory of a compromised machine from the underlying hypervisor, so some rootkits will avoid infecting virtual machines for this reason.

Removal

Manual removal of a rootkit is often too difficult for a typical computer user, but a number of security-software vendors offer tools to automatically detect and remove some rootkits, typically as part of an antivirus suite. As of 2005, Microsoft's monthly Windows Malicious Software Removal Tool is able to detect and remove some classes of rootkits. Also, Windows Defender Offline can remove rootkits, as it runs from a trusted environment before the operating system starts. Some antivirus scanners can bypass file system APIs, which are vulnerable to manipulation by a rootkit. Instead, they access raw file system structures directly, and use this information to validate the results from the system APIs to identify any differences that may be caused by a rootkit. There are experts who believe that the only reliable way to remove them is to re-install the operating system from trusted media. This is because antivirus and malware removal tools running on an untrusted system may be ineffective against well-written kernel-mode rootkits. Booting an alternative operating system from trusted media can allow an infected system volume to be mounted and potentially safely cleaned and critical data to be copied off—or, alternatively, a forensic examination performed. Lightweight operating systems such as Windows PE, Windows Recovery Console, Windows Recovery Environment, BartPE, or Live Distros can be used for this purpose, allowing the system to be "cleaned". Even if the type and nature of a rootkit is known, manual repair may be impractical, while re-installing the operating system and applications is safer, simpler and quicker.

Defenses

System hardening represents one of the first layers of defence against a rootkit, to prevent it from being able to install. Applying security patches, implementing the principle of least privilege, reducing the attack surface and installing antivirus software are some standard security best practices that are effective against all classes of malware. New secure boot specifications like Unified Extensible Firmware Interface have been designed to address the threat of bootkits, but even these are vulnerable if the security features they offer are not utilized. For server systems, remote server attestation using technologies such as Intel Trusted Execution Technology (TXT) provide a way of verifying that servers remain in a known good state. For example, Microsoft Bitlocker's encryption of data-at-rest verifies that servers are in a known "good state" on bootup. PrivateCore vCage is a software offering that secures data-in-use (memory) to avoid bootkits and rootkits by verifying servers are in a known "good" state on bootup. The PrivateCore implementation works in concert with Intel TXT and locks down server system interfaces to avoid potential bootkits and rootkits.

KEYSTROKE LOGGING

Keystroke logging, often referred to as keylogging or keyboard capturing, is the action of recording (logging) the keys struck on a keyboard, typically covertly, so that person using the keyboard is unaware that their actions are being monitored. Data can then be retrieved by the person operating the logging program. A keylogger can be either software or hardware.

While the programs themselves are legal, with many of them being designed to allow employers to oversee the use of their computers, keyloggers are most often used for stealing passwords and other confidential information.

Keylogging can also be used to study human-computer interaction. Numerous keylogging methods exist: They range from hardware and software-based approaches to acoustic analysis.

Application

Software-based Keyloggers

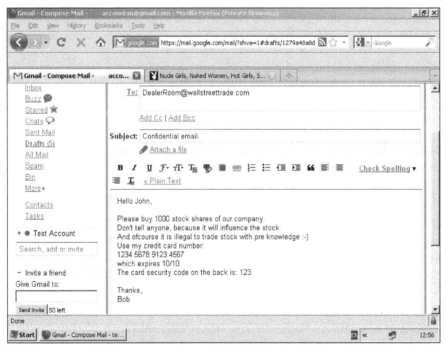

A keylogger example of a screen capture, which holds potentially confidential and private information. The image below holds the corresponding keylogger text result.

Software-based keyloggers are computer programs designed to work on the target computer's software. Keyloggers are used in IT organizations to troubleshoot technical problems with computers and business networks. Families and business people use keyloggers legally to monitor network usage without their users' direct knowledge. Even Microsoft publicly admitted that Windows 10 operation system has a built-in keylogger in its final version "to improve typing and writing services". However, malicious individuals can use keyloggers on public computers to steal passwords or credit card information. Most keyloggers are not stopped by HTTPS encryption because that only protects data in transit between computers, thus the threat being from the user's computer.

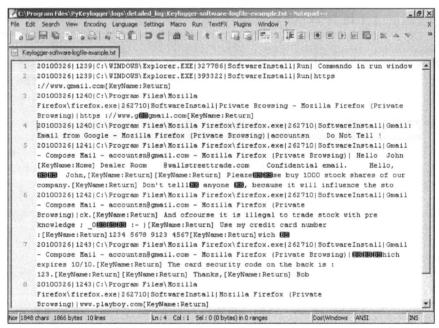

A logfile from a software-based keylogger, based on the screen capture above.

From a technical perspective, there are several categories:

- Hypervisor-based: The keylogger can theoretically reside in a malware hypervisor running underneath the operating system, which thus remains untouched. It effectively becomes a virtual machine. Blue Pill is a conceptual example.

- Kernel-based: A program on the machine obtains root access to hide in the OS and intercepts keystrokes that pass through the kernel. This method is difficult both to write and to combat. Such keyloggers reside at the kernel level, which makes them difficult to detect, especially for user-mode applications that don't have root access. They are frequently implemented as rootkits that subvert the operating system kernel to gain unauthorized access to the hardware. This makes them very powerful. A keylogger using this method can act as a keyboard device driver, for example, and thus gain access to any information typed on the keyboard as it goes to the operating system.

- API-based: These keyloggers hook keyboard APIs inside a running application. The keylogger registers keystroke events as if it was a normal piece of the application instead of malware. The keylogger receives an event each time the user presses or releases a key. The keylogger simply records it.

  ○ Windows APIs such as `GetAsyncKeyState()`, `GetForegroundWindow()`, etc. are used to poll the state of the keyboard or to subscribe to keyboard events. A more recent example simply polls the BIOS for pre-boot authentication PINs that have not been cleared from memory.

- Form grabbing based: Form grabbing-based keyloggers log web form submissions by re-cording the web browsing on submit events. This happens when the user completes a form and submits it, usually by clicking a button or hitting enter. This type of keylogger records forms data before it is passed over the Internet.

- Javascript-based: A malicious script tag is injected into a targeted web page, and listens for key events such as `onKeyUp()`. Scripts can be injected via a variety of methods, including cross-site scripting, man-in-the-browser, man-in-the-middle, or a compromise of the re-mote web site.

- Memory-injection-based: Memory Injection (MitB)-based keyloggers perform their log-ging function by altering the memory tables associated with the browser and other system functions. By patching the memory tables or injecting directly into memory, this technique can be used by malware authors to bypass Windows UAC (User Account Control). The Zeus and SpyEye trojans use this method exclusively. Non-Windows systems have protection mechanisms that allow access to locally recorded data from a remote location. Remote communication may be achieved when one of these methods is used:

  ○ Data is uploaded to a website, database or an FTP server.

  ○ Data is periodically emailed to a pre-defined email address.

  ○ Data is wirelessly transmitted employing an attached hardware system.

  ○ The software enables a remote login to the local machine from the Internet or the local network, for data logs stored on the target machine.

Keystroke Logging in Writing Process Research

Keystroke logging is now an established research method for the study of writing processes. Dif-ferent programs have been developed to collect online process data of writing activities, including Inputlog, Scriptlog, and Translog.

Keystroke logging is legitimately used as a suitable research instrument in several writing con-texts. These include studies on cognitive writing processes, which include:

- Descriptions of writing strategies; the writing development of children (with and without writing difficulties),

- Spelling,

- First and second language writing,

- Specialist skill areas such as translation and subtitling.

Keystroke logging can be used to research writing, specifically. It can also be integrated into edu-cational domains for second language learning, programming skills, and typing skills.

Related Features

Software keyloggers may be augmented with features that capture user information without relying on keyboard key presses as the sole input. Some of these features include:

- Clipboard logging: Anything that has been copied to the clipboard can be captured by the program.

- Screen logging: Screenshots are taken to capture graphics-based information. Applications with screen logging abilities may take screenshots of the whole screen, of just one application, or even just around the mouse cursor. They may take these screenshots periodically or in response to user behaviors (for example, when a user clicks the mouse). A practical application that is used by some keyloggers with this screen logging ability, is to take small screenshots around where a mouse has just clicked; thus defeating web-based keyboards (for example, the web-based screen keyboards that are often used by banks), and any web-based on-screen keyboard without screenshot protection.

- Programmatically capturing the text in a control: The Microsoft Windows API allows programs to request the text 'value' in some controls. This means that some passwords may be captured, even if they are hidden behind password masks (usually asterisks).

- The recording of every program/folder/window opened including a screenshot of every website visited.

- The recording of search engines queries, instant messenger conversations, FTP downloads and other Internet-based activities (including the bandwidth used).

Hardware-based Keyloggers

A hardware-based keylogger.

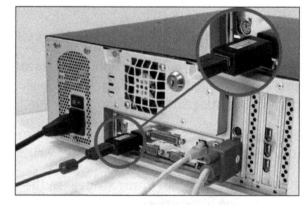

A connected hardware-based keylogger.

Hardware-based keyloggers do not depend upon any software being installed as they exist at a hardware level in a computer system.

- Firmware-based: BIOS-level firmware that handles keyboard events can be modified to record these events as they are processed. Physical and root-level access is required to the machine, and the software loaded into the BIOS needs to be created for the specific hardware that it will be running on.

- Keyboard hardware: Hardware keyloggers are used for keystroke logging utilizing a hardware circuit that is attached somewhere in between the computer keyboard and the computer, typically inline with the keyboard's cable connector. There are also USB connectors based Hardware keyloggers as well as ones for Laptop computers (the Mini-PCI card plugs into the expansion slot of a laptop). More stealthy implementations can be installed or built into standard keyboards so that no device is visible on the external cable. Both types log all keyboard activity to their internal memory, which can be subsequently accessed, for example, by typing in a secret key sequence. A hardware keylogger has an advantage over a software solution: it is not dependent on being installed on the target computer's operating system and therefore will not interfere with any program running on the target machine or be detected by any software. However, its physical presence may be detected if, for example, it is installed outside the case as an inline device between the computer and the keyboard. Some of these implementations can be controlled and monitored remotely using a wireless communication standard.

- Wireless keyboard and mouse sniffers: These passive sniffers collect packets of data being transferred from a wireless keyboard and its receiver. As encryption may be used to secure the wireless communications between the two devices, this may need to be cracked beforehand if the transmissions are to be read. In some cases, this enables an attacker to type arbitrary commands into a victim's computer.

- Keyboard overlays: Criminals have been known to use keyboard overlays on ATMs to capture people's PINs. Each keypress is registered by the keyboard of the ATM as well as the criminal's keypad that is placed over it. The device is designed to look like an integrated part of the machine so that bank customers are unaware of its presence.

- Acoustic keyloggers: Acoustic cryptanalysis can be used to monitor the sound created by someone typing on a computer. Each key on the keyboard makes a subtly different acoustic signature when struck. It is then possible to identify which keystroke signature relates to which keyboard character via statistical methods such as frequency analysis. The repetition frequency of similar acoustic keystroke signatures, the timings between different keyboard strokes and other context information such as the probable language in which the user is writing are used in this analysis to map sounds to letters. A fairly long recording (1000 or more keystrokes) is required so that a big enough sample is collected.

- Electromagnetic emissions: It is possible to capture the electromagnetic emissions of a wired keyboard from up to 20 metres (66 ft) away, without being physically wired to it. In 2009, Swiss researchers tested 11 different USB, PS/2 and laptop keyboards in a semi-anechoic chamber and found them all vulnerable, primarily because of the prohibitive cost of adding shielding during manufacture. The researchers used a wideband receiver to tune into the specific frequency of the emissions radiated from the keyboards.

- Optical surveillance: Optical surveillance, while not a keylogger in the classical sense, is nonetheless an approach that can be used to capture passwords or PINs. A strategically placed camera, such as a hidden surveillance camera at an ATM, can allow a criminal to watch a PIN or password being entered.

- Physical evidence: For a keypad that is used only to enter a security code, the keys which are in actual use will have evidence of use from many fingerprints. A passcode of four digits, if the four digits in question are known, is reduced from 10,000 possibilities to just 24 possibilities (10^4 versus 4! (factorial of 4)). These could then be used on separate occasions for a manual "brute force attack".

- Smartphone sensors: Researchers have demonstrated that it is possible to capture the keystrokes of nearby computer keyboards using only the commodity accelerometer found in smartphones. The attack is made possible by placing a smartphone near a keyboard on the same desk. The smartphone's accelerometer can then detect the vibrations created by typing on the keyboard and then translate this raw accelerometer signal into readable sentences with as much as 80 percent accuracy. The technique involves working through probability by detecting pairs of keystrokes, rather than individual keys. It models "keyboard events" in pairs and then works out whether the pair of keys pressed is on the left or the right side of the keyboard and whether they are close together or far apart on the QWERTY keyboard. Once it has worked this out, it compares the results to a preloaded dictionary where each word has been broken down in the same way. Similar techniques have also been shown to be effective at capturing keystrokes on touchscreen keyboards while in some cases, in combination with gyroscope or with the ambient-light sensor.

Cracking

Writing simple software applications for keylogging can be trivial, and like any nefarious computer program, can be distributed as a trojan horse or as part of a virus. What is not trivial for an attacker, however, is installing a covert keystroke logger without getting caught and downloading data that has been logged without being traced. An attacker that manually connects to a host machine to download logged keystrokes risks being traced. A trojan that sends keylogged data to a fixed e-mail address or IP address risks exposing the attacker.

Trojans

Researchers devised several methods for solving this problem. They presented a deniable password snatching attack in which the keystroke logging trojan is installed using a virus or worm. An attacker who is caught with the virus or worm can claim to be a victim. The cryptotrojan asymmetrically encrypts the pilfered login/password pairs using the public key of the trojan author and covertly broadcasts the resulting ciphertext. They mentioned that the ciphertext can be steganographically encoded and posted to a public bulletin board such as Usenet.

Use by Police

In 2000, the FBI used FlashCrest iSpy to obtain the PGP passphrase of Nicodemo Scarfo, Jr., son of mob boss Nicodemo Scarfo. Also in 2000, the FBI lured two suspected Russian cybercriminals to the US in an elaborate ruse, and captured their usernames and passwords with a keylogger that was covertly installed on a machine that they used to access their computers in Russia. The FBI then used these credentials to hack into the suspects' computers in Russia to obtain evidence to prosecute them.

Countermeasures

The effectiveness of countermeasures varies because keyloggers use a variety of techniques to capture data and the countermeasure needs to be effective against the particular data capture technique. In the case of Windows 10 keylogging from Microsoft it is enough to change some privacy settings on your computer. For example, an on-screen keyboard will be effective against hardware keyloggers, transparency will defeat some—but not all—screen loggers and an anti-spyware application that can only disable hook-based keyloggers will be ineffective against kernel-based keyloggers.

Also, keylogger program authors may be able to update the code to adapt to countermeasures that may have proven to be effective against them.

Anti-keyloggers

An anti-keylogger is a piece of software specifically designed to detect keyloggers on a computer, typically comparing all files in the computer against a database of keyloggers looking for similarities which might signal the presence of a hidden keylogger. As anti-keyloggers have been designed specifically to detect keyloggers, they have the potential to be more effective than conventional antivirus software; some antivirus software do not consider keyloggers to be malware, as under some circumstances a keylogger can be considered a legitimate piece of software.

Live CD/USB

Rebooting the computer using a Live CD or write-protected Live USB is a possible countermeasure against software keyloggers if the CD is clean of malware and the operating system contained on it is secured and fully patched so that it cannot be infected as soon as it is started. Booting a different operating system does not impact the use of a hardware or BIOS based keylogger.

Anti-spyware/Anti-virus Programs

Many anti-spyware applications can detect some software based keyloggers and quarantine, disable or cleanse them. However, because many keylogging programs are legitimate pieces of software under some circumstances, anti-spyware often neglects to label keylogging programs as spyware or a virus. These applications can detect software-based keyloggers based on patterns in executable code, heuristics and keylogger behaviors (such as the use of hooks and certain APIs).

No software-based anti-spyware application can be 100% effective against all keyloggers. Also, software-based anti-spyware cannot defeat non-software keyloggers (for example, hardware keyloggers attached to keyboards will always receive keystrokes before any software-based anti-spyware application).

However, the particular technique that the anti-spyware application uses will influence its potential effectiveness against software keyloggers. As a general rule, anti-spyware applications with higher privileges will defeat keyloggers with lower privileges. For example, a hook-based anti-spyware application cannot defeat a kernel-based keylogger (as the keylogger will receive the keystroke messages before the anti-spyware application), but it could potentially defeat hook- and API-based keyloggers.

Network Monitors

Network monitors (also known as reverse-firewalls) can be used to alert the user whenever an application attempts to make a network connection. This gives the user the chance to prevent the keylogger from "phoning home" with his or her typed information.

Automatic Form Filler Programs

Automatic form-filling programs may prevent keylogging by removing the requirement for a user to type personal details and passwords using the keyboard. Form fillers are primarily designed for web browsers to fill in checkout pages and log users into their accounts. Once the user's account and credit card information has been entered into the program, it will be automatically entered into forms without ever using the keyboard or clipboard, thereby reducing the possibility that private data is being recorded. However, someone with physical access to the machine may still be able to install software that can intercept this information elsewhere in the operating system or while in transit on the network. (Transport Layer Security (TLS) reduces the risk that data in transit may be intercepted by network sniffers and proxy tools).

One-time Passwords (OTP)

Using one-time passwords may be keylogger-safe, as each password is invalidated as soon as it is used. This solution may be useful for someone using a public computer. However, an attacker who has remote control over such a computer can simply wait for the victim to enter his/her credentials before performing unauthorized transactions on their behalf while their session is active.

Security Tokens

Use of smart cards or other security tokens may improve security against replay attacks in the face of a successful keylogging attack, as accessing protected information would require both the (hardware) security token *as well as* the appropriate password/passphrase. Knowing the keystrokes, mouse actions, display, clipboard, etc. used on one computer will not subsequently help an attacker gain access to the protected resource. Some security tokens work as a type of hardware-assisted one-time password system, and others implement a cryptographic challenge-response authentication, which can improve security in a manner conceptually similar to one time passwords. Smartcard readers and their associated keypads for PIN entry may be vulnerable to keystroke logging through a so-called supply chain attack where an attacker substitutes the card reader/PIN entry hardware for one which records the user's PIN.

On-screen Keyboards

Most on-screen keyboards (such as the on-screen keyboard that comes with Windows XP) send normal keyboard event messages to the external target program to type text. Software key loggers can log these typed characters sent from one program to another. Additionally, keylogging software can take screenshots of what is displayed on the screen (periodically, and upon each mouse click), which means that although certainly a useful security measure, an on-screen keyboard will not protect from all keyloggers.

Keystroke Interference Software

Keystroke interference software is also available. These programs attempt to trick keyloggers by introducing random keystrokes, although this simply results in the keylogger recording more information than it needs to. An attacker has the task of extracting the keystrokes of interest—the security of this mechanism, specifically how well it stands up to cryptanalysis, is unclear.

Speech Recognition

Similar to on-screen keyboards, speech-to-text conversion software can also be used against keyloggers, since there are no typing or mouse movements involved. The weakest point of using voice-recognition software may be how the software sends the recognized text to target software after the recognition took place.

Handwriting Recognition and Mouse Gestures

Also, many PDAs and lately tablet PCs can already convert pen (also called stylus) movements on their touchscreens to computer understandable text successfully. Mouse gestures use this principle by using mouse movements instead of a stylus. Mouse gesture programs convert these strokes to user-definable actions, such as typing text. Similarly, graphics tablets and light pens can be used to input these gestures, however, these are less common every day.

The same potential weakness of speech recognition applies to this technique as well.

Macro Expanders/Recorders

With the help of many programs, a seemingly meaningless text can be expanded to a meaningful text and most of the time context-sensitively can be expanded when a web browser window has the focus. The biggest weakness of this technique is that these programs send their keystrokes directly to the target program. However, this can be overcome by using the 'alternating', i.e. sending mouse clicks to non-responsive areas of the target program, sending meaningless keys, sending another mouse click to the target area (e.g. password field) and switching back-and-forth.

Deceptive Typing

Alternating between typing the login credentials and typing characters somewhere else in the focus window can cause a keylogger to record more information than they need to, although this could easily be filtered out by an attacker. Similarly, a user can move their cursor using the mouse during typing, causing the logged keystrokes to be in the wrong order e.g., by typing a password beginning with the last letter and then using the mouse to move the cursor for each subsequent letter. Lastly, someone can also use context menus to remove, cut, copy, and paste parts of the typed text without using the keyboard. An attacker who can capture only parts of a password will have a larger key space to attack if he chose to execute a brute-force attack.

Another very similar technique uses the fact that any selected text portion is replaced by the next key typed. e.g., if the password is "secret", one could type "s", then some dummy keys "asdf". Then, these dummies could be selected with the mouse, and the next character from the password "e" is typed, which replaces the dummies "asdf".

These techniques assume incorrectly that keystroke logging software cannot directly monitor the clipboard, the selected text in a form, or take a screenshot every time a keystroke or mouse click occurs. They may, however, be effective against some hardware keyloggers.

RANSOMWARE

Ransomware is a type of malware from cryptovirology that threatens to publish the victim's data or perpetually block access to it unless a ransom is paid. While some simple ransomware may lock the system in a way which is not difficult for a knowledgeable person to reverse, more advanced malware uses a technique called cryptoviral extortion, in which it encrypts the victim's files, making them inaccessible, and demands a ransom payment to decrypt them. In a properly implemented cryptoviral extortion attack, recovering the files without the decryption key is an intractable problem – and difficult to trace digital currencies such as Ukash or Bitcoin and other cryptocurrency are used for the ransoms, making tracing and prosecuting the perpetrators difficult.

Ransomware attacks are typically carried out using a Trojan that is disguised as a legitimate file that the user is tricked into downloading or opening when it arrives as an email attachment. However, one high-profile example, the "WannaCry worm", travelled automatically between computers without user interaction.

Starting from around 2012 the use of ransomware scams has grown internationally. There were 181.5 million ransomware attacks in the first six months of 2018. This marks a 229% increase over this same time frame in 2017. In June 2014, vendor McAfee released data showing that it had collected more than double the number of samples of ransomware that quarter than it had in the same quarter of the previous year. CryptoLocker was particularly successful, procuring an estimated US $3 million before it was taken down by authorities, and CryptoWall was estimated by the US Federal Bureau of Investigation (FBI) to have accrued over US $18 million by June 2015.

Operation

The concept of file-encrypting ransomware was invented and implemented by Young and Yung at Columbia University and was presented at the 1996 IEEE Security & Privacy conference. It is called *cryptoviral extortion* and it was inspired by the fictional facehugger in the movie *Alien*. Cryptoviral extortion is the following three-round protocol carried out between the attacker and the victim:

1. [attacker→victim]- The attacker generates a key pair and places the corresponding public key in the malware. The malware is released.

2. [victim→attacker]- To carry out the cryptoviral extortion attack, the malware generates a random symmetric key and encrypts the victim's data with it. It uses the public key in the malware to encrypt the symmetric key. This is known as hybrid encryption and it results in a small asymmetric ciphertext as well as the symmetric ciphertext of the victim's data. It zeroizes the symmetric key and the original plaintext data to prevent recovery. It puts up a message to the user that includes the asymmetric ciphertext and how to pay the ransom. The victim sends the asymmetric ciphertext and e-money to the attacker.

3. [attacker→victim]- The attacker receives the payment, deciphers the asymmetric ciphertext with the attacker's private key, and sends the symmetric key to the victim. The victim deciphers the encrypted data with the needed symmetric key thereby completing the cryptovirology attack.

The symmetric key is randomly generated and will not assist other victims. At no point is the attacker's private key exposed to victims and the victim need only send a very small ciphertext (the encrypted symmetric-cipher key) to the attacker.

Ransomware attacks are typically carried out using a Trojan, entering a system through, for example, a malicious attachment, embedded link in a Phishing email, or a vulnerability in a network service. The program then runs a payload, which locks the system in some fashion, or claims to lock the system but does not (e.g., a scareware program). Payloads may display a fake warning purportedly by an entity such as a law enforcement agency, falsely claiming that the system has been used for illegal activities, contains content such as pornography and "pirated" media.

Some payloads consist simply of an application designed to lock or restrict the system until payment is made, typically by setting the Windows Shell to itself, or even modifying the master boot record and partition table to prevent the operating system from booting until it is repaired. The most sophisticated payloads encrypt files, with many using strong encryption to encrypt the victim's files in such a way that only the malware author has the needed decryption key.

Payment is virtually always the goal, and the victim is coerced into paying for the ransomware to be removed either by supplying a program that can decrypt the files, or by sending an unlock code that undoes the payload's changes. While the attacker may simply take the money without returning the victim's files, it is in the attacker's best interest to perform the decryption as agreed, since victims will stop sending payments if it becomes known that they serve no purpose. A key element in making ransomware work for the attacker is a convenient payment system that is hard to trace. A range of such payment methods have been used, including wire transfers, premium-rate text messages, pre-paid voucher services such as paysafecard, and the digital currency bitcoin.

Notable Examples

Reveton

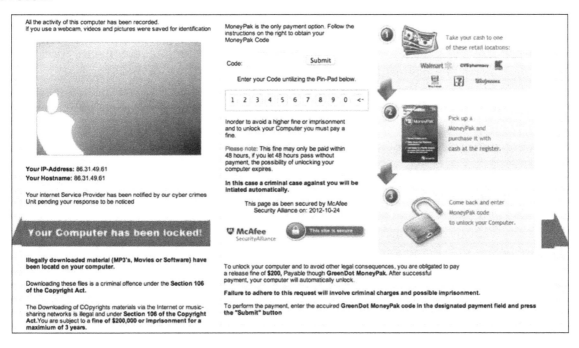

In 2012, a major ransomware Trojan known as Reveton began to spread. Based on the Citadel Trojan (which itself, is based on the Zeus Trojan), its payload displays a warning purportedly from a law enforcement agency claiming that the computer has been used for illegal activities, such as downloading unlicensed software or child pornography. Due to this behaviour, it is commonly referred to as the "Police Trojan". The warning informs the user that to unlock their system, they would have to pay a fine using a voucher from an anonymous prepaid cash service such as Ukash or paysafecard. To increase the illusion that the computer is being tracked by law enforcement, the screen also displays the computer's IP address, while some versions display footage from a victim's webcam to give the illusion that the user is being recorded.

Reveton initially began spreading in various European countries in early 2012. Variants were localized with templates branded with the logos of different law enforcement organizations based on the user's country; for example, variants used in the United Kingdom contained the branding of organizations such as the Metropolitan Police Service and the Police National E-Crime Unit. Another version contained the logo of the royalty collection society PRS for Music, which specifically accused the user of illegally downloading music. In a statement warning the public about the malware, the Metropolitan Police clarified that they would never lock a computer in such a way as part of an investigation.

In May 2012, Trend Micro threat researchers discovered templates for variations for the United States and Canada, suggesting that its authors may have been planning to target users in North America. By August 2012, a new variant of Reveton began to spread in the United States, claiming to require the payment of a $200 fine to the FBI using a MoneyPak card. In February 2013, a Russian citizen was arrested in Dubai by Spanish authorities for his connection to a crime ring that had been using Reveton; ten other individuals were arrested on money laundering charges. In August 2014, Avast Software reported that it had found new variants of Reveton that also distribute password-stealing malware as part of its payload.

CryptoLocker

Encrypting ransomware reappeared in September 2013 with a Trojan known as *CryptoLocker*, which generated a 2048-bit RSA key pair and uploaded in turn to a command-and-control server, and used to encrypt files using a whitelist of specific file extensions. The malware threatened to delete the private key if a payment of Bitcoin or a pre-paid cash voucher was not made within 3 days of the infection. Due to the extremely large key size it uses, analysts and those affected by the Trojan considered CryptoLocker extremely difficult to repair. Even after the deadline passed, the private key could still be obtained using an online tool, but the price would increase to 10 BTC— which cost approximately US$2300 as of November 2013.

CryptoLocker was isolated by the seizure of the Gameover ZeuS botnet as part of Operation Tovar, as officially announced by the U.S. Department of Justice on 2 June 2014. The Department of Justice also publicly issued an indictment against the Russian hacker Evgeniy Bogachev for his alleged involvement in the botnet. It was estimated that at least US$3 million was extorted with the malware before the shutdown.

CryptoLocker.F and TorrentLocker

In September 2014, a wave of ransomware Trojans surfaced that first targeted users in Australia, under the names *CryptoWall* and *CryptoLocker* (which is, as with CryptoLocker 2.0, unrelated to the original CryptoLocker). The Trojans spread via fraudulent e-mails claiming to be failed parcel delivery notices from Australia Post; to evade detection by automatic e-mail scanners that follow all links on a page to scan for malware, this variant was designed to require users to visit a web page and enter a CAPTCHA code before the payload is actually downloaded, preventing such automated processes from being able to scan the payload. Symantec determined that these new variants, which it identified as *CryptoLocker.F*, were again, unrelated to the original CryptoLocker due to differences in their operation. A notable victim of the Trojans was the Australian Broadcasting Corporation; live programming on its television news channel ABC News 24 was disrupted for half an hour and shifted to Melbourne studios due to a CryptoWall infection on computers at its Sydney studio.

Another Trojan in this wave, TorrentLocker, initially contained a design flaw comparable to CryptoDefense; it used the same keystream for every infected computer, making the encryption trivial to overcome. However, this flaw was later fixed. By late-November 2014, it was estimated that over 9,000 users had been infected by TorrentLocker in Australia alone, trailing only Turkey with 11,700 infections.

CryptoWall

Another major ransomware Trojan targeting Windows, CryptoWall, first appeared in 2014. One strain of CryptoWall was distributed as part of a malvertising campaign on the Zedo ad network in late-September 2014 that targeted several major websites; the ads redirected to rogue websites that used browser plugin exploits to download the payload. A Barracuda Networks researcher also noted that the payload was signed with a digital signature in an effort to appear trustworthy to security software. CryptoWall 3.0 used a payload written in JavaScript as part of an email attachment, which downloads executables disguised as JPG images. To further evade detection, the malware creates new instances of explorer.exe and svchost.exe to communicate with its servers. When encrypting files, the malware also deletes volume shadow copies and installs spyware that steals passwords and Bitcoin wallets.

The FBI reported in June 2015 that nearly 1,000 victims had contacted the bureau's Internet Crime Complaint Center to report CryptoWall infections, and estimated losses of at least $18 million.

The most recent version, CryptoWall 4.0, enhanced its code to avoid antivirus detection, and encrypts not only the data in files but also the file names.

Fusob

Fusob is one of the major mobile ransomware families. Between April 2015 and March 2016, about 56 percent of accounted mobile ransomware was Fusob.

Like a typical mobile ransomware, it employs scare tactics to extort people to pay a ransom. The program pretends to be an accusatory authority, demanding the victim to pay a fine from $100 to $200 USD or otherwise face a fictitious charge. Rather surprisingly, Fusob suggests using iTunes gift cards for payment. Also, a timer clicking down on the screen adds to the users' anxiety as well.

In order to infect devices, Fusob masquerades as a pornographic video player. Thus, victims, thinking it is harmless, unwittingly download Fusob.

When Fusob is installed, it first checks the language used in the device. If it uses Russian or certain Eastern European languages, Fusob does nothing. Otherwise, it proceeds on to lock the device and demand ransom. Among victims, about 40% of them are in Germany with the United Kingdom and the United States following with 14.5% and 11.4% respectively.

Fusob has lots in common with Small, which is another major family of mobile ransomware. They represented over 93% of mobile ransomware between 2015 and 2016.

WannaCry

In May 2017, the WannaCry ransomware attack spread through the Internet, using an exploit vector named EternalBlue, which was allegedly leaked from the U.S. National Security Agency. The ransomware attack, unprecedented in scale, infected more than 230,000 computers in over 150 countries, using 20 different languages to demand money from users using Bitcoin cryptocurrency. WannaCry demanded US$300 per computer. The attack affected Telefónica and several other large companies in Spain, as well as parts of the British National Health Service (NHS), where at least 16 hospitals had to turn away patients or cancel scheduled operations, FedEx, Deutsche Bahn, Honda, Renault, as well as the Russian Interior Ministry and Russian telecom MegaFon. The attackers gave their victims a 7-day deadline from the day their computers got infected, after which the encrypted files would be deleted.

Petya

Petya was first discovered in March 2016; unlike other forms of encrypting ransomware, the malware aimed to infect the master boot record, installing a payload which encrypts the file tables of the NTFS file system the next time that the infected system boots, blocking the system from booting into Windows at all until the ransom is paid. Check Point reported that despite what it believed to be an innovative evolution in ransomware design, it had resulted in relatively-fewer infections than other ransomware active around the same time frame.

On 27 June 2017, a heavily modified version of Petya was used for a global cyberattack primarily targeting Ukraine (but affecting many countries). This version had been modified to propagate using the same EternalBlue exploit that was used by WannaCry. Due to another design change, it is also unable to actually unlock a system after the ransom is paid; this led to security analysts speculating that the attack was not meant to generate illicit profit, but to simply cause disruption.

Bad Rabbit

On 24 October 2017, some users in Russia and Ukraine reported a new ransomware attack, named "Bad Rabbit", which follows a similar pattern to WannaCry and Petya by encrypting the user's file tables and then demands a BitCoin payment to decrypt them. ESET believed the ransomware to have been distributed by a bogus update to Adobe Flash software. Among agencies that were affected by the ransomware were: Interfax, Odessa International Airport, Kiev Metro, and the Ministry of Infrastructure of Ukraine. As it used corporate network structures to spread, the ransomware was also discovered in other countries, including Turkey, Germany, Poland, Japan, South Korea, and the United States. Experts believed the ransomware attack was tied to the Petya attack in Ukraine (especially because Bad Rabbit's code has many overlapping and analogical elements to the code of Petya/NotPetya, appending to CrowdStrike Bad Rabbit and NotPetya's DLL (dynamic link library) share 67 percent of the same code) though the only identity to the culprits are the names of characters from the *Game of Thrones* series embedded within the code.

Security experts found that the ransomware did not use the EternalBlue exploit to spread, and a simple method to vaccinate an unaffected machine running older Windows versions was found by 24 October 2017. Further, the sites that had been used to spread the bogus Flash updating have gone offline or removed the problematic files within a few days of its discovery, effectively killing off the spread of Bad Rabbit.

SamSam

In 2016, a new strain of ransomware emerged that was targeting JBoss servers. This strain, named "SamSam", was found to bypass the process of phishing or illicit downloads in favor of exploiting vulnerabilities on weak servers. The malware uses a Remote Desktop Protocol brute-force attack to guess weak passwords until one is broken. The virus has been behind attacks on government and healthcare targets, with notable hacks occurring against the town of Farmington, New Mexico, the Colorado Department of Transportation, Davidson County, North Carolina, and most recently, a major breach of security on the infrastructure of Atlanta.

Mohammad Mehdi Shah Mansouri (born in Qom, Iran in 1991) and Faramarz Shahi Savandi (born in Shiraz, Iran, in 1984) are wanted by the FBI for allegedly launching SamSam ransomware. The two have allegedly made $6 million from extortion and caused over $30 million in damages using the malware.

Mitigation

As with other forms of malware, security software (antivirus software) might not detect a ransomware payload, or, especially in the case of encrypting payloads, only after encryption is under way or complete, particularly if a new version unknown to the protective software is distributed. If an attack is suspected or detected in its early stages, it takes some time for encryption to take place; immediate removal of the malware (a relatively simple process) before it has completed would stop further damage to data, without salvaging any already lost.

Security experts have suggested precautionary measures for dealing with ransomware. Using software or other security policies to block known payloads from launching will help to prevent infection, but will not protect against all attacks Keeping "offline" backups of data stored in locations inaccessible from any potentially infected computer, such as external storage drives or devices that do not have any access to any network (including the Internet), prevents them from being accessed by the ransomware. Installing security updates issued by software vendors can mitigate the vulnerabilities leveraged by certain strains to propagate. Other measures include cyber hygiene – exercising caution when opening e-mail attachments and links, network segmentation, and keeping critical computers isolated from networks. Furthermore, to mitigate the spread of ransomware measures of infection control can be applied. Such may include disconnecting infected machines from all networks, educational programs, effective communication channels, malware surveillance and ways of collective participation.

File System Defenses against Ransomware

A number of file systems keep snapshots of the data they hold, which can be used to recover the contents of files from a time prior to the ransomware attack in the event the ransomware doesn't disable it.

- On Windows, the Volume shadow copy (VSS) is often used to store backups of data; ransomware often targets these snapshots to prevent recovery and therefore it is often advisable to disable user access to the user tool *VSSadmin.exe* to reduce the risk that ransomware can disable or delete past copies.

- On Windows 10, users can add specific directories or files to Controlled Folder Access in Windows Defender to protect them from ransomware. It is advised to add backup and other important directories to Controlled Folder Access.

- File servers running ZFS are almost universally immune to ransomware, because ZFS is capable of snapshotting even a large file system many times an hour, and these snapshots are immutable (read only) and easily rolled back or files recovered in the event of data corruption. In general, only an administrator can delete (but cannot modify) snapshots.

File Decryption and Recovery

There are a number of tools intended specifically to decrypt files locked by ransomware, although successful recovery may not be possible. If the same encryption key is used for all files, decryption tools use files for which there are both uncorrupted backups and encrypted copies (a known-plaintext attack in the jargon of cryptanalysis. But, it only works when the cipher the attacker used was weak to begin with, being vulnerable to known-plaintext attack); recovery of the key, if it is possible, may take several days. Free ransomware decryption tools can help decrypt files encrypted by the following forms of ransomware: AES_NI, Alcatraz Locker, Apocalypse, BadBlock, Bart, BTCWare, Crypt888, CryptoMix, CrySiS, EncrypTile, FindZip, Globe, Hidden Tear, Jigsaw, LambdaLocker, Legion, NoobCrypt, Stampado, SZFLocker, TeslaCrypt, XData.

In addition, old copies of files may exist on the disk, which has been previously deleted. In some cases, these deleted versions may still be recoverable using software designed for that purpose.

The Growing Threat of Malware

Ransomware malicious software has evolved since its beginnings when it was confined to one or two countries in Eastern Europe which then spread across the Atlantic to the United States and Canada. The first versions of this type of malware used various techniques to disable the computers by locking the victims system machine (Locker Ransomware) . Some examples of how this ransomware works, include; locking the screen by displaying a message from a branch of local law enforcement indicating the user's lines like "You have browsed illicit materials and must pay a fine". They were first seen in Russia by year 2009 claiming to be a message from Microsoft. They also used to request a payment by sending an SMS message to a premium rate number. The next variant displayed pornographic image content and demanded payment for the removal of it.

In 2011 the tactics changed, the attackers started to use electronic payment methods and they added more languages to the messages which also changed based on the user's location which was obtained by geo-locating the user's IP addresses.

Not only end users are affected by these attacks. Corporations, private entities, government, and even hospitals are also affected. For example, in healthcare (although 2015 was the year in which the largest ePHI data breaches occurred according to the ONC) 2016 was the year that ransomware started to increase exponentially in this market. According to the 2017 Internet Security Threat Report from Symantec Corp, ransomware affects not only IT systems but also patient care, clinical operations, and billing. Online criminals have found "there was easy money to be made in healthcare," according to the Symantec report, which was developed with data from insurance claims and the U.S. Department of Health and Human Services (HHS).

Ransomware is growing rapidly across the internet users but also for the IoT environment which creates a challenging problem to the INFOSEC while increasing the attack surface area. They are evolving into more sophisticated attacks and, they are becoming more resistant; at the same time, they are also more accessible than ever. Today, for a cheap price, the attackers have access to ransomware as a service. The big problem is that millions of dollars are lost by some organizations and industries that have decided to pay, such as the Hollywood Presbyterian Medical Center and the MedStar Health. At the end, the pressure to offer services to the patients and keep their lives is so critical that they are forced to pay, and the attacker knows that. The problem here is that by paying the ransom, they are funding the cybercrime.

According to Symantec 2019 ISTR report, for the first time since 2013, in 2018 there was an observed decrease in ransomware activity with a drop of 20 percent. Before 2017, consumers were the preferred victims, but in 2017 this changed dramatically, it moved to the enterprises. In 2018 this path accelerated with 81 percent infections which represented a 12 percent increase. The common distribution method today is based on email campaigns.

Cyber awareness training is crucial to detecting attacks, whereas technology cannot protect against careless or foolish behavior. It is important for organizations to help their users recognize malicious contact whereas ransomware is typically introduced through email and social engineering techniques to either download a file, provide key sensitive information or take some action that will bring harm to the organization. According to KnowBe4 Osterman report, there are number of approaches to security awareness training that are practiced by organizations and managed by security teams. There is the break room approach which are special meetings periodically held to talk about security; monthly security videos with short snippets of security information; simulated phishing tests which target users with internal phishing messages; human firewall approach where everyone is subject to simulated phishing and those employees that are prone to attack are identified; and then there is the do-nothing approach where cyber awareness training does not exist in the organization.

An effective and successful cyber awareness training program must be sponsored from the top of the organization with supporting policies and procedures which effectively outline ramifications of non-compliance, frequency of training and a process for acknowledgement of training. Without sponsorship from the "C-level" executives the training cannot be ignored. Other factors that are key to a successful Cyber Awareness Training program is to establish a baseline identifying the level of knowledge of the organization to establish where the users are in their knowledge prior to training and after. Whichever approach an organization decides to implement, it is important that the organization has policies and procedures in place that provide training that is up to date, performed frequently and has the backing of the entire organization from the top down.

Investment in technology to detect and stop these threats must be maintained, but along with that we need to remember and focus on our weakest link, which is the user.

PHISHING

Phishing is the fraudulent attempt to obtain sensitive information such as usernames, passwords and credit card details by disguising oneself as a trustworthy entity in an electronic communication. Typically carried out by email spoofing or instant messaging, it often directs users to enter personal information at a fake website which matches the look and feel of the legitimate site.

TrustedBank™

Dear valued customer of TrustedBank,

We have recieved notice that you have recently attempted to withdraw the following amount from your checking account while in another country: $135.25.

If this information is not correct, someone unknown may have access to your account. As a safety measure, please visit our website via the link below to verify your personal information:

http://www.trustedbank.com/general/custverifyinfo.asp

Once you have done this, our fraud department will work to resolve this discrepency. We are happy you have chosen us to do business with.

Thank you,
TrustedBank

An example of a phishing email, disguised as an official email from a (fictional) bank.

Phishing is an example of social engineering techniques being used to deceive users. Users are often lured by communications purporting to be from trusted parties such as social web sites, auction sites, banks, online payment processors or IT administrators.

Attempts to deal with phishing incidents include legislation, user training, public awareness, and technical security measures (the latter being due to phishing attacks frequently exploiting weaknesses in current web security).

The word itself is a neologism created as a homophone of *fishing*.

Technique

Phishing Types

1. Spear Phishing:

Phishing attempts directed at specific individuals or companies have been termed *spear phishing*. In contrast to bulk phishing, spear phishing attackers often gather and use personal information about their target to increase their probability of success.

Threat Group-4127 (Fancy Bear) used spear phishing tactics to target email accounts linked to Hillary Clinton's 2016 presidential campaign. They attacked more than 1,800 Google accounts and implemented the accounts-google.com domain to threaten targeted users.

2. Whaling:

The term whaling refers to spear phishing attacks directed specifically at senior executives and other high-profile targets. In these cases, the content will be crafted to target an upper manager and the person's role in the company. The content of a whaling attack email may be an executive issue such as a subpoena or customer complaint.

3. Clone Phishing:

Clone phishing is a type of phishing attack whereby a legitimate, and previously delivered, email containing an attachment or link has had its content and recipient address(es) taken and used to create an almost identical or cloned email. The attachment or link within the email is replaced with a malicious version and then sent from an email address spoofed to appear to come from the original sender. It may claim to be a resend of the original or an updated version to the original. Typically this requires either the sender or recipient to have been previously hacked for the malicious third party to obtain the legitimate email.

Link Manipulation

Most methods of phishing use some form of technical deception designed to make a link in an email (and the spoofed website it leads to) appear to belong to the spoofed organization. Misspelled URLs or the use of subdomains are common tricks used by phishers. In the following example URL, `http://www.yourbank.example.com/`, it appears as though the URL will take you to the *example* section of the *yourbank* website; actually this URL points to the "*yourbank*" (i.e. phishing) section of the *example* website. Another common trick is to make the displayed text for a link (the text between the <A> tags) suggest a reliable destination, when the link actually goes to the phishers' site. Many desktop email clients and web browsers will show a link's target URL in the status bar while hovering the mouse over it. This behavior, however, may in some circumstances be overridden by the phisher. Equivalent mobile apps generally do not have this preview feature.

Internationalized domain names (IDN) can be exploited via IDN spoofing or homograph attacks, to create web addresses visually identical to a legitimate site, that lead instead to malicious version. Phishers have taken advantage of a similar risk, using open URL redirectors on the websites of trusted organizations to disguise malicious URLs with a trusted domain. Even digital certificates do not solve this problem because it is quite possible for a phisher to purchase a valid certificate and subsequently change content to spoof a genuine website, or, to host the phish site without SSL at all.

Filter Evasion

Phishers have sometimes used images instead of text to make it harder for anti-phishing filters to detect the text commonly used in phishing emails. In response, more sophisticated anti-phishing filters are able to recover hidden text in images using OCR (optical character recognition).

Website Forgery

Some phishing scams use JavaScript commands in order to alter the address bar of the website they lead to. This is done either by placing a picture of a legitimate URL over the address bar, or by closing the original bar and opening up a new one with the legitimate URL.

An attacker can also potentially use flaws in a trusted website's own scripts against the victim. These types of attacks (known as cross-site scripting) are particularly problematic, because they direct the user to sign in at their bank or service's own web page, where everything from the web address to the security certificates appears correct. In reality, the link to the website is crafted to carry out the attack, making it very difficult to spot without specialist knowledge. Such a flaw was used in 2006 against PayPal.

To avoid anti-phishing techniques that scan websites for phishing-related text, phishers sometimes use Flash-based websites (a technique known as phlashing). These look much like the real website, but hide the text in a multimedia object.

Covert Redirect

Covert redirect is a subtle method to perform phishing attacks that makes links appear legitimate, but actually redirect a victim to an attacker's website. The flaw is usually masqueraded under a log-in popup based on an affected site's domain. It can affect OAuth 2.0 and OpenID based on well-known exploit parameters as well. This often makes use of open redirect and XSS vulnerabilities in the third-party application websites. Users may also be redirected to phishing websites covertly through malicious browser extensions.

Normal phishing attempts can be easy to spot because the malicious page's URL will usually be different from the real site link. For covert redirect, an attacker could use a real website instead by corrupting the site with a malicious login popup dialogue box. This makes covert redirect different from others.

For example, suppose a victim clicks a malicious phishing link beginning with Facebook. A popup window from Facebook will ask whether the victim would like to authorize the app. If the victim chooses to authorize the app, a "token" will be sent to the attacker and the victim's personal sensitive information could be exposed. These information may include the email address, birth date, contacts, and work history. In case the "token" has greater privilege, the attacker could obtain more sensitive information including the mailbox, online presence, and friends list. Worse still, the attacker may possibly control and operate the user's account. Even if the victim does not choose to authorize the app, he or she will still get redirected to a website controlled by the attacker. This could potentially further compromise the victim.

This vulnerability was discovered by Wang Jing, a Mathematics Ph.D. student at School of Physical and Mathematical Sciences in Nanyang Technological University in Singapore. Covert redirect is a notable security flaw, though it is not a threat to the Internet worth significant attention.

Social Engineering

Users can be encouraged to click on various kinds of unexpected content for a variety of technical and social reasons. For example, a malicious attachment might masquerade as a benign linked

Google doc. Alternatively users might be outraged by a fake news story, click a link and become infected.

Voice Phishing

Not all phishing attacks require a fake website. Messages that claimed to be from a bank told users to dial a phone number regarding problems with their bank accounts. Once the phone number (owned by the phisher, and provided by a voice over IP service) was dialed, prompts told users to enter their account numbers and PIN. Vishing (voice phishing) sometimes uses fake caller-ID data to give the appearance that calls come from a trusted organization.

Other Techniques

- Another attack used successfully is to forward the client to a bank's legitimate website, then to place a popup window requesting credentials on top of the page in a way that makes many users think the bank is requesting this sensitive information.

- Tabnabbing takes advantage of tabbed browsing, with multiple open tabs. This method silently redirects the user to the affected site. This technique operates in reverse to most phishing techniques in that it does not directly take the user to the fraudulent site, but instead loads the fake page in one of the browser's open tabs.

Anti-phishing

There are anti-phishing websites which publish exact messages that have been recently circulating the internet, such as FraudWatch International and Millersmiles. Such sites often provide specific details about the particular messages.

As recently as 2007, the adoption of anti-phishing strategies by businesses needing to protect personal and financial information was low. Now there are several different techniques to combat phishing, including legislation and technology created specifically to protect against phishing. These techniques include steps that can be taken by individuals, as well as by organizations. Phone, web site, and email phishing can now be reported to authorities.

User Training

People can be trained to recognize phishing attempts, and to deal with them through a variety of approaches. Such education can be effective, especially where training emphasises conceptual knowledge and provides direct feedback.

Many organisations run regular simulated phishing campaigns targeting their staff to measure the effectiveness of their training.

People can take steps to avoid phishing attempts by slightly modifying their browsing habits. When contacted about an account needing to be "verified" (or any other topic used by phishers), it is a sensible precaution to contact the company from which the email apparently originates to check that the email is legitimate. Alternatively, the address that the individual knows is the company's genuine website can be typed into the address bar of the browser, rather than trusting any hyperlinks in the suspected phishing message.

Nearly all legitimate e-mail messages from companies to their customers contain an item of information that is not readily available to phishers. Some companies, for example PayPal, always address their customers by their username in emails, so if an email addresses the recipient in a generic fashion ("*Dear PayPal customer*") it is likely to be an attempt at phishing. Furthermore, PayPal offers various methods to determine spoof emails and advises users to forward suspicious emails to their spoof@PayPal.com domain to investigate and warn other customers. However it is it unsafe to assume that the presence of personal information alone guarantees that a message is legitimate, and some studies have shown that the presence of personal information does not significantly affect the success rate of phishing attacks; which suggests that most people do not pay attention to such details.

Emails from banks and credit card companies often include partial account numbers. However, recent research has shown that the public do not typically distinguish between the first few digits and the last few digits of an account number—a significant problem since the first few digits are often the same for all clients of a financial institution. The Anti-Phishing Working Group produces regular report on trends in phishing attacks.

Technical Approaches

A wide range of technical approaches are available to prevent phishing attacks reaching users or to prevent them from successfully capturing sensitive information.

Filtering out Phishing Mail

Specialized spam filters can reduce the number of phishing emails that reach their addressees' inboxes. These filters use a number of techniques including machine learning and natural language processing approaches to classify phishing emails, and reject email with forged addresses.

Browsers Alerting Users to Fraudulent Websites

Another popular approach to fighting phishing is to maintain a list of known phishing sites and to check websites against the list. One such service is the Safe Browsing service. Web browsers such as Google Chrome, Internet Explorer 7, Mozilla Firefox 2.0, Safari 3.2, and Opera all contain this type of anti-phishing measure. Firefox 2 used Google anti-phishing software. Opera 9.1 uses live blacklists from Phishtank, cyscon and GeoTrust, as well as live whitelists from GeoTrust. Some implementations of this approach send the visited URLs to a central service to be checked, which has raised concerns about privacy. According to a report by Mozilla in late 2006, Firefox 2 was found to be more effective than Internet Explorer 7 at detecting fraudulent sites in a study by an independent software testing company.

Screenshot of Firefox 2.0.0.1 Phishing suspicious site warning.

An approach introduced in mid-2006 involves switching to a special DNS service that filters out known phishing domains: this will work with any browser, and is similar in principle to using a hosts file to block web adverts.

To mitigate the problem of phishing sites impersonating a victim site by embedding its images (such as logos), several site owners have altered the images to send a message to the visitor that a site may be fraudulent. The image may be moved to a new filename and the original permanently replaced, or a server can detect that the image was not requested as part of normal browsing, and instead send a warning image.

Augmenting Password Logins

The Bank of America website is one of several that asks users to select a personal image (marketed as SiteKey) and displays this user-selected image with any forms that request a password. Users of the bank's online services are instructed to enter a password only when they see the image they selected. However, several studies suggest that few users refrain from entering their passwords when images are absent. In addition, this feature (like other forms of two-factor authentication) is susceptible to other attacks, such as those suffered by Scandinavian bank Nordea in late 2005, and Citibank in 2006.

A similar system, in which an automatically generated "Identity Cue" consisting of a colored word within a colored box is displayed to each website user, is in use at other financial institutions.

Security skins are a related technique that involves overlaying a user-selected image onto the login form as a visual cue that the form is legitimate. Unlike the website-based image schemes, however, the image itself is shared only between the user and the browser, and not between the user and the website. The scheme also relies on a mutual authentication protocol, which makes it less vulnerable to attacks that affect user-only authentication schemes.

Still another technique relies on a dynamic grid of images that is different for each login attempt. The user must identify the pictures that fit their pre-chosen categories (such as dogs, cars and flowers). Only after they have correctly identified the pictures that fit their categories are they allowed to enter their alphanumeric password to complete the login. Unlike the static images used on the Bank of America website, a dynamic image-based authentication method creates a one-time passcode for the login, requires active participation from the user, and is very difficult for a phishing website to correctly replicate because it would need to display a different grid of randomly generated images that includes the user's secret categories.

Monitoring and Takedown

Several companies offer banks and other organizations likely to suffer from phishing scams round-the-clock services to monitor, analyze and assist in shutting down phishing websites. Individuals can contribute by reporting phishing to both volunteer and industry groups, such as cyscon or PhishTank. Individuals can also contribute by reporting phone phishing attempts to Phone Phishing, Federal Trade Commission. Phishing web pages and emails can be reported to Google. The Internet Crime Complaint Center noticeboard carries phishing and ransomware alerts.

Transaction Verification and Signing

Solutions have also emerged using the mobile phone (smartphone) as a second channel for verification and authorization of banking transactions.

Multi Factor Authentication

Organisations can implement two factor or multi-factor authentication (MFA), which requires a user to use at least 2 factors when logging in. (For example, a user must both present a smart card and a password). This mitigates some risk, in the event of a successful phishing attack, the stolen password on its own cannot be reused to further breach the protected system. However, there are several attack methods which can defeat many of the typical systems. MFA schemes such as WebAuthn address this issue by design.

Email Content Redaction

Organizations that prioritize security over convenience can require users of its computers to use an email client that redacts URLs from email messages, thus making it impossible for the reader of the email to click on a link, or even copy a URL. While this may result in an inconvenience, it does almost completely eliminate email phishing attacks.

Limitations of Technical Responses

An article in *Forbes* in August 2014 argues that the reason phishing problems persist even after a decade of anti-phishing technologies being sold is that phishing is "a technological medium to exploit human weaknesses" and that technology cannot fully compensate for human weaknesses.

INFORMATION PROTECTION METHODS

There are several groups of protection methods, including:

- Obstacle to the alleged intruder through physical and software means.

- Management or influence on the elements of a protected system.

- Masking or data transformation with the use of cryptographic methods.

- Regulation or the development of legislation and a set of measures aimed at encouraging proper behavior of users working with databases.

- Enforcement or creation of conditions under which a user will be forced to comply with the rules for handling data.

- Encouragement or buildup of an environment that motivates users to act properly.

Each method is implemented through various means.

CRYPTOGRAPHY

German Lorenz cipher machine, used in World War II to encrypt very-high-level general staff messages.

Cryptography or cryptology is the practice and study of techniques for secure communication in the presence of third parties called adversaries. More generally, cryptography is about constructing and analyzing protocols that prevent third parties or the public from reading private messages; various aspects in information security such as data confidentiality, data integrity, authentication, and non-repudiation are central to modern cryptography. Modern cryptography exists at the intersection of the disciplines of mathematics, computer science, electrical engineering, communication science, and physics. Applications of cryptography include electronic commerce, chip-based payment cards, digital currencies, computer passwords, and military communications.

Cryptography prior to the modern age was effectively synonymous with *encryption*, the conversion of information from a readable state to apparent nonsense. The originator of an encrypted message shares the decoding technique only with intended recipients to preclude access from adversaries. The cryptography literature often uses the names Alice ("A") for the sender, w Bob ("B") for the intended recipient, and Eve ("eavesdropper") for the adversary. Since the development of rotor cipher machines in World War I and the advent of computers in World War II, the methods used to carry out cryptology have become increasingly complex and its application more widespread.

Modern cryptography is heavily based on mathematical theory and computer science practice; cryptographic algorithms are designed around computational hardness assumptions, making such algorithms hard to break in practice by any adversary. It is theoretically possible to break such a system, but it is infeasible to do so by any known practical means. These schemes are therefore termed computationally secure; theoretical advances, e.g., improvements in integer factorization algorithms, and faster computing technology require these solutions to be continually adapted. There exist information-theoretically secure schemes that provably cannot be broken even with unlimited computing power—an example is the one-time pad—but these schemes are more difficult to use in practice than the best theoretically breakable but computationally secure mechanisms.

The growth of cryptographic technology has raised a number of legal issues in the information age. Cryptography's potential for use as a tool for espionage and sedition has led many governments to classify it as a weapon and to limit or even prohibit its use and export. In some jurisdictions where the use of cryptography is legal, laws permit investigators to compel the disclosure of encryption keys for documents relevant to an investigation. Cryptography also plays a major role in digital rights management and copyright infringement of digital media.

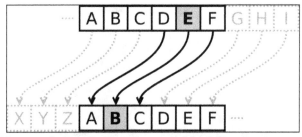

Alphabet shift ciphers are believed to have been used by Julius Caesar over 2,000 years ago. This is an example with k=3. In other words, the letters in the alphabet are shifted three in one direction to encrypt and three in the other direction to decrypt.

The first use of the term *cryptograph* (as opposed to *cryptogram*) dates back to the 19th century—originating from *The Gold-Bug*, a novel by Edgar Allan Poe.

Until modern times, cryptography referred almost exclusively to *encryption*, which is the process of converting ordinary information (called plaintext) into unintelligible form (called ciphertext). Decryption is the reverse, in other words, moving from the unintelligible ciphertext back to plaintext. A *cipher* (or *cypher*) is a pair of algorithms that create the encryption and the reversing decryption. The detailed operation of a cipher is controlled both by the algorithm and in each instance by a "key". The key is a secret (ideally known only to the communicants), usually a short string of characters, which is needed to decrypt the ciphertext. Formally, a "cryptosystem" is the ordered list of elements of finite possible plaintexts, finite possible cyphertexts, finite possible keys, and the encryption and decryption algorithms which correspond to each key. Keys are important both formally and in actual practice, as ciphers without variable keys can be trivially broken with only the knowledge of the cipher used and are therefore useless (or even counter-productive) for most purposes.

Historically, ciphers were often used directly for encryption or decryption without additional procedures such as authentication or integrity checks. There are two kinds of cryptosystems: symmetric and asymmetric. In symmetric systems the same key (the secret key) is used to encrypt and decrypt a message. Data manipulation in symmetric systems is faster than asymmetric systems as they generally use shorter key lengths. Asymmetric systems use a public key to encrypt a message and a private key to decrypt it. Use of asymmetric systems enhances the security of communication. Examples of asymmetric systems include RSA (Rivest–Shamir–Adleman), and ECC (Elliptic Curve Cryptography). Symmetric models include the commonly used AES (Advanced Encryption Standard) which replaced the older DES (Data Encryption Standard).

In colloquial use, the term "code" is often used to mean any method of encryption or concealment of meaning. However, in cryptography, *code* has a more specific meaning. It means the replacement of a unit of plaintext (i.e., a meaningful word or phrase) with a code word (for example, "wallaby" replaces "attack at dawn").

Cryptanalysis is the term used for the study of methods for obtaining the meaning of encrypted information without access to the key normally required to do so; i.e., it is the study of how to crack encryption algorithms or their implementations.

Some use the terms *cryptography* and *cryptology* interchangeably in English, while others (including US military practice generally) use *cryptography* to refer specifically to the use and practice of cryptographic techniques and *cryptology* to refer to the combined study of cryptography and cryptanalysis. English is more flexible than several other languages in which *cryptology* (done by cryptologists) is always used in the second sense above. RFC 2828 advises that steganography is sometimes included in cryptology.

The study of characteristics of languages that have some application in cryptography or cryptology (e.g. frequency data, letter combinations, universal patterns, etc.) is called cryptolinguistics.

Modern Cryptography

The modern field of cryptography can be divided into several areas of study.

Symmetric-key Cryptography

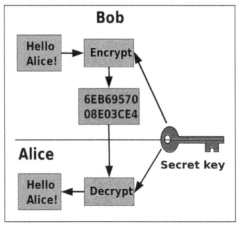

Symmetric-key cryptography, where a single key is used for encryption and decryption.

Symmetric-key cryptography refers to encryption methods in which both the sender and receiver share the same key (or, less commonly, in which their keys are different, but related in an easily computable way). This was the only kind of encryption publicly known until June 1976.

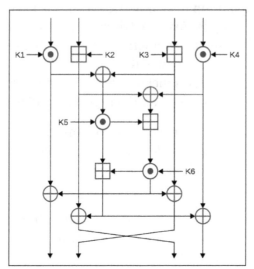

One round (out of 8.5) of the IDEA cipher, used in most versions of PGP and OpenPGP compatible software for time-efficient encryption of messages.

Symmetric key ciphers are implemented as either block ciphers or stream ciphers. A block cipher enciphers input in blocks of plaintext as opposed to individual characters, the input form used by a stream cipher.

The Data Encryption Standard (DES) and the Advanced Encryption Standard (AES) are block cipher designs that have been designated cryptography standards by the US government (though DES's designation was finally withdrawn after the AES was adopted). Despite its deprecation as an official standard, DES (especially its still-approved and much more secure triple-DES variant) remains quite popular; it is used across a wide range of applications, from ATM encryption to e-mail privacy and secure remote access. Many other block ciphers have been designed and released, with considerable variation in quality. Many, even some designed by capable practitioners, have been thoroughly broken, such as FEAL.

Stream ciphers, in contrast to the 'block' type, create an arbitrarily long stream of key material, which is combined with the plaintext bit-by-bit or character-by-character, somewhat like the one-time pad. In a stream cipher, the output stream is created based on a hidden internal state that changes as the cipher operates. That internal state is initially set up using the secret key material. RC4 is a widely used stream cipher. Block ciphers can be used as stream ciphers.

Cryptographic hash functions are a third type of cryptographic algorithm. They take a message of any length as input, and output a short, fixed length hash, which can be used in (for example) a digital signature. For good hash functions, an attacker cannot find two messages that produce the same hash. MD4 is a long-used hash function that is now broken; MD5, a strengthened variant of MD4, is also widely used but broken in practice. The US National Security Agency developed the Secure Hash Algorithm series of MD5-like hash functions: SHA-0 was a flawed algorithm that the agency withdrew; SHA-1 is widely deployed and more secure than MD5, but cryptanalysts have identified attacks against it; the SHA-2 family improves on SHA-1, but is vulnerable to clashes as of

2011; and the US standards authority thought it "prudent" from a security perspective to develop a new standard to "significantly improve the robustness of NIST's overall hash algorithm toolkit." Thus, a hash function design competition was meant to select a new U.S. national standard, to be called SHA-3, by 2012. The competition ended on October 2, 2012 when the NIST announced that Keccak would be the new SHA-3 hash algorithm. Unlike block and stream ciphers that are invertible, cryptographic hash functions produce a hashed output that cannot be used to retrieve the original input data. Cryptographic hash functions are used to verify the authenticity of data retrieved from an untrusted source or to add a layer of security.

Message authentication codes (MACs) are much like cryptographic hash functions, except that a secret key can be used to authenticate the hash value upon receipt; this additional complication blocks an attack scheme against bare digest algorithms, and so has been thought worth the effort.

Public-key Cryptography

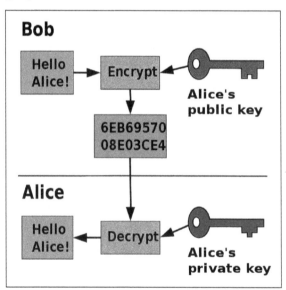

Public-key cryptography, where different keys are used for encryption and decryption.

Symmetric-key cryptosystems use the same key for encryption and decryption of a message, although a message or group of messages can have a different key than others. A significant disadvantage of symmetric ciphers is the key management necessary to use them securely. Each distinct pair of communicating parties must, ideally, share a different key, and perhaps for each ciphertext exchanged as well. The number of keys required increases as the square of the number of network members, which very quickly requires complex key management schemes to keep them all consistent and secret.

In a groundbreaking 1976 paper, Whitfield Diffie and Martin Hellman proposed the notion of *public-key* (also, more generally, called *asymmetric key*) cryptography in which two different but mathematically related keys are used—a *public* key and a *private* key. A public key system is so constructed that calculation of one key (the 'private key') is computationally infeasible from the other (the 'public key'), even though they are necessarily related. Instead, both keys are generated secretly, as an interrelated pair. The historian David Kahn described public-key cryptography as "the most revolutionary new concept in the field since polyalphabetic substitution emerged in the Renaissance".

Whitfield Diffie and Martin Hellman, authors of the
first published paper on public-key cryptography.

In public-key cryptosystems, the public key may be freely distributed, while its paired private key must remain secret. In a public-key encryption system, the *public key* is used for encryption, while the *private* or *secret key* is used for decryption. While Diffie and Hellman could not find such a system, they showed that public-key cryptography was indeed possible by presenting the Diffie–Hellman key exchange protocol, a solution that is now widely used in secure communications to allow two parties to secretly agree on a shared encryption key. The X.509 standard defines the most commonly used format for public key certificates.

Diffie and Hellman's publication sparked widespread academic efforts in finding a practical public-key encryption system. This race was finally won in 1978 by Ronald Rivest, Adi Shamir, and Len Adleman, whose solution has since become known as the RSA algorithm.

The Diffie–Hellman and RSA algorithms, in addition to being the first publicly known examples of high quality public-key algorithms, have been among the most widely used. Other asymmetric-key algorithms include the Cramer–Shoup cryptosystem, ElGamal encryption, and various elliptic curve techniques.

A document published in 1997 by the Government Communications Headquarters (GCHQ), a British intelligence organization, revealed that cryptographers at GCHQ had anticipated several academic developments. Reportedly, around 1970, James H. Ellis had conceived the principles of asymmetric key cryptography. In 1973, Clifford Cocks invented a solution that very similar in design rationale to RSA. And in 1974, Malcolm J. Williamson is claimed to have developed the Diffie–Hellman key exchange.

Public-key cryptography is also used for implementing digital signature schemes. A digital signature is reminiscent of an ordinary signature; they both have the characteristic of being easy for a user to produce, but difficult for anyone else to forge. Digital signatures can also be permanently tied to the content of the message being signed; they cannot then be 'moved' from one document to another, for any attempt will be detectable. In digital signature schemes, there are two algorithms: one for *signing*, in which a secret key is used to process the message (or a hash of the message, or both), and one for *verification*, in which the matching public key is used with the message to check the validity of the signature. RSA and DSA are two of the most popular digital signature schemes. Digital signatures are central to the operation of public key infrastructures and many network security schemes (e.g., SSL/TLS, many VPNs, etc.).

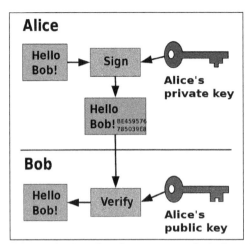

In this example the message is only signed and not encrypted. 1) Alice signs a message with her private key. 2) Bob can verify that Alice sent the message and that the message has not been modified.

Public-key algorithms are most often based on the computational complexity of "hard" problems, often from number theory. For example, the hardness of RSA is related to the integer factorization problem, while Diffie–Hellman and DSA are related to the discrete logarithm problem. The security of elliptic curve cryptography is based on number theoretic problems involving elliptic curves. Because of the difficulty of the underlying problems, most public-key algorithms involve operations such as modular multiplication and exponentiation, which are much more computationally expensive than the techniques used in most block ciphers, especially with typical key sizes. As a result, public-key cryptosystems are commonly hybrid cryptosystems, in which a fast high-quality symmetric-key encryption algorithm is used for the message itself, while the relevant symmetric key is sent with the message, but encrypted using a public-key algorithm. Similarly, hybrid signature schemes are often used, in which a cryptographic hash function is computed, and only the resulting hash is digitally signed.

Cryptanalysis

Variants of the Enigma machine, used by Germany's military and civil authorities from the late 1920s through World War II, implemented a complex electro-mechanical polyalphabetic cipher.

Breaking and reading of the Enigma cipher at Poland's Cipher Bureau, for 7 years before the war, and subsequent decryption at Bletchley Park, was important to Allied victory.

The goal of cryptanalysis is to find some weakness or insecurity in a cryptographic scheme, thus permitting its subversion or evasion.

It is a common misconception that every encryption method can be broken. In connection with his WWII work at Bell Labs, Claude Shannon proved that the one-time pad cipher is unbreakable, provided the key material is truly random, never reused, kept secret from all possible attackers, and of equal or greater length than the message. Most ciphers, apart from the one-time pad, can be broken with enough computational effort by brute force attack, but the amount of effort needed may be exponentially dependent on the key size, as compared to the effort needed to make use of the cipher. In such cases, effective security could be achieved if it is proven that the effort required (i.e., "work factor", in Shannon's terms) is beyond the ability of any adversary. This means it must be shown that no efficient method (as opposed to the time-consuming brute force method) can be found to break the cipher. Since no such proof has been found to date, the one-time-pad remains the only theoretically unbreakable cipher.

There are a wide variety of cryptanalytic attacks, and they can be classified in any of several ways. A common distinction turns on what Eve (an attacker) knows and what capabilities are available. In a ciphertext-only attack, Eve has access only to the ciphertext (good modern cryptosystems are usually effectively immune to ciphertext-only attacks). In a known-plaintext attack, Eve has access to a ciphertext and its corresponding plaintext (or to many such pairs). In a chosen-plaintext attack, Eve may choose a plaintext and learn its corresponding ciphertext (perhaps many times); an example is gardening, used by the British during WWII. In a chosen-ciphertext attack, Eve may be able to *choose* ciphertexts and learn their corresponding plaintexts. Finally in a man-in-the-middle attack Eve gets in between Alice (the sender) and Bob (the recipient), accesses and modifies the traffic and then forwards it to the recipient. Also important, often overwhelmingly so, are mistakes (generally in the design or use of one of the protocols involved.

Poznań monument (*center*) to Polish cryptanalysts whose breaking of Germany's Enigma machine ciphers, beginning in 1932, altered the course of World War II.

Cryptanalysis of symmetric-key ciphers typically involves looking for attacks against the block ciphers or stream ciphers that are more efficient than any attack that could be against a perfect cipher. For example, a simple brute force attack against DES requires one known plaintext and 2^{55} decryptions, trying approximately half of the possible keys, to reach a point at which chances are better than even that the key sought will have been found. But this may not be enough assurance;

a linear cryptanalysis attack against DES requires 2^{43} known plaintexts (with their corresponding ciphertexts) and approximately 2^{43} DES operations. This is a considerable improvement over brute force attacks.

Public-key algorithms are based on the computational difficulty of various problems. The most famous of these are the difficulty of integer factorization of semiprimes and the difficulty of calculating discrete logarithms, both of which are not yet proven to be solvable in polynomial time using only a classical Turing-complete computer. Much public-key cryptanalysis concerns designing algorithms in P that can solve these problems, or using other technologies, such as quantum computers. For instance, the best known algorithms for solving the elliptic curve-based version of discrete logarithm are much more time-consuming than the best known algorithms for factoring, at least for problems of more or less equivalent size. Thus, other things being equal, to achieve an equivalent strength of attack resistance, factoring-based encryption techniques must use larger keys than elliptic curve techniques. For this reason, public-key cryptosystems based on elliptic curves have become popular since their invention in the mid-1990s.

While pure cryptanalysis uses weaknesses in the algorithms themselves, other attacks on cryptosystems are based on actual use of the algorithms in real devices, and are called *side-channel attacks*. If a cryptanalyst has access to, for example, the amount of time the device took to encrypt a number of plaintexts or report an error in a password or PIN character, he may be able to use a timing attack to break a cipher that is otherwise resistant to analysis. An attacker might also study the pattern and length of messages to derive valuable information; this is known as traffic analysis and can be quite useful to an alert adversary. Poor administration of a cryptosystem, such as permitting too short keys, will make any system vulnerable, regardless of other virtues. Social engineering and other attacks against humans (e.g., bribery, extortion, blackmail, espionage, torture) are usually employed due to being more cost-effective and feasible to perform in a reasonable amount of time compared to pure cryptanalysis by a high margin.

Cryptographic Primitives

Much of the theoretical work in cryptography concerns cryptographic *primitives*—algorithms with basic cryptographic properties—and their relationship to other cryptographic problems. More complicated cryptographic tools are then built from these basic primitives. These primitives provide fundamental properties, which are used to develop more complex tools called *cryptosystems* or *cryptographic protocols*, which guarantee one or more high-level security properties. Note however, that the distinction between cryptographic *primitives* and cryptosystems, is quite arbitrary; for example, the RSA algorithm is sometimes considered a cryptosystem, and sometimes a primitive. Typical examples of cryptographic primitives include pseudorandom functions, one-way functions, etc.

Cryptosystems

One or more cryptographic primitives are often used to develop a more complex algorithm, called a cryptographic system, or *cryptosystem*. Cryptosystems (e.g., El-Gamal encryption) are designed to provide particular functionality (e.g., public key encryption) while guaranteeing certain security properties (e.g., chosen-plaintext attack (CPA) security in the random oracle model). Cryptosystems use the properties of the underlying cryptographic primitives to support the system's security properties. As the distinction between primitives and cryptosystems is somewhat arbitrary, a sophisticated cryptosystem can be derived from a combination of several more primitive cryptosystems. In many cases, the cryptosystem's structure involves back and forth communication among two or more parties in space (e.g., between the sender of a secure message and its receiver) or across time (e.g., cryptographically protected backup data). Such cryptosystems are sometimes called *cryptographic protocols*.

Some widely known cryptosystems include RSA encryption, Schnorr signature, El-Gamal encryption, PGP, etc. More complex cryptosystems include electronic cash systems, signcryption systems, etc. Some more 'theoretical' cryptosystems include interactive proof systems, (like zero-knowledge proofs), systems for secret sharing, etc.

Encryption

In cryptography, encryption is the process of encoding a message or information in such a way that only authorized parties can access it and those who are not authorized cannot. Encryption does not itself prevent interference, but denies the intelligible content to a would-be interceptor. In an encryption scheme, the intended information or message, referred to as plaintext, is encrypted using an encryption algorithm – a cipher – generating ciphertext that can be read only if decrypted. For technical reasons, an encryption scheme usually uses a pseudo-random encryption key generated by an algorithm. It is in principle possible to decrypt the message without possessing the key, but, for a well-designed encryption scheme, considerable computational resources and skills are required. An authorized recipient can easily decrypt the message with the key provided by the originator to recipients but not to unauthorized users.

Types

Symmetric Key

In symmetric-key schemes, the encryption and decryption keys are the same. Communicating parties must have the same key in order to achieve secure communication. An example of a symmetric key is the German military's Enigma Machine. There were key settings for each day. When the Allies figured out how the machine worked, they were able to decipher the information encoded within the messages as soon as they could discover the encryption key for a given day's transmissions.

Public Key

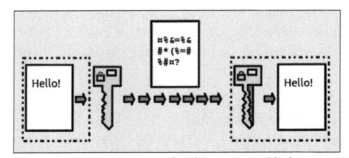

Illustration of how encryption is used within servers Public key encryption.

In public-key encryption schemes, the encryption key is published for anyone to use and encrypt messages. However, only the receiving party has access to the decryption key that enables messages to be read. Public-key encryption was first described in a secret document in 1973; before then all encryption schemes were symmetric-key (also called private-key). Although published subsequently, the work of Diffie and Hellman, was published in a journal with a large readership, and the value of the methodology was explicitly described and the method became known as the Diffie Hellman key exchange.

A publicly available public key encryption application called Pretty Good Privacy (PGP) was written in 1991 by Phil Zimmermann, and distributed free of charge with source code; it was purchased by Symantec in 2010 and is regularly updated.

Uses

Encryption has long been used by militaries and governments to facilitate secret communication. It is now commonly used in protecting information within many kinds of civilian systems. For example, the Computer Security Institute reported that in 2007, 71% of companies surveyed utilized encryption for some of their data in transit, and 53% utilized encryption for some of their data in storage. Encryption can be used to protect data "at rest", such as information stored on computers and storage devices (e.g. USB flash drives). In recent years, there have been numerous reports of confidential data, such as customers' personal records, being exposed through loss or theft of laptops or backup drives; encrypting such files at rest helps protect them if physical security measures fail. Digital rights management systems, which prevent unauthorized use or reproduction of copyrighted material and protect software against reverse engineering, is another somewhat different example of using encryption on data at rest.

Encryption is also used to protect data in transit, for example data being transferred via networks (e.g. the Internet, e-commerce), mobile telephones, wireless microphones, wireless intercom systems, Bluetooth devices and bank automatic teller machines. There have been numerous reports of data in transit being intercepted in recent years. Data should also be encrypted when transmitted across networks in order to protect against eavesdropping of network traffic by unauthorized users.

Data Erasure

Conventional methods for deleting data permanently from a storage device involve overwriting its whole content with zeros, ones or other patterns – a process which can take a significant amount of time, depending on the capacity and the type of the medium. Cryptography offers a way of making the erasure almost instantaneous. This method is called crypto-shredding. An example implementation of this method can be found on iOS devices, where the cryptographic key is kept in a dedicated 'Effaceable Storage'. Because the key is stored on the same device, this setup on its own does not offer full confidentiality protection in case an unauthorized person gains physical access to the device.

Limitations, Attacks and Countermeasures

Encryption is an important tool but is not sufficient alone to ensure the security or privacy of sensitive information throughout its lifetime. Most applications of encryption protect information only at rest or in transit, leaving sensitive data in cleartext and potentially vulnerable to improper disclosure during processing, such as by a cloud service for example. Homomorphic encryption and secure multi-party computation are emerging techniques to compute on encrypted data; these techniques are general and Turing complete but incur high computational and communication costs.

In response to encryption of data at rest, cyber-adversaries have developed new types of attacks. These more recent threats to encryption of data at rest include cryptographic attacks, stolen ciphertext attacks, attacks on encryption keys, insider attacks, data corruption or integrity attacks, data destruction attacks, and ransomware attacks. Data fragmentation and active defense data protection technologies attempt to counter some of these attacks, by distributing, moving, or mutating ciphertext so it is more difficult to identify, steal, corrupt, or destroy.

Integrity Protection of Ciphertexts

Encryption, by itself, can protect the confidentiality of messages, but other techniques are still needed to protect the integrity and authenticity of a message; for example, verification of a message authentication code (MAC) or a digital signature. Authenticated encryption algorithms are designed to provide both encryption and integrity protection together. Standards for cryptographic software and hardware to perform encryption are widely available, but successfully using encryption to ensure security may be a challenging problem. A single error in system design or execution can allow successful attacks. Sometimes an adversary can obtain unencrypted information without directly undoing the encryption.

Integrity protection mechanisms such as MACs and digital signatures must be applied to the ciphertext when it is first created, typically on the same device used to compose the message, to protect a message end-to-end along its full transmission path; otherwise, any node between the sender and the encryption agent could potentially tamper with it. Encrypting at the time of creation is only secure if the encryption device itself has correct keys and has not been tampered with. If an endpoint device has been configured to trust a root certificate that an attacker controls, for example, then the attacker can both inspect and tamper with encrypted data by performing a man-in-the-middle attack anywhere along the message's path. The common practice of TLS interception by network operators represents a controlled and institutionally sanctioned form of such an attack, but countries have also attempted to employ such attacks as a form of control and censorship.

Ciphertext Length and Padding

Even when encryption correctly hides a message's content and it cannot be tampered with at rest or in transit, a message's *length* is a form of metadata that can still leak sensitive information about the message. The well-known CRIME and BREACH attacks against HTTPS were side-channel attacks that relied on information leakage via the length of encrypted content, for example. Traffic analysis is a broad class of techniques that often employs message lengths to infer sensitive implementation about traffic flows from many messages in aggregate.

padding a message's payload before encrypting it can help obscure the cleartext's true length, at a cost of increasing the ciphertext's size and introducing bandwidth overhead. Messages may be padded randomly or deterministically, each approach having different tradeoffs. Encrypting and padding messages to form padded uniform random blobs or PURBs is a practice guaranteeing that the cipher text leaks no metadata about its cleartext's content, and leaks asymptotically minimal $O(\log \log M)$ information via its length.

ELECTRONIC AUTHENTICATION

Electronic authentication is the process of establishing confidence in user identities electronically presented to an information system. Digital authentication or e-authentication may be used synonymously when referring to the authentication process that confirms or certifies a person's identity and works. When used in conjunction with an electronic signature, it can provide evidence whether data received has been tampered with after being signed by its original sender. In a time where fraud and identity theft has become rampant, electronic authentication can be a more secure method of verifying that a person is who they say they are when performing transactions online.

There are various e-authentication methods that can be used to authenticate a user's identify ranging from a password to higher levels of security that utilize multifactor authentication (MFA). Depending on the level of security used, the user might need to prove his or her identity through the use of security tokens, challenge questions or being in possession of a certificate from a third-party certificate authority that attests to their identity.

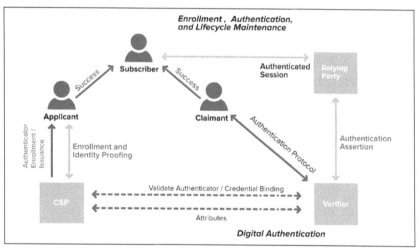

Digital enrollment and authentication reference process by the American National Institute of Standards and Technology (NIST).

The American National Institute of Standards and Technology (NIST) has developed a generic electronic authentication model that provides a basic framework on how the authentication process is accomplished regardless of jurisdiction or geographic region. According to this model, the enrollment process begins with an individual applying to a Credential Service Provider (CSP). The CSP will need to prove the applicant's identity before proceeding with the transaction. Once the applicant's identity has been confirmed by the CSP, he or she receives the status of "subscriber", is given an authenticator, such as a token and a credential, which may be in the form of a username.

The CSP is responsible for managing the credential along with the subscriber's enrollment data for the life of the credential. The subscriber will be tasked with maintaining the authenticators. An example of this is when a user normally uses a specific computer to do their online banking. If he or she attempts to access their bank account from another computer, the authenticator will not be present. In order to gain access, the subscriber would need to verify their identity to the CSP, which might be in the form of answering a challenge question successfully before being given access.

Authentication Factors

There are three generally accepted factors that are used to establish a digital identity for electronic authentication, including:

- Knowledge factor, which is something that the user knows, such as a password, answers to challenge questions, ID numbers or a PIN.

- Possession factor, which is something that the user has, such as mobile phone, PC or token.

- Biometric factor, which is something that the user is, such as his or her fingerprints, eye scan or voice pattern.

Out of the three factors, the biometric factor is the most convenient and convincing to prove an individual's identity. However, having to rely on this sole factor can be expensive to sustain. Although having their own unique weaknesses, by combining two or more factors allows for reliable authentication. It is always recommended to use multifactor authentication for that reason.

Methods

Authentication systems are often categorized by the number of factors that they incorporate. The three factors often considered as the cornerstone of authentication are: Something you know (for example, a password) Something you have (for example, an ID badge or a cryptographic key). Something you are (for example, a voice print, thumb print or other biometric).

Multifactor authentication is generally more secure than single-factor authentication. But, some multi-factor authentication approaches are still vulnerable to cases like man-in-the-middle attacks and Trojan attacks.

Token

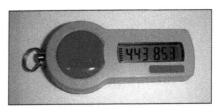

A sample of token.

Tokens generically are something the claimant possesses and controls that may be used to authenticate the claimant's identity. In e-authentication, the claimant authenticates to a system or application over a network. Therefore, a token used for e-authentication is a secret and the token must be protected. The token may, for example, be a cryptographic key, that is protected by encrypting it under a password. An impostor must steal the encrypted key and learn the password to use the token.

Passwords and PIN-based Authentication

Passwords and PINs are categorized as "something you know" method. A combination of numbers, symbols, and mixed cases are considered to be stronger than all-letter password. Also, the adoption of Transport Layer Security (TLS) or Secure Socket Layer (SSL) features during the information transmission process will as well create an encrypted channel for data exchange and to further protect information delivered. Currently, most security attacks target on password-based authentication systems.

Public-key Authentication

This type of authentication has two parts. One is a public key, the other is a private key. A public key is issued by a Certification Authority and is available to any user or server. A private key is known by the user only.

Symmetric-key Authentication

The user shares a unique key with an authentication server. When the user sends a randomly generated message (the challenge) encrypted by the secret key to the authentication server, if the message can be matched by the server using its shared secret key, the user is authenticated. When implemented together with the password authentication, this method also provides a possible solution for two-factor authentication systems.

SMS-based Authentication

Biometric Authentication.

The user receives password by reading the message in the cell phone, and types back the password to complete the authentication. Short Message Service (SMS) is very effective when cell phones are commonly adopted. SMS is also suitable against man-in-the-middle (MITM) attacks, since the use of SMS does not involve the Internet.

Biometric Authentication

Biometric authentication is the use of unique physical attributes and body measurements as the intermediate for better identification and access control. Physical characteristics that are often used for authentication include fingerprints, voice recognition, face, recognition, and iris scans because all of these are unique to every individual separately. Traditionally, Biometric Authentication based on token-based identification systems, such as passport, and nowadays becomes one of the most secure identification systems to user protections. A new technological innovation which provides a wide variety of either behavioral or physical characteristics which are defining the proper concept of Biometric Authentication.

Digital Identity Authentication

Digital identity authentication refers to the combined use of device, behavior, location and other data, including email address, account and credit card information, to authenticate online users in real time.

Electronic Credentials

Paper credentials are documents that attest to the identity or other attributes of an individual or entity called the subject of the credentials. Some common paper credentials include passports, birth certificates, driver's licenses, and employee identity cards. The credentials themselves are authenticated in a variety of ways: traditionally perhaps by a signature or a seal, special papers and inks, high quality engraving, and today by more complex mechanisms, such as holograms, that make the credentials recognizable and difficult to copy or forge. In some cases, simple possession of the credentials is sufficient to establish that the physical holder of the credentials is indeed the subject of the credentials. More commonly, the credentials contain biometric information such as the subject's description, a picture of the subject or the handwritten signature of the subject that can be used to authenticate that the holder of the credentials is indeed the subject of the credentials. When these paper credentials are presented in-person, authentication biometrics contained in those credentials can be checked to confirm that the physical holder of the credential is the subject.

Electronic identity credentials bind a name and perhaps other attributes to a token. There are a variety of electronic credential types in use today, and new types of credentials are constantly being created (eID, electronic voter ID card, biometric passports, bank cards, etc.) At a minimum, credentials include identifying information that permits recovery of the records of the registration associated with the credentials and a name that is associated with the subscriber.

Verifiers

In any authenticated on-line transaction, the verifier is the party that verifies that the claimant has possession and control of the token that verifies his or her identity. A claimant authenticates his or her identity to a verifier by the use of a token and an authentication protocol. This is called Proof of Possession (PoP). Many PoP protocols are designed so that a verifier, with no knowledge of the token before the authentication protocol run, learns nothing about the token from the run. The verifier and CSP may be the same entity, the verifier and relying party may be the same entity or they may all three be separate entities. It is undesirable for verifiers to learn shared secrets unless they are a part of the same entity as the CSP that registered the tokens. Where the verifier and the relying party are separate entities, the verifier must convey the result of the authentication protocol to the relying party. The object created by the verifier to convey this result is called an assertion.

Authentication Schemes

There are four types of authentication schemes: local authentication, centralized authentication, global centralized authentication, global authentication and web application (portal).

When using a local authentication scheme, the application retains the data that pertains to the user's credentials. This information is not usually shared with other applications. The onus is on the user to maintain and remember the types and number of credentials that are associated with the service in which they need to access. This is a high risk scheme because of the possibility that the storage area for passwords might become compromised.

Using the central authentication scheme allows for each user to use the same credentials to access various services. Each application is different and must be designed with interfaces and the ability to interact with a central system to successfully provide authentication for the user. This allows the user to access important information and be able to access private keys that will allow him or her to electronically sign documents.

Using a third party through a global centralized authentication scheme allows the user direct access to authentication services. This then allows the user to access the particular services they need.

The most secure scheme is the global centralized authentication and web application (portal). It is ideal for E-Government use because it allows a wide range of services. It uses a single authentication mechanism involving a minimum of two factors to allow access to required services and the ability to sign documents.

Authentication and Digital Signing Working Together

Often, authentication and digital signing are applied in conjunction. In advanced electronic signatures, the signatory has authenticated and uniquely linked to a signature. In the case of a qualified electronic signature as defined in the eIDAS-regulation, the signer's identity is even certified by a qualified trust service provider. This linking of signature and authentication firstly supports the probative value of the signature – commonly referred to as non-repudiation of origin. The protection of the message on the network-level is called non-repudiation of emission. The authenticated sender and the message content are linked to each other. If a 3rd party tries to change the message content, the signature loses validity.

Characteristics of Biometric Authentication

Homogenization and Decoupling

Biometric authentication can be defined by many different procedures and sensors which are being used to produce security. Biometric can be separated into physical or behavioral security. Physical protection is based on identification through fingerprint, face, hand, iris, etc. On the other hand, behavioral safety is succeeded by keystroke, signature, and voice. The main point is that all of these different procedures and mechanism that exist, produce the same homogeneous result, namely the security of the system and users. When thinking of the decoupling of hardware, the hardware is not coded in the same form by digitization which directly makes decoupling more difficult. Because of unlinkability and irreversibility of biometric templates, this technology can secure user authentication.

Digital Traces

Biometric authentication has a substantial impact on digital traces. For example when the user decides to use his fingerprint to protect his data on his smartphone, then the system memorizes the input so it will be able to be re-used again. During this procedure and many other similar applications proves that the digital trace is vital and exist on biometric authentication.

Connectivity

Another characteristic of biometric authentication is that it combines different components such as security tokens with computer systems to protect the user. Another example is the connection between devices, such as camera and computer systems to scan the user's retina and produce new ways of security. So biometric authentication could be defined by connectivity as long it connects different applications or components and through these users are getting connected and can work under the same roof and especially on a safe environment on the cyber world.

Reprogrammable and Smart

As new kinds of cybercrime are appearing, the ways of authentication must be able to adapt. This adaptation means that it is always ready for evolution and updating, and so it will be able to protect the users at any time. At first biometric authentication started in the sampler form of user's access and defining user profiles and policies. Over time the need of biometric authentication became more complex, so cybersecurity organizations started reprogramming their products/technology from simple personal user's access to allow interoperability of identities across multiple solutions. Through this evolution, business value also rises.

Risk Assessment

When developing electronic systems, there are some industry standards requiring United States agencies to ensure the transactions provide an appropriate level of assurance. Generally, servers adopt the US' Office of Management and Budget's (OMB's) E-Authentication Guidance for Federal Agencies (M-04-04) as a guideline, which is published to help federal agencies provide secure electronic services that protect individual privacy. It asks agencies to check whether their transactions require e-authentication, and determine a proper level of assurance.

It established four levels of assurance:

- Assurance Level 1: Little or no confidence in the asserted identity's validity.

- Assurance Level 2: Some confidence in the asserted identity's validity.

- Assurance Level 3: High confidence in the asserted identity's validity.

- Assurance Level 4: Very high confidence in the asserted identity's validity.

Determining Assurance Levels

The OMB proposes a five-step process to determine the appropriate assurance level for their applications:

- Conduct a risk assessment, which measures possible negative impacts.

- Compare with the five assurance levels and decide which one suits this case.

- Select technology according to the technical guidance issued by NIST.

- Confirm the selected authentication process satisfies requirements.

- Reassess the system regularly and adjust it with changes.

The required level of authentication assurance are assessed through the factors below:

- Inconvenience, distress, or damage to standing or reputation;

- Financial loss or agency liability;

- Harm to agency programs or public interests;

- Unauthorized release of sensitive information;

- Personal safety; and civil or criminal violations.

Determining Technical Requirements

National Institute of Standards and Technology (NIST) guidance defines technical requirements for each of the four levels of assurance in the following areas:

- Tokens are used for proving identity. Passwords and symmetric cryptographic keys are private information that the verifier needs to protect. Asymmetric cryptographic keys have a private key (which only the subscriber knows) and a related public key.

- Identity proofing, registration, and the delivery of credentials that bind an identity to a token. This process can involve a far distance operation.

- Credentials, tokens, and authentication protocols can also be combined together to identify that a claimant is in fact the claimed subscriber.

- An assertion mechanism that involves either a digital signature of the claimant or is acquired directly by a trusted third party through a secure authentication protocol.

Other Applications

Apart from government services, e-authentication is also widely used in other technology and industries. These new applications combine the features of authorizing identities in traditional database and new technology to provide a more secure and diverse use of e-authentication.

Mobile Authentication

Mobile authentication is the verification of a user's identity through the use a mobile device. It can be treated as an independent field or it can also be applied with other multifactor authentication schemes in the e-authentication field.

For mobile authentication, there are five levels of application sensitivity from Level 0 to Level 4. Level 0 is for public use over a mobile device and requires no identity authentications, while level 4 has the most multi-procedures to identify users. For either level, mobile authentication is relatively easy to process. Firstly, users send a one-time password (OTP) through offline channels. Then, a server identifies the information and makes adjustment in the database. Since only the user has the access to a PIN code and can send information through their mobile devices, there is a low risk of attacks.

E-commerce Authentication

In the early 1980s, electronic data interchange (EDI) systems was implemented, which was considered as an early representative of E-commerce. But ensuring its security is not a significant issue since the systems are all constructed around closed networks. However, more recently, business-to-consumer transactions have transformed. Remote transacting parties have forced the implementation of E-commerce authentication systems.

Generally speaking, the approaches adopted in E-commerce authentication are basically the same as e-authentication. The difference is E-commerce authentication is a more narrow field that focuses on the transactions between customers and suppliers. A simple example of E-commerce authentication includes a client communicating with a merchant server via the Internet. The merchant server usually utilizes a web server to accept client requests, a database management system to manage data and a payment gateway to provide online payment services.

AUTHORIZATION

Authorization is the function of specifying access rights/privileges to resources, which is related to information security and computer security in general and to access control in particular. More formally, "to authorize" is to define an access policy. For example, human resources staff are normally authorized to access employee records and this policy is usually formalized as access control rules in a computer system. During operation, the system uses the access control rules to decide whether access requests from (authenticated) consumers shall be approved (granted) or disapproved (rejected). Resources include individual files or an item's data, computer programs, computer devices and functionality provided by computer applications. Examples of consumers are computer users, computer Software and other Hardware on the computer.

Access control in computer systems and networks rely on access policies. The access control process can be divided into the following phases: policy definition phase where access is authorized, and policy enforcement phase where access requests are approved or disapproved. Authorization is the function of the policy definition phase which precedes the policy enforcement phase where access requests are approved or disapproved based on the previously defined authorizations.

Most modern, multi-user operating systems include access control and thereby rely on authorization. Access control also uses authentication to verify the identity of consumers. When a consumer tries to access a resource, the access control process checks that the consumer has been authorized to use that resource. Authorization is the responsibility of an authority, such as a department manager, within the application domain, but is often delegated to a custodian such as a system administrator. Authorizations are expressed as access policies in some types of "policy definition application", e.g. in the form of an access control list or a capability, or a policy administration point e.g. XACML. On the basis of the "principle of least privilege": consumers should only be authorized to access whatever they need to do their jobs. Older and single user operating systems often had weak or non-existent authentication and access control systems.

"Anonymous consumers" or "guests", are consumers that have not been required to authenticate. They often have limited authorization. On a distributed system, it is often desirable to grant access without requiring a unique identity. Familiar examples of access tokens include keys, certificates and tickets: they grant access without proving identity.

Trusted consumers are often authorized for unrestricted access to resources on a system, but must be verified so that the access control system can make the access approval decision. "Partially trusted" and guests will often have restricted authorization in order to protect resources against improper access and usage. The access policy in some operating systems, by default, grant all consumers full access to all resources. Others do the opposite, insisting that the administrator explicitly authorizes a consumer to use each resource.

Even when access is controlled through a combination of authentication and access control lists, the problems of maintaining the authorization data is not trivial, and often represents as much administrative burden as managing authentication credentials. It is often necessary to change or remove a user's authorization: this is done by changing or deleting the corresponding access rules on the system. Using atomic authorization is an alternative to per-system authorization management, where a trusted third party securely distributes authorization information.

INTRUSION DETECTION SYSTEM

An Intrusion Detection System (IDS) is a system that monitors network traffic for suspicious activity and issues alerts when such activity is discovered. It is a software application that scans a network or a system for harmful activity or policy breaching. Any malicious venture or violation is normally reported either to an administrator or collected centrally using a security information and event management (SIEM) system. A SIEM system integrates outputs from multiple sources and uses alarm filtering techniques to differentiate malicious activity from false alarms.

Although intrusion detection systems monitor networks for potentially malicious activity, they are also disposed to false alarms. Hence, organizations need to fine-tune their IDS products when they first install them. It means properly setting up the intrusion detection systems to recognize what normal traffic on the network looks like as compared to malicious activity.

Intrusion prevention systems also monitor network packets inbound the system to check the malicious activities involved in it and at once sends the warning notifications.

Classification of Intrusion Detection System

IDS is basically classified into 2 types:

Network Intrusion Detection System (NIDS)

Network intrusion detection systems (NIDS) are set up at a planned point within the network to examine traffic from all devices on the network. It performs an observation of passing traffic on the entire subnet and matches the traffic that is passed on the subnetts to the collection of known attacks. Once an attack is identified or abnormal behavior is observed, the alert can be sent to the administrator. An example of an NIDS is installing it on the subnet where firewalls are located in order to see if someone is trying crack the firewall.

Host Intrusion Detection System (HIDS)

Host intrusion detection systems (HIDS) run on independent hosts or devices on the network. A HIDS monitors the incoming and outgoing packets from the device only and will alert the administrator if suspicious or malicious activity is detected. It takes a snapshot of existing system files and compares it with the previous snapshot. If the analytical system files were edited or deleted, an alert is sent to the administrator to investigate. Anexample of HIDS usage can be seen on mission critical machines, which are not expected to change their layout.

Detection Method of IDS

Signature-based Method

Signature-based IDS detects the attacks on the basis of the specific patterns such as number of bytes or number of 1's or number of 0's in the network traffic. It also detects on the basis of the already known malicious instruction sequence that is used by the malware. The detected patterns in the IDS are known as signatures.

Signature-based IDS can easily detect the attacks whose pattern (signature) already exists in system but it is quite difficult to detect the new malware attacks as their pattern (signature) is not known.

Anomaly-based Method

Anomaly-based IDS was introduced to detect the unknown malware attacks as new malware are developed rapidly. In anomaly-based IDS there is use of machine learning to create a trustful activity model and anything coming is compared with that model and it is declared suspicious if it is not found in model. Machine learning based method has a better generalized property in comparison to signature-based IDS as these models can be trained according to the applications and hardware configurations.

Benefits of Intrusion Detection Systems

Intrusion detection systems offer organizations a number of benefits, starting with the ability to identify security incidents. An IDS can be used to help analyze the quantity and types of attacks, and organizations can use this information to change their security systems or implement more effective controls. An intrusion detection system can also help companies identify bugs or problems with their network device configurations. These metrics can then be used to assess future risks.

Intrusion detection systems can also help the enterprise attain regulatory compliance. An IDS gives companies greater visibility across their networks, making it easier to meet security regulations. Additionally, businesses can use their IDS logs as part of the documentation to show they are meeting certain compliance requirements.

Intrusion detection systems can also improve security response. Since IDS sensors can detect network hosts and devices, they can also be used to inspect data within the network packets, as well as identify the operating systems of services being used. Using an IDS to collect this information can be much more efficient that manual censuses of connected systems.

References

- What-is-information-security: geeksforgeeks.org, Retrieved 19 April, 2019

- "under cyberthreat: defense contractors". Businessweek. July 6, 2009. Archived from the original on 11 january 2010. Retrieved 2010-01-20

- What-is-information-security, newsroom: snhu.edu, Retrieved 17 May, 2019

- Joaquin jay gonzalez iii, rogerl.kemp (2019-01-16). Cybersecurity: current writings on threats and protection. Mcfarland, 2019. P. 69. Isbn 9781476674407

- Kovacs, eduard. "miniduke malware used against european government organizations". Softpedia. Retrieved 27 february 2013

- Andrew hay; daniel cid; rory bray (2008). Ossec host-based intrusion detection guide. Syngress. P. 276. Isbn 978-1-59749-240-9

- Methods-to-protect-information, data-protection, infosec-blog: searchinform.com, Retrieved 14 July, 2019

- Russinovich, mark (2005-10-31). "sony, rootkits and digital rights management gone too far". Technet blogs. Microsoft. Retrieved 2010-08-16

- Intrusion-detection-system-ids: geeksforgeeks.org, Retrieved 31 March, 2019

Permissions

Index

Printed in the USA
CPSIA information can be obtained
at www.ICGtesting.com
JSHW051422221024
72173JS00006B/1390

9 781682 858974